60 HIKES WITHIN 60 MILES

4TH Edition

CHICAGO

Including Wisconsin and Northwest Indiana

Ted Villaire

MENASHA RIDGE PRESS
Your Guide to the Outdoors

D0814205

60 Hikes Within 60 Miles: Chicago

Project editor: Ritchey Halphen
Cover and interior design: Jonathan Norberg
Photos: Credits as noted below and throughout
Cartography: Scott McGrew and Ted Villaire

Cover photos/credits: (Front) Kaskaskia Canyon, Starved Rock State Park (see Hike 58, page 272); wildnerdpix/ Shutterstock. (Back, top) Miller Woods, Indiana Dunes National Lakeshore (see Hike 42, page 203); Ted Villaire. (Back, bottom, left–right) Goose Lake Prairie State Natural Area (see Hike 50, page 239); Openlands Lakeshore Preserve (see Hike 28, Nearby Activities, page 143); and Humboldt Park, Chicago (see Hike 5, page 38); all by Ted Villaire.

Back cover and page 286: Arc of Nature, Openlands Lakeshore Preserve; © 2010 by Augustina Droze and Ginny Sykes in collaboration with Jim Brenner, Julia Sowles-Barlow, and others

Library of Congress Cataloging-in-Publication Data

Names: Villaire, Ted, 1969– author.
Title: 60 hikes within 60 miles : Chicago : including Wisconsin and Northwest Indiana / Ted Villaire.
Other titles: Sixty hikes within sixty miles
Description: Fourth Edition. | Birmingham, Alabama : Menasha Ridge Press, [2018] | "Distributed by
    Publishers Group West"—T.p. verso. | Includes index.
Identifiers: LCCN 2017050891| ISBN 9781634040860 (paperback) | ISBN 9781634040877 (ebook)
    ISBN 9781634041607 (hardcover)
Subjects: LCSH: Hiking—Illinois—Chicago Region—Guidebooks. | Walking—Illinois—Chicago Region—
    Guidebooks. | Trails—Illinois—Chicago Region—Guidebooks. | Backpacking—Illinois—Chicago
    Region—Guidebooks. | Chicago Region (Ill.)—Guidebooks.
Classification: LCC GV199.42.I32 C478 2018 | DDC 796.5109773—dc23
LC record available at lccn.loc.gov/2017050891

MENASHA RIDGE PRESS
An imprint of AdventureKEEN
2204 First Ave. S., Ste. 102
Birmingham, Alabama 35233

Visit menasharidge.com for a complete listing of our books and for ordering information. Contact us at our website, at facebook.com/menasharidge, or at twitter.com/menasharidge with questions or comments. To find out more about who we are and what we're doing, visit blog.menasharidge.com.

Dedication

This book is dedicated to my father, someone who knew that regularly taking a walk in the woods is a necessary part of a healthy, happy life.

60 Hikes Within 60 Miles: Chicago

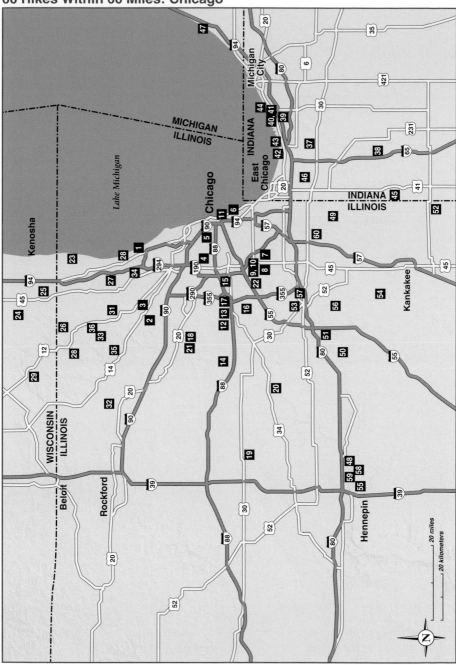

TABLE OF CONTENTS

SOUTH CHICAGOLAND AND THE ILLINOIS RIVER VALLEY   231

↔ ➡ Directional arrows	—— Featured trail	⋯⋯ Alternate trail
▬▬ Freeway	▭▬▭ Highway with bridge	▭▭ Minor road
▥▥ Boardwalk	▭▭▭ Unpaved road	⋯⋯ Stairs
┼┼┼ Railroad	▬·▬·▬ Boundary line	
Park/forest	Water body	River/creek/ intermittent stream

✈ Airport	🎣 Fishing	🏕 Picnic shelter
🏃 Baseball field	✖ Footbridge	👫 Playground
🏀 Basketball court	✳ Garden	⚠ Primitive campsite
🏄 Beach access	•— Gate	🗼 Radio tower
⌐ Bench	● General point of interest	🚻 Restroom
🚲 Bicycle trail	🏌 Golf course	🅷 Scenic view
⛵ Boat launch	⑦ Information/kiosk	⊂ Shelter
▲ Campground	⚘ Marsh/bog	🛷 Sledding hill
🛶 Canoe launch	Ⓜ Metra station	⚽ Soccer field
✝ Cemetery	◀ One-way (road)	○ Spring
🍴 Concessions	⚠ Overlook	🎾 Tennis court
/ Dam	🅿 Parking	🏃 Trailhead
🚰 Drinking water	🏠 Park office	⌒ Tunnel (pedestrian)
🗼 Electrical tower	🔺 Peak/hill	🏳 Viewing platform
🐎 Equestrian trail	⊤ Picnic area	// Waterfall
$ Fee station		

ACKNOWLEDGMENTS

My gratitude goes to all the staff and volunteers who provide the essential service of maintaining the parks and trails in the Chicago area—particularly when resources for doing so are scarce. Without these committed individuals, our local sanctuaries wouldn't exist. Thanks to all the readers who have contacted me with suggestions for improving the book, and thanks to reader Erica Tesla for creating a Google map showing locations and characteristics for all the hikes. Thanks to the hundreds of people who've shared their thoughts and interests with me at the dozens of hiking presentations I've done over the years in public libraries throughout the region. Thanks to friends, coworkers, and family for their support and encouragement during the book's research and writing. And thanks to my wife, Christine, for being a greater fan than I deserve and for being the best hiking companion I could ask for.

—Ted Villaire

FOREWORD

Welcome to Menasha Ridge Press's 60 Hikes Within 60 Miles, a series designed to provide hikers with the information they need to find and hike the very best trails surrounding metropolitan areas.

Our strategy is simple: First, find a hiker who knows the area and loves to hike. Second, ask that person to spend a year researching the most popular and very best trails around. And third, have that person describe each trail in terms of difficulty, scenery, condition, elevation change, and other categories of information that are important to hikers. "Pretend you've just completed a hike and met up with other hikers at the trailhead," we told each author. "Imagine their questions, and be clear in your answers."

An experienced hiker and writer, author Ted Villaire has selected 60 of the best hikes in and around the Chicago metropolitan area. This fourth edition includes new hikes, as well as additional sections and new routes for some of the existing hikes. Villaire provides hikers (and walkers) with a great variety of hikes, all within roughly 60 miles of Chicago—from urban strolls on city sidewalks to aerobic outings in the Indiana Dunes.

You'll get more out of this book if you take a moment to read the Introduction, which explains how to read the trail listings. The "Maps" section will help you understand how useful topographic maps are on a hike and will also tell you where to get them. And though this is a where-to, not a how-to, guide, readers who have not hiked extensively will find the Introduction of particular value.

As much for the opportunity to free the spirit as to free the body, let these hikes elevate you above the urban hurry.

All the best,
The Editors at Menasha Ridge Press

PREFACE

There's no arguing with the benefits of wandering through the woods. Whatever we're looking for—fresh air, exercise, time with (or away from) your family or friends, a bit of adventure, or a momentary escape from the concrete grid—traipsing through the local landscape helps us take stock of ourselves and the world around us.

The best thing about hiking in the Chicago area is the variety of scenic spots, each with a distinctive topographical flavor, its own combination of plants and wildlife, and its unique seasonal ambience. When it's time to dodge city living for a while, a short trip to Lake Michigan is the first idea in the minds of many. Mesmerizing us every chance it gets, the Big Lake's endless blue horizon is no small part of the region's allure. Profoundly intertwined with the area's weather, economic and social history, and, of course, its visual charm, this exquisite diversion is in Chicagoans' own front yard. Heading inland away from the lake, there is no shortage of patches of parkland that can provide us with a respite from our daily routines. These are places that invite us to trace the routes of meandering rivers, wander through expansive prairies, and scramble up steep, wooded hills. These are places we go to enjoy a picnic in a dappled oak savanna, or where we can sit on the edge of a quiet lake while admiring a field of water lilies beyond the weeping willows.

Spring and fall provide some of the best times to explore local trails: temperatures are moderate, bugs are dormant, the number of visitors is minimal, and lovely surprises often present themselves to those who look. Spring, of course, brings a sensory banquet as buds pop, wildflowers bloom, and the landscape becomes braided with intermittent streams. The only thing more pleasurable than the awakening of spring is getting hit with a Technicolor blast in fall. Places such as Deer Grove Forest Preserve, Morton Arboretum, and the Bailly–Chellberg Hike at the Indiana Dunes are a few spots where one can witness brilliant displays of autumn's leaves. Fall also offers opportunities to swim through a sea of prairie grass as the mauve stalks of big bluestem reach heights of 8–10 feet at places such as Goose Lake Prairie State Park and Chain O' Lakes State Park.

Destinations swarming with visitors in the warmer months usually supply a pleasing solitude during winter. While the dead grasses, naked trees, and frozen streams of winter can seem stark and barren, the snowy landscape is alive with opportunities to follow the comings and goings of elusive creatures such as raccoons, opossums, and coyotes. Winter serves up other delights, too. Opportunities for sledding and outdoor ice skating can be found at places such as Lakewood and Goodenow Grove Forest Preserves.

Winter's fleeting daylight hours need not prevent you from seeking treatment for your cabin fever; many of the destinations listed in this book stay open after dark. Just bring a headlamp or flashlight, or better yet, take a hike under the glow of a full moon.

Many people prefer hiking in summer, when the sun is warm, the greenery is lush, and kids are searching for something to do. Lake Michigan excursions such as the Cowles Bog and Dead River hikes are particularly fun for the family on hot summer days when you can kick off your shoes and float in the lake at the hikes' halfway points. It's true, summer is the most conducive season for combining your hike with a myriad of other outdoor pursuits such as picnicking, playing Frisbee, casting a fishing line, or practicing your tai chi. It's also the time of year to combine hiking with a night or two of sleeping under the stars at places like Chain O' Lakes and Illinois Beach State Parks and Shabbona Lake State Recreation Area.

Whatever the season, I can't stress enough the advantages of getting out on the trail early in the day. Early morning—the time of day when sightings of wildlife outnumber sightings of people—delivers the most captivating moments: a line of deer leaping over a fence, steam rising off a pond on a cool spring morning, or a great blue heron fishing for frogs.

City on the Prairie

At the time of European settlement, the landscape of the Chicago region was mostly tallgrass prairie, an especially fertile type of grassland due to thousands of years of tall grasses decomposing. While this eastern edge of the nation's grassland is known for being productive farmland, farmers were initially in for an unpleasant surprise when they struggled to plow soil that seemed to have more roots than dirt. But once the sod was turned over and seeds were planted, their efforts were rewarded. To this day, Illinois continues to be a top producer of national staples such as corn and soybeans. While nearly all of the tallgrass prairie has been cultivated, the remnants described in this book provide a taste of what it was like to trek through prairie grass growing as high as a horse's head.

Even though much of the native landscape was gently rolling prairie, numerous hilly wooded exceptions could always be found. Among those places spared from the steamrolling effect of the last glacier were the steep hills scattered throughout McHenry and Lake Counties, the wooded bluffs within the Palos and Sag Valley Forest Preserves, and the sandstone cliffs and canyons along the Illinois and Kankakee Rivers. And later, after the last glacier began to recede some 14,000 years ago, the colossal sand dunes formed at the south edge of Lake Michigan.

Under Threat

Unfortunately, this rich bounty of natural places in Chicagoland is not guaranteed. The state of Illinois has dramatically cut its park staff in recent years, and a long list of park maintenance and improvement projects has been ignored and delayed. This neglect means that trails are not cleared of deadfall as quickly as they once were. It means that park nature centers have cut back hours and, in some cases, closed completely, which is a substantial loss for school programs that rely on such places to expose kids to the natural world. It means that there are fewer park staff around to make sure visitors are following the rules.

Now throw climate change into the mix. Wetter weather in the Midwest means more trail flooding and erosion—problems that take longer to fix with a skeleton crew. And forget about much in the way of new trails opening. While some of the so-called collar counties are able to adequately maintain their parks and trails and occasionally add to them, natural areas operated by the state and Cook County often seem neglected and sometimes appear to be in jeopardy of closing.

So what can you do about it? Get involved. Local agencies are responsive to the needs of residents, but they have to know about your concerns—that you want not only well-maintained natural spaces, but that you also want to see local park systems expanded and improved. Let your political representatives know you care. While you'll often hear that no money is available for such things, there are always opportunities for reallocating public tax dollars.

Another way you can make a difference is by minimizing your carbon footprint on your hiking trip. With transportation now accounting for one-third of the carbon dioxide entering our atmosphere, it's time to think carefully about using cleaner, healthier modes of transportation. For nearly half of these hikes, I've included directions for accessing the park by public transit. If one of the reasons you're hiking is for exercise, then taking public transit will likely contribute to that goal. If the trailhead is a bikeable distance from a train station, bring your bike on the train. Metra has long allowed bikes on its trains, and the South Shore Line, serving both Chicago and northwest Indiana, has recently started allowing them—take advantage of it.

Around Chicagoland, many thousands of people volunteer regularly at their local forest preserve. You can learn about these opportunities on map boards at the parks or at the websites operated by the countless "friends of" groups that exist throughout the region. Many local parks and forest preserves rely on donations and volunteers to regularly remove the invasive plants that crowd out the native species. Once you've seen the dramatic difference it makes when acres of an invasive plant like buckthorn is removed from a preserve, you may just want to sign up.

Pick a Trail, Any Trail

Even though the focus of this book is hiking, much of the information will be useful to trail runners, cross-country skiers, snowshoers, parents with strollers, and wheelchair users. With a growing number of trails classified as multiuse, many people are seeing that there's more than one way to follow a trail. One mother I know, for example, runs along multiuse trails while her 10-year-old son rides his bike beside her. Hitting the trails is a great way for them to stay active and fit while spending time together outdoors.

Local hikers will want to keep an eye on the growing network of multiuse trails within the region. Hikers should also watch for changes at Midewin National Tallgrass Prairie (see Hike 56, page 264). Each year, a few more miles of trails are opening within the 19,000-acre preserve, which once hosted the largest ammunition-production plant in the world. Also in south Chicagoland, keep an eye on Kankakee Sands, a Nature Conservancy–owned preserve that will serve as the anchor for a huge area of publicly accessible land near where the Kankakee River crosses the Indiana–Illinois border.

As digital screens and constant connectivity become more and more interwoven into our lives, making regular escapes to the natural world seems more crucial than ever. These escapes allow us to slow down and enjoy the sound of a shallow stream flowing over its rocky bottom, watch a turkey vulture gradually lifted by an updraft, and study a butterfly as it extracts nectar from a milkweed flower. It's a time for us to temporarily unburden ourselves from lives that seem to be moving faster by the day. It provides a time to walk and talk with people we care about.

As you explore the hikes in this book, good wishes to you and your trail companions as you embark on your adventures.   *—T. V.*

OPPOSITE: Family fun at Kankakee River State Park (see Hike 54, page 256)
Photo: Lotzman Katzman/Flickr

60 HIKES BY CATEGORY

REGION / Hike Number/Hike Name	Page	Less Than 3 Miles	3-6 Miles	More Than 6 Miles	Kids	Public Transport	Hilly Terrain	Urban Hike	Solitude	Wildlife	Wildflowers	River Hike	Lake Hike	Beach Hike
COOK COUNTY														
1 Chicago Botanic Garden Hike	20	E			✓	✓		✓		✓	✓	✓		
2 Crabtree Nature Center Hike	25	E			✓				✓	✓	✓		✓	
3 Deer Grove Loop	29		E			✓	✓							
4 Des Plaines River Trail: North Avenue to Chevalier Woods	33			S		✓		✓	✓			✓		
5 Humboldt Park Lagoon and Prairie River Loop	38	E			✓	✓		✓			✓	✓		
6 Jackson Park Loop	43	E			✓	✓		✓					✓	
7 Lake Katherine Hike	48		M		✓	✓	✓	✓		✓	✓	✓		
8 Palos–Sag Valley Trail System: Cap Sauers and Swallow Cliff Loop	52		M						✓	✓	✓			
9 Palos–Sag Valley Trail System: Country Lane Loop	56		M				✓		✓	✓	✓			
10 Palos–Sag Valley Trail System: Little Red Schoolhouse Hike	61	E			✓					✓		✓		
11 South Lakefront Trail	65		M			✓		✓					✓	✓
DuPAGE COUNTY AND DESTINATIONS WEST														
12 Blackwell Forest Preserve Hike	72			M	✓					✓		✓		
13 Danada Forest Preserve Hike	76		E		✓					✓	✓			
14 Dick Young Forest Preserve Hike	80		E						✓			✓		
15 Fullersburg Woods Forest Preserve Loop	84		E		✓					✓	✓			
16 Greene Valley Forest Preserve Loop	88		E							✓				
17 Morton Arboretum: East Hike	92		E		✓	✓				✓				
18 Pratt's Wayne Loop	97		M									✓		
19 Shabonna State Recreation Area Loop	101		M									✓		
20 Silver Springs State Park Loop	105	M			✓		✓			✓	✓	✓		
21 Tekakwitha–Fox River Hike	109	E			✓		✓	✓		✓	✓	✓		
22 Waterfall Glen Forest Preserve Loop	113			M			✓							
NORTH CHICAGOLAND AND WISCONSIN														
23 Adeline Jay Geo-Karis Illinois Beach State Park: Dead River Loop	120	E			✓	✓				✓	✓	✓	✓	✓
24 Bong State Recreation Area Loop	124		M									✓		
25 Bristol Woods Hike	128	E			✓		✓		✓					
26 Chain O' Lakes State Park Hike	132			E	✓					✓		✓		
27 Des Plaines River Trail: Old School to Independence Grove	136			M	✓			✓				✓		
28 Fort Sheridan Forest Preserve Hike	140	M			✓					✓			✓	✓
29 Geneva Lake: North Shore Hike	145			S			✓	✓					✓	✓
30 Glacial Park Loop	150		E							✓		✓		
31 Lakewood Forest Preserve Loop	154	E							✓	✓		✓		
32 Marengo Ridge Hike	158		E				✓		✓		✓			

REGION / Hike Number/Hike Name	Page	Less Than 6 Miles	3–6 Miles	More Than 6 Miles	Kids	Public Transport	Hilly Terrain	Urban Hike	Solitude	Wildlife	Wildflowers	River Hike	Lake Hike	Beach Hike
NORTH CHICAGOLAND AND WISCONSIN *(continued)*														
33 Moraine Hills State Park Hike	162			M			✓				✓		✓	
34 Ryerson Woods Hike	166		E			✓				✓		✓		
35 Veteran Acres–Sterne's Woods Hike	171		M		✓	✓	✓	✓		✓				
36 Volo Bog State Natural Area Hike	175		M		✓					✓				
NORTHWEST INDIANA AND ENVIRONS														
37 Deep River Hike	182	E			✓				✓		✓	✓		
38 Grand Kankakee Marsh County Park Hike	186			S					✓	✓		✓		
39 Indiana Dunes National Lakeshore: Bailly–Chellberg Hike	190		E		✓	✓			✓		✓	✓		
40 Indiana Dunes National Lakeshore: Cowles Bog Loop	194		M		✓	✓	✓		✓		✓		✓	✓
41 Indiana Dunes National Lakeshore: Glenwood Dunes Hike	198			S	✓				✓					
42 Indiana Dunes National Lakeshore: Miller Woods Hike	203		M		✓	✓			✓	✓	✓		✓	✓
43 Indiana Dunes National Lakeshore: West Beach Loop	208		M		✓		✓				✓		✓	✓
44 Indiana Dunes State Park: Dune Ridge Loop	212		M		✓	✓	✓			✓			✓	✓
45 LaSalle Fish and Wildlife Area Loop	216		M						✓	✓	✓	✓		
46 Oak Ridge Prairie Loop	220	E			✓						✓		✓	
47 Warren Dunes State Park Loop	224		M		✓			✓						✓
SOUTH CHICAGOLAND AND THE ILLINOIS RIVER VALLEY														
48 Buffalo Rock State Park Hike	232	E			✓							✓	✓	
49 Goodenow Grove Hike	236	E			✓				✓	✓		✓		
50 Goose Lake Prairie State Natural Area Loop	239	E			✓				✓	✓	✓			
51 I&M Canal State Trail and McKinley Woods Hike	243			M		✓				✓		✓		
52 Iroquois County State Wildlife Area Hike	248	E							✓	✓	✓			
53 Joliet Iron Works Hike	252	E				✓		✓						
54 Kankakee River State Park Hike	256		E									✓		
55 Matthiessen State Park: Dells Area Hike	260	M			✓		✓				✓	✓		
56 Midewin National Tallgrass Prairie Hike	264			S	✓				✓	✓	✓			
57 Pilcher Park Loop	268		E		✓	✓				✓	✓	✓		
58 Starved Rock State Park: East Hike	272			M			✓				✓	✓		
59 Starved Rock State Park: West Hike	276	S					✓					✓		
60 Thorn Creek Woods Hike	280	M			✓				✓			✓		

DIFFICULTY RATINGS		
E = Easy	M = Moderate	S = Strenuous

A stately tree canopy at Blackwell Forest Preserve (see Hike 12, page 72)   *Photo: Ted Villaire*

INTRODUCTION

Welcome to *60 Hikes Within 60 Miles: Chicago.* If you're new to hiking or even if you're a seasoned trailsmith, take a few minutes to read the following introduction. We explain how this book is organized and how to use it.

About This Book

The destinations in this book are organized into five chapters: **Cook County, DuPage County and Destinations West, North Chicagoland and Wisconsin, Northwest Indiana and Environs,** and **South Chicagoland and the Illinois River Valley.** These 60 hikes are scattered across four states and more than a dozen counties, but a few areas in particular contain high concentrations of trails.

The most accessible trails lie in the vicinity of the Palos–Sag Valley Trail System (southwest of downtown Chicago) and the Indiana Dunes (southeast of downtown). In the far northeastern corner of Illinois is an assortment of good destinations in McHenry and Lake Counties. Southwest of the city, beyond Joliet, a great collection of trails lies near the Illinois River and the Illinois & Michigan (I&M) Canal.

PALOS AREA

The **Palos–Sag Valley Trail System** hosts about 35 miles of trails that branch out and converge within 14,000 acres of woodland, lakes, ponds, sloughs, and rugged glacial terrain. Families visiting Palos will enjoy the **Little Red Schoolhouse Nature Center,** where they can take a short hike along the banks of Long John Slough and through groves of stately oaks, and then visit a nature center featuring a menagerie of birds, snakes, and frogs. Across the Des Plaines River, at **Waterfall Glen Forest Preserve,** a 10-mile loop trail through rugged wooded terrain winds around the Argonne National Laboratory. To the east, **Lake Katherine Nature Center** provides an unrivaled spot for a casual urban stroll. The most scenic and remote hiking destination in the Palos area is **Cap Sauers Holding**—the largest roadless area in Cook County and one of the largest state-designated nature preserves in Illinois.

INDIANA DUNES

Located on the southern tip of Lake Michigan, the Indiana Dunes offer great stretches of sandy beach, dense bottomland forests, and soaring mountains of sand overlooking the lake. Even though the dunes are bounded by steel mills, residential areas, and a power plant, the 17,200 acres that make up the national and state parks can feel surprisingly remote. At the state park and at the national lakeshore's **West Beach** and **Cowles Bog Trails,** you'll encounter curious dune formations know as "blowouts," where forceful lake winds have scooped out huge bowls in the sand. Other hikes in the area, such as the **Glenwood Dunes Trail, Miller Woods Hike,** and **Bailly–Chellberg**

Hike, feature rolling oak savannas, gentle dune ridges, winding streams, and marshland active with birds. With access via the South Shore Line, the dunes are an especially attractive destination for individuals using public transit.

McHENRY AND LAKE COUNTIES

Thanks to a glacier that dumped enormous heaps of dirt and gravel as it retreated from the area some 14,000 years ago, McHenry and Lake Counties possess hills galore. Situated side by side in Illinois's far northeast comer, these counties are where you'll find destinations with names like **Glacial Park, Moraine Hills State Park,** and **Marengo Ridge Conservation Area,** which hint at the area's geological legacy. The glacial heritage is also evident in the many types of wetlands dotting the landscape. When glaciers retreated, chunks of ice often would get left behind, leaving depressions in the ground that eventually became lakes, ponds, marshes, or bogs. This process created extensive wetlands at places such as Volo Bog, Chain O' Lakes State Park, and Moraine Hills State Park.

THE ILLINOIS RIVER

Perhaps the most important development that led to Chicago becoming the economic and cultural capital of the Midwest was the digging of the I&M Canal in 1848. Running parallel to the Illinois and Des Plaines Rivers, the canal provided a link between the Great Lakes and the Mississippi River. After the canal was completed, the task of getting grain from the Midwest's breadbasket to markets in Chicago and beyond suddenly became easier, and in the larger picture, shipping traffic could travel from the Atlantic Ocean to the Gulf of Mexico. For much of the canal's lifespan, boats were pulled by mules along an accompanying towpath.

Today, 60 miles of the old towpath between Joliet and LaSalle has been preserved as a multiuse trail. This trail and its surrounding environs now offer some of the best hiking in the Chicago region. Sprinkled in the vicinity of the trail and the Illinois River are the high bluffs of **McKinley Woods;** sandstone cliffs and canyons of **Starved Rock, Buffalo Rock,** and **Matthiessen State Parks;** and the largest tract of tallgrass prairie in the state, at **Goose Lake Prairie State Park.**

As I mulled over the trails to include in this edition, I sometimes found it difficult to eliminate one hike in favor of another. As much as possible, I leaned toward variety in terms of length, location, and scenic attractions. And while I hope you enjoy the hikes I've laid out, keep in mind that there are many more excellent hikes that are not among these 60. Some are included in the "Nearby Activities" sections of the various profiles, but many are not.

How to Use This Guidebook

The following information walks you through this guidebook's organization to make it easy and convenient for planning great hikes.

OVERVIEW MAP, REGIONAL MAPS, AND MAP LEGEND

Use the overview map, opposite the table of contents on page iv, to assess the location of each hike's primary trailhead. Thanks to a resourceful reader named Erica Tesla, you can also view a Google map showing all 60 hikes at tinyurl.com/60hikeschicagomap. On this map, Erica has labeled all of the hikes according to length and difficulty. It's wonderful to have readers helping to share these hikes!

Each hike's number appears on the overview map; in the table of contents; at the beginning of each regional chapter, which has its own overview map and list of hikes; and in the hike profiles themselves. The regional maps provide more detail than the main overview map, bringing you closer to the hikes in that chapter. As you flip through the book, a hike's full profile is easy to locate by watching for the hike number at the top of each left-hand page.

A map legend that details the symbols found on trail maps follows the table of contents, on page viii.

TRAIL MAPS

A detailed map of each hike's route accompanies its profile. On each map, symbols indicate the trailhead; the complete route; significant features and facilities; and geographic landmarks such as creeks, overlooks, and peaks. But despite the high quality of the maps in this guidebook, we strongly recommend that you always carry an additional map, such as the ones noted in each entry's Key Information listing for "Maps."

THE HIKE PROFILE

Each hike contains a brief overview of the trail, a detailed description of the route, from start to finish; key at-a-glance information, from the trail's distance and configuration to contacts for local information; GPS trailhead coordinates; and directions for driving to the trailhead area. Each profile also includes a map (see "Trail Maps," above). Many (but not all) hike profiles also include notes on nearby activities.

In Brief

Think of this section as a taste of the trail, a snapshot focused on the historical landmarks, beautiful vistas, and other sights you may encounter on the hike.

Key Information

The information in this box gives you an at-a-glance rundown of each hike.

DISTANCE & CONFIGURATION *Distance* notes the length of the hike from start to finish. If the hike description includes options to shorten or extend the hike, those distances will also be factored here. *Configuration* defines the trail as a loop, an out-and-back (taking you in and out along the same route), a point-to-point (one-way) route, a figure eight, a balloon, or some combination of these.

DIFFICULTY The degree of effort that a typical hiker should expect on a given route. For simplicity, the trails are rated as *easy, moderate,* or *strenuous.*

SCENERY A short summary of the attractions offered by the hike and what to expect in terms of plant life, wildlife, natural wonders, and historical features.

EXPOSURE A quick check of how much sun you can expect on your shoulders during the hike.

TRAIL TRAFFIC Indicates how busy the trail might be on an average day. Trail traffic, of course, varies from day to day and season to season. Weekend days typically see the most visitors. Other trail users that may be encountered on the trail are also noted here.

TRAIL SURFACE Indicates whether the trail surface is pavement, grass, gravel, dirt, boardwalk, or a mixture of elements.

HIKING TIME How long it takes to hike the trail. A slow but steady hiker will average 2–3 miles an hour, depending on the terrain.

DRIVING DISTANCE The mileage to the trail from a familiar place: in this case, Millennium Park in downtown Chicago. Not that you'd necessarily want to start from here, but the mileages should give you a good estimate of the travel time from where you live (or where you're staying if you're a visitor). Also, with Chicagoland being such a sprawling metropolis, note that a few hikes are slightly to considerably farther than 60 miles from Millennium Park versus, say, the far western suburbs.

ACCESS Fees or permits required to hike the trail are detailed here—and noted if there are none. Trail-access hours are also listed here.

MAPS Resources for maps, in addition to those in this guidebook, are listed here. (As previously noted, we recommend that you carry more than one map—and that you consult those maps before heading out on the trail.)

FACILITIES Alerts you to restrooms, water, picnic tables, and other basics at or near the trailhead.

WHEELCHAIR ACCESS Lets you know if there are paved sections or other areas where persons with disabilities can safely use a wheelchair.

CONTACT Listed here are phone numbers and website addresses for checking trail conditions and gleaning other day-to-day information.

LOCATION Where available, the full street address of the park or trailhead is listed here; otherwise, just the city and state are listed.

COMMENTS Here you'll find assorted nuggets of information, such as whether or not dogs are allowed on the trails.

Description

The heart of each hike. Here, the author provides a summary of the trail's essence and highlights any special traits the hike has to offer. The route is clearly outlined, including landmarks, side trips, and possible alternative routes along the way.

Nearby Activities

Look here for information on things to do or points of interest: nearby parks, museums, restaurants, and the like. Note that not every hike has a listing.

Directions

Used in conjunction with the GPS coordinates (see next page), the driving directions will help you locate each trailhead.

If you're visiting from out of state, from outside of Illinois and Indiana in particular, know that toll roads are a fact of life in these parts. Bring cash with you in case you encounter toll roads en route to your hike—most toll booths take credit cards, but some don't. Also check illinoistollway.com or indianatollroad.org to see if there will be tolls on your trip; you might also invest in an **I-Pass** (getipass.com) or **E-ZPass** (indianatollroad.org/e-zpass). Using the GPS coordinates and a mapping tool such as Google Maps, you can also create your own toll-free alternative routes.

For hikes that are accessible by public transportation, the distance from the closest rail or bus line to the trailhead is usually given. To cover the final stretch to the trailhead, you may consider taking a bicycle along on the train or bus. Most Chicago-area commuter-rail and bus lines now allow passengers to board with bicycles. **Metra** restricts hours for bicycles on board trains, as does Indiana's **South Shore Line,** so be sure to visit metrarail.com or mysouthshoreline.com before your journey. The websites for the **Chicago Transit Authority** (transitchicago.com) and the **Regional Transportation Authority** (rta.org) will connect you with information about Chicagoland's extensive public-transportation system.

Other resources to help you get to the trail car-free include the **Active Transportation Alliance**'s *Chicagoland Bicycle Map* ($8; activetransreg.org/shop), the **Illinois Department of Transportation**'s collection of PDF bike maps (idot.illinois.gov /travel-information/recreation/trails-paths-streets/index), and the **Northwest Indiana Regional Planning Commission**'s *Greenways & Blueways Map* (go to nirpc.org and mouse over the "Transportation" pull-down menu; choose "Non-Motorized" and then "Greenways & Blueways Map").

GPS TRAILHEAD COORDINATES

As noted in "Trail Maps," page 3, I used a handheld GPS unit to obtain geographic data and sent the information to Menasha Ridge's cartographers. The trailhead coordinates, the intersection of latitude (north) and longitude (west), will orient you from the trailhead. In some cases, you can drive within viewing distance of a trailhead. Other hiking routes require a short walk to the trailhead from a parking area.

This book lists GPS coordinates as latitude and longitude, in degree–decimal minute format. As an example specific to this book, the GPS coordinates for Hike 1, Chicago Botanic Garden Hike (page 20), are as follows:

N42° 08.958' W87° 47.342'

The latitude–longitude grid system is likely already familiar to you, but here's a refresher:

Imaginary lines of latitude—called *parallels* and approximately 69 miles apart from each other—run horizontally around the globe. The equator is established to be 0°, and each parallel is indicated by degrees from the equator: up to 90°N at the North Pole, and down to 90°S at the South Pole.

Imaginary lines of longitude—called *meridians*—run perpendicular to latitude lines. Longitude lines are likewise indicated by degrees. Starting from 0° at the Prime Meridian in Greenwich, England, they continue to the east and west until they meet 180° later at the International Date Line in the Pacific Ocean. At the equator, longitude lines are also approximately 69 miles apart, but that distance narrows as the meridians converge toward the North and South Poles.

To convert GPS coordinates given in degrees, minutes, and seconds to the format shown above in degrees and decimal minutes, the seconds are divided by 60. For more on GPS technology, visit usgs.gov.

TOPOGRAPHIC MAPS

The maps in this book have been produced with great care and, used in conjunction with the hike text, will direct you to the trail and help you stay on course. However, you'll find superior detail and valuable information in the U.S. Geological Survey's

7.5-minute-series topographic maps. At **MyTopo.com,** for example, you can view and print free USGS topos of the entire United States. Online services such as **Trails .com** charge annual fees for additional features such as shaded relief, which makes the topography stand out more. If you expect to print out many topo maps each year, it might be worth paying for such extras.

The downside to USGS maps is that most are outdated, having been created 20–30 years ago; nevertheless, they provide excellent topographic detail. Of course, **Google Earth** (earth.google.com) does away with topo maps and their inaccuracies . . . replacing them with satellite imagery and *its* inaccuracies. Regardless, what one lacks, the other augments.

If you're new to hiking, you might be wondering, "What's a topo map?" In short, it indicates not only linear distance but elevation as well, using contour lines. These lines spread across the map like dozens of intricate spiderwebs. Each line represents a particular elevation, and at the base of each topo a contour's interval designation is given. If, for example, the contour interval is 20 feet, then the distance between each contour line is 20 feet. Follow five contour lines up on the same map, and the elevation has increased by 100 feet.

In addition to the sources listed previously and in Appendix B, you'll find topos at major universities, outdoors shops, and some public libraries, as well as online at nationalmap.gov and store.usgs.gov.

Weather

During an average year in Chicago, the mercury slides up and down the full length of the thermometer, spending two weeks above the 90°F mark and nearly the same amount of time below 0°F. While few will want to linger outside during the extremes of local weather, the rest of the year is great for outdoor activities. Extremes aside, summer and winter are full of mild days that provide excellent opportunities for hiking. And for those who like to watch leaves change, flowers bloom, and birds migrate, spring and fall are favorite times for a ramble.

While the seasons provide a bounty of possible weather conditions, there are sometimes major weather variations within the region. The most important factor contributing to local variations is the freshwater sea outside our front door: Lake Michigan absorbs heat more quickly and releases it more slowly than the land. As a result, the phrase "cooler by the lake" habitually rolls off the tongues of our weather forecasters. This phenomenon is most noticeable on summer days when a cool breeze is sweeping the lakeshore, but several blocks away the city feels like a sauna because of the heat-absorbing properties of asphalt.

Lake effect—another way in which Lake Michigan influences local weather patterns—occurs when an air mass absorbs moisture as it passes over the lake and then releases precipitation upon reaching land. Lake effect explains why snow often falls heaviest on the eastern and southern shores of Lake Michigan compared with the western shore.

With all of these variations in Chicagoland weather, the word to remember is *adaptability*. Especially in spring, winter, and fall, consider bringing one or two more layers than you think you'll need. Even on a warm summer day, know that a trip to the lakeshore may require a sweater or a light windbreaker. Adaptability, however, isn't just a question of wearing sandals or snowshoes, hiking shorts or ski pants—it's also an attitude. It means thinking less about how the weather ought to be and thinking more about ways to find pleasure in a variety of conditions.

The following chart lists average temperatures and precipitation by month for the Chicagoland region. For each month, "Hi Temp" is the average daytime high, "Lo Temp" is the average nighttime low, and "Rain or Snow" is the average precipitation in inches.

	January	February	March	April	May	June
HI TEMP	30°F	35°F	46°F	58°F	70°F	79°F
LO TEMP	14°F	19°F	28°F	38°F	59°F	68°F
RAIN or SNOW	1.7"	1.7"	2.5"	3.3"	3.6"	3.4"
	July	August	September	October	November	December
HI TEMP	84°F	81°F	74°F	62°F	47 F	34°F
LO TEMP	63°F	62°F	54°F	42°F	32°F	20°F
RAIN or SNOW	3.7"	4.9"	3.2"	3.2"	3.2"	2.3"
Source: USClimateData.com						

Water

How much is enough? Well, one simple physiological fact should convince you to err on the side of excess when deciding how much water to pack: a hiker walking steadily in 90° heat needs approximately 10 quarts of fluid per day. That's 2.5 gallons. A good rule of thumb is to hydrate prior to your hike, carry (and drink) 6 ounces of water for every mile you plan to hike, and hydrate again after the hike. For most people, the pleasures of hiking make carrying water a relatively minor price to pay to remain safe and healthy. So pack more water than you think you'll need, even for short hikes.

If you find yourself tempted to drink "found" water, in a word, **don't.** Other titles in the 60 Hikes Within 60 Miles series advise that hikers invest in a chemical- or filtration-based water-purification system; unfortunately, the Chicagoland area is simply too developed and too heavily populated for hikers to risk coming in contact with—much less drinking—water from streams or rivers, which could be tainted with not only biological contaminants such as untreated sewage but also chemical pollutants such as agricultural and industrial runoff.

Clothing

Weather, unexpected trail conditions, fatigue, extended hiking duration, and wrong turns can individually or collectively turn a great outing into a very uncomfortable one at best and a life-threatening one at worst. Therefore, the right attire plays a key role in staying comfortable—and sometimes it can be crucial to staying alive. Here are some helpful guidelines:

➤ Choose silk, wool, or synthetics for maximum comfort in all of your hiking attire—from hats to socks and in between. Cotton is fine if the weather remains dry and stable, but it makes for misery in rainy or hot, humid conditions.

➤ Always wear a hat, or at least tuck one into your day pack or hitch it to your belt. Hats offer all-weather sun and wind protection as well as warmth if it turns cold.

➤ Be ready to layer up or down as the day progresses and the mercury rises or falls. Today's outdoor wear makes layering easy, with such designs as jackets that convert to vests and zip-off or button-up legs.

➤ Wear comfortable shoes. Hiking boots or sturdy hiking sandals with toe protection work great, but for most of the hikes in this book, running shoes work just fine. If you're hiking alongside a river or the weather has been wet, boots will do a better job of keeping your feet dry. Flip-flops and other shoes not designed for comfortable walking can turn an enjoyable outing into a joyless slog.

➤ Pair that footwear with good socks. Even if you prefer to let your toes breathe when wearing hiking sandals, tuck some socks into your day pack; you may need them if the weather plummets or if you hit rocky turf. And in a cold-weather emergency, socks can become makeshift mittens in case you left your gloves at home.

➤ Don't leave rainwear behind, even if the day dawns clear and sunny. Tuck into your day pack, or tie around your waist, a jacket that is breathable and either water-resistant or waterproof. Investigate different choices at your local outdoors retailer. If you are a frequent hiker, ideally you'll have more than one rainwear weight, material, and style in your closet to protect you in all seasons in your regional climate and hiking microclimates.

Essential Gear

Today you can buy outdoor vests that have up to 20 pockets shaped and sized to carry everything from toothpicks to binoculars. Or, if you don't aspire to feel like a burro, you can neatly stow all of these items in your day pack or backpack. The following list showcases never-hike-without-them items, in alphabetical order, as all are important:

➤ **Extra clothes:** raingear, wide-brim hat, gloves, and a change of socks and shirt.

➤ **Extra food:** trail mix, granola bars, or other high-energy foods.

➤ **Flashlight or headlamp** with extra bulb and batteries.

➤ **Insect repellent.** For some areas and seasons, this is vital.

➤ **Maps and a high-quality compass.** Even if you know the terrain from previous hikes, don't leave home without these. As previously recommended, bring maps in addition to those in this guidebook, and consult those maps before you hike. If you're GPS-savvy, bring that device too, but don't rely on it as your sole navigational tool—battery life is limited, after all—and be sure to compare its guidance with that of your maps.

➤ **Pocketknife and/or multitool.**

➤ **Sunscreen.** (Note the expiration date on the tube or bottle; it's usually embossed on the top.)

➤ **Water.** As emphasized more than once in this book, you should bring more than you think you'll drink.

➤ **Whistle.** This little gadget could be your best friend in an emergency.

➤ **Windproof matches and/or a lighter,** as well as a fire starter.

First Aid Kit

In addition to the aforementioned items, the ones below may seem like overkill for a day hike. But any paramedic will tell you that these products—listed in alphabetical order, because all are important—are just the basics. The reality of hiking is that you can be out for a week of backpacking and acquire only a mosquito bite. Or you can hike for an hour, slip, and suffer a cut, scrape, or broken bone. Fortunately, these listed items will collapse into a very small space. Convenient prepackaged kits are also available at your pharmacy or online.

➤ **Adhesive bandages**

➤ **Antibiotic ointment** (Neosporin or the generic equivalent)

➤ **Athletic tape**

➤ **Blister kit** (such as Moleskin or Spenco 2nd Skin)

➤ **Butterfly-closure bandages**

➤ **Diphenhydramine** (Benadryl or generic), in case of allergic reactions

➤ **Elastic bandages** or joint wraps

➤ **Epinephrine** in a prefilled syringe (EpiPen), typically available by prescription only, for people known to have severe allergic reactions to hiking mishaps such as bee stings

➤ **Gauze** (one roll and a half-dozen 4-by-4-inch pads)

➤ **Hydrogen peroxide** or iodine

➤ **Ibuprofen** (Advil) **or acetaminophen** (Tylenol)

Note: Consider your intended terrain and the number of hikers in your party before you exclude any article cited above. A botanical-garden stroll may not inspire you to carry a complete kit, but anything beyond that warrants precaution. When hiking alone, you should always be prepared for a medical need. And if you're a two-some or with a group, one or more people in your party should be equipped with first aid material.

General Safety

The following tips may have the familiar ring of your mom's voice as you take note of them.

➤ **Let someone know where you'll be hiking and how long you expect to be gone.** Give that person a copy of your route, particularly if you're headed into an isolated area. Let him or her know when you return.

➤ **Sign in and out of any trail registers provided.** Don't hesitate to comment on the trail condition if space is provided; that's your opportunity to alert others to any problems you encounter.

➤ **Don't count on a cell phone for your safety.** Reception may be spotty or nonexistent on the trail, even on an urban walk—especially one embraced by towering trees.

➤ **Always carry food and water, even for a short hike.** And bring more water than you think you will need. (We can't emphasize this enough.)

➤ **Ask questions.** State forest and park employees are on hand to help.

➤ **Stay on designated trails.** Even on the most clearly marked trails, you usually reach a point where you have to stop and consider in which direction to head. If you become disoriented, don't panic. As soon as you think you may be off-track, stop, assess your current direction, and then retrace your steps to the point where you went astray. Using a map, a compass, and this book, and keeping in mind what you have passed thus far, reorient yourself and trust your judgment on which way to continue. If you become absolutely unsure of how to continue, return to your vehicle the way you came in. Should you become completely lost and have no idea how to find the trailhead, remaining in place along the trail and waiting for help is most often the best option for adults and always the best option for children.

➤ **Always carry a whistle,** another precaution that we can't overemphasize. It may be a lifesaver if you get lost or hurt.

➤ **Be especially careful when crossing streams,** especially after monsoon rains. Whether you're fording the stream or crossing on a log, make every step count. If you're unsure that you can maintain your balance on a log, ford the stream instead: use a trekking pole or stout stick for balance, and *face upstream as you cross.* If a stream seems too deep to ford, don't chance it—whatever is on the other side isn't worth the risk.

➤ **Be careful at overlooks.** While these areas may provide spectacular views, they're potentially hazardous. Stay back from the edge of outcrops, and make absolutely sure of your footing; a misstep could mean a nasty or possibly fatal fall.

➤ **Standing dead trees and storm-damaged living trees pose a significant hazard to hikers.** These trees may have loose or broken limbs that could fall at any time. While walking beneath trees, and when choosing a spot to rest or enjoy your snack, *look up.*

➤ **Know the symptoms of subnormal body temperature, or hypothermia.** Shivering and forgetfulness are the two most common indicators of this stealthy killer. Hypothermia can occur at any elevation, even in the summer, especially when the hiker is wearing lightweight cotton clothing. If symptoms develop, seek shelter, hot liquids, and dry clothes as soon as possible.

➤ **Likewise, know the symptoms of heat exhaustion, or hyperthermia.** Lightheadedness and weakness are the first two indicators. If you feel these symptoms, find some shade, drink some water, remove as many layers of clothing as practical, and stay put until you cool down. Marching through heat exhaustion leads to heatstroke—which can be fatal. If you should be sweating and you're not, that's the signature warning sign. Your hike is over at that point—heatstroke is a life-threatening condition that can cause seizures, convulsions, and eventually death. If you or a hiking partner is experiencing heatstroke, do whatever you can to get cool and find help.

In summary: Plan ahead. Watch your step. Avoid accidents before they happen.

WATCHWORDS FOR FLORA AND FAUNA

Hikers should be aware of the following concerns regarding plants and wildlife, described in alphabetical order.

MOSQUITOES While it happens only rarely, individuals can become infected with the West Nile virus by being bitten by an infected mosquito. Culex mosquitoes, the primary species that can transmit West Nile virus to humans, thrive in urban rather than natural areas. They lay their eggs in stagnant water and can breed in any standing water that remains for more than five days. Most people infected with West Nile virus have no symptoms of illness, but some may become ill, usually 3–15 days after being bitten.

In the Chicago area, August and September are likely to be the highest-risk periods for West Nile. At this time of year and anytime you expect mosquitoes to be buzzing around, you may want to wear protective clothing such as long sleeves, long pants, and socks. Loose-fitting, light-colored clothing is best. Spray clothing with insect repellent. Remember to follow the instructions on the repellent carefully, and take extra care with children.

POISON IVY, OAK, AND SUMAC Recognizing and avoiding poison ivy, oak, and sumac are the most effective ways to prevent the painful, itchy rashes associated with these plants. Poison ivy (*top right*) occurs as a vine or ground cover, 3 leaflets to a leaf; poison oak (*center right*) occurs as either a vine or shrub, also with 3 leaflets; and poison sumac (*bottom right*) flourishes in swampland, each leaf having 7–13 leaflets. Urushiol, the oil in the sap of these plants, is responsible for the rash. Within 14 hours of exposure, raised lines and/or blisters will appear on the affected area, accompanied by a terrible itch. Try to refrain from scratching, as bacteria under your fingernails could cause an infection. Wash and dry the affected area thoroughly, applying a calamine lotion to help dry out the rash. If itching or blistering is severe, seek medical attention.

Photo: Tom Watson

Photo: Jane Huber

If you knowingly touch the plant, you have a window of about 15–20 minutes to remove the oil before it causes a reaction. Rinsing it off with cool water is impractical on the trail, but commercial products such as Tecnu are effective at removing urushiol from your skin. To keep from spreading the misery to someone else, wash not only any exposed parts of your body but also any oil-contaminated clothes, hiking gear, or pets.

Photo: Kevin Hansen

13

Photo: Jane Huber

SNAKES If you spend any time hiking in Chicagoland, you may be surprised by the variety of snakes that inhabit the area. Most encounters will be with garter snakes, water snakes, brown snakes, and perhaps an Eastern hognose snake (which, while not venomous, can be intimidating as it hisses and puts on a cobralike display). The only venomous snake found in the Chicago region is the massasauga rattlesnake; fortunately, sightings of this small rattler are extremely rare. The best rule is to leave all snakes alone, give them a wide berth as you hike past, and make sure any hiking companions (including dogs) do the same.

TICKS These arachnids are often found on brush and tall grass, where they seem to be waiting to hitch a ride on a warm-blooded passerby. While adult ticks are most active April–May and again October–November, you should be on the lookout for them throughout spring, summer, and fall.

Among the local varieties of ticks, deer ticks and dog ticks are the ones that can transmit diseases; both need several hours of attachment before they can do that. The deer, or black-legged, tick, the primary carrier of Lyme disease, is very small, sometimes the size of a poppy seed.

You can use several strategies to reduce your chances of ticks getting under your skin. Some people choose to wear light-colored clothing so they can spot ticks before they migrate to your skin. An insect repellent containing DEET or picaridin (20%–30%) is an effective deterrent.

If it's prime tick season, you may want to perform a quick visual check every hour or so during your hike. When I wear shorts, for example, I often find ticks hiding under the top edge of my socks (ticks need some type of backstop to start drilling into the skin). In any case, be sure to check your hair, back of neck, armpits, and socks after your hike, and take a moment to do a more complete body check during your posthike shower.

Use tweezers to remove ticks that are already embedded: grasp the tick close to your skin, and remove it by pulling straight out firmly. Do your best to remove the head, but don't twist. Apply disinfectant solution to the wound.

Hunting

In fall and winter, be mindful that a few parks in the area may be closed for hunting, while others may provide restricted access and still others allow hikers and hunters to coexist. During hunting season, it's never a bad idea to call the park to ask about access and safety precautions.

Trail Etiquette

Always treat the trail, wildlife, and fellow hikers with respect. Here are some reminders.

- ➤ **Plan ahead in order to be self-sufficient at all times**. For example, carry necessary supplies for changes in weather or other conditions.

- ➤ **Hike on open trails only.**

- ➤ **In seasons or areas** where road or trail closures may be a possibility, use the websites or phone numbers in the "Contacts" line for each of this guidebook's hikes to check conditions before you head out. And don't attempt to circumvent such closures.

- ➤ **Avoid trespassing on private land,** and obtain all permits and authorization as required. Also, leave gates as you found them or as directed by signage.

- ➤ **Be courteous to other hikers,** bikers, equestrians, and others you encounter on the trails.

- ➤ **Never spook wild animals or pets.** An unannounced approach, a sudden movement, or a loud noise startles most critters, and a surprised animal can be dangerous to you, to others, and to itself. Give animals plenty of space.

- ➤ **Observe any YIELD signs you see on the trail.** Typically they advise bikers to yield to hikers. Per common courtesy on hills, both hikers and bikers yield to any uphill traffic.

- ➤ **Stay on the existing trail,** and don't blaze any new trails.

- ➤ **Pack out what you pack in,** leaving only your footprints. Nobody likes to see the trash someone else has left behind.

Tips on Enjoying Hiking in the Chicago Area

Before you hike at a state park, national park, or county forest preserve, visit its corresponding website to help yourself get oriented to its roads, features, and attractions. General and detailed park maps are often available online or, if you're visiting a state park, at the park office. It's never a bad to call a park ahead of you visit, just to make sure that its trails aren't temporarily closed or restricted because of erosion, repairs, or hunting season.

In addition, the following tips will help make your hike more enjoyable and more rewarding:

➤ **Chicago is notorious for its frigid winters,** but its summers are occasionally brutally hot. If you don't want to miss out on a hike because of the heat, go early in the morning. Temperatures on the trail can be 10–20 degrees lower at dawn than they'll be later in the day, and there's no better way to start your hike than listening to the cheerful singing of birds.

➤ **Take your time on the trail.** Pace yourself. The Chicago region is filled with wonders both big and small. Don't rush past a bluebird to get to the lakeshore. Stop and smell the wildflowers. Peer into a clear creek for minnows. Don't miss the trees for the forest. Allow yourself plenty of time for those moments when you simply feel like stopping and taking it all in.

➤ **Consider hiking during the week** and avoiding busy seasons, if possible. Trails that are packed in the spring and fall are often clear during the hotter or colder months. If you're hiking on a busy day, go early in the morning; it'll enhance your chances of seeing wildlife. And, of course, trails really clear out on rainy days (but don't hike during a thunderstorm).

➤ **Investigate different areas around the region.** The scenery you'll find hiking through grasslands is pleasantly different from the riparian forest alongside the Des Plaines and Fox Rivers. Sample a few of each to see what the area has to offer and what most appeals to you.

➤ **Hike during different seasons.** Trails change dramatically from spring to winter and can transform themselves into something you might not even recognize. If you found a trail you particularly liked—or didn't—try it in a different season.

➤ **No one is too young for a hike in the outdoors.** Flat, short, and shaded trails are best for infants. Toddlers who haven't quite mastered walking can still tag along, riding on an adult's back in a child carrier. Use common sense to judge a child's capacity to hike a particular trail and always expect that the child will tire quickly and need to be carried. Kids dehydrate quickly, so make sure you have plenty of fluid for everyone. Hikes suitable for children are listed in "60 Hikes by Category" (pages xvi–xvii).

➤ **Think about safety when hiking in Chicagoland.** While crime is extremely rare in our parks and preserves, it doesn't hurt to call ahead or research online if you're wondering how safe a particular place is. If you're still unsure, choose a destination where you'll have plenty of company versus a secluded park or preserve, and hike with a friend or a group rather than going solo.

OPPOSITE: A sandy path at Indiana Dunes State Park (see Hike 44, page 212)   *Photo: Dorothy Weatherly*

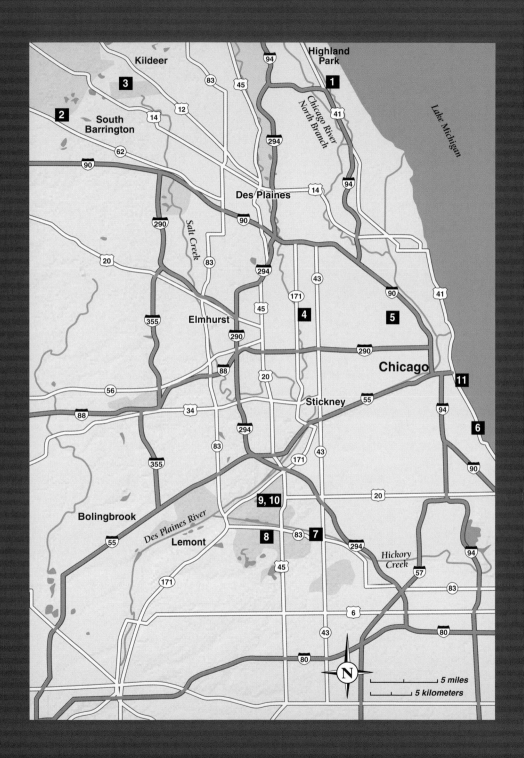

Kildeer

94

Highland
Park

3

83

45

1

2

South
Barrington

14

12

41

62

90

294

*Chicago River
North Branch*

14

94

Des Plaines

Salt Creek

290

90

20

83

294

355

43

171

90

41

45

4

5

Elmhurst

290

88

Chicago

11

20

56

Stickney

55

88

34

94

294

6

83

43

90

171

43

20

9, 10

Bolingbrook

Des Plaines River

8

83

7

294

*Hickory
Creek*

55

Lemont

45

57

83

171

6

94

43

80

80

N

5 miles

5 kilometers

COOK COUNTY

Attractive bridges connect the islands that make up the Chicago Botanic Garden. *Photo: Tim Putala*

IF YOU LOVE to see carefully selected flowers, trees, and bushes growing in perfectly landscaped environments, the Chicago Botanic Garden is a slice of heaven. While the interior gardens are admittedly the main attraction here, many visitors miss the additional gardens, the prairie and woodland, and the striking views that accompany a walk along the outer perimeter of the garden, highlighted on this hike.

DESCRIPTION

Among the Botanic Garden's 305 acres of artfully landscaped grounds are 23 distinct gardens, including Japanese- and English-style gardens, rose and bulb gardens, fruit and vegetable gardens, and gardens specially designed for children and wheelchair users. Along with this excess of gardens, there are attractive bridges, statues, fountains, and plenty of scenic spots situated among the nine islands and the surrounding shoreline. Owned by the Cook County Forest Preserve District and managed by the Chicago Horticultural Society, the gardens are just part of what goes on here. The Botanic Garden has programs in education and research and offers a number of special events and services, such as classes, plant sales, opportunities to consult master gardeners, concerts, and speakers.

DISTANCE & CONFIGURATION: 2.7 miles, large loop plus a few short loops

DIFFICULTY: Easy

SCENERY: Islands, prairie, oak woodland, marsh, and acres of pristine gardens of every stripe

EXPOSURE: Mostly exposed

TRAIL TRAFFIC: Most of this hike will be busy during the warmer months.

TRAIL SURFACE: Pavement, gravel, wood chips

HIKING TIME: 1 hour

DRIVING DISTANCE: 24 miles from Millennium Park

ACCESS: Daily, 7 a.m.–9 p.m., June 3–September 4; hours scaled back slightly the rest of the year. Garden admission is free, but parking costs $25/car on weekdays and $30/car on weekends. See page 24 for public-transportation alternatives to the hefty parking fee.

MAPS: Pick up a map at the visitor center or print one out at chicagobotanic.org/visit/map; USGS *Highland Park, IL*

FACILITIES: Visitor center, café, restrooms, gift shop, library, ATM, and wheelchair rentals, among others. A tram tour follows much of the route of this hike.

WHEELCHAIR ACCESS: Most of the hike is accessible; the parts that aren't—Mary Mix McDonald Woods, Evening Island, and Marsh Island—are easily skipped.

CONTACT: 847-835-5440, chicagobotanic.org

LOCATION: 1000 Lake Cook Road, Glencoe, IL 60022

COMMENTS: Pets prohibited but service animals welcome. Two different tram tours run seasonally. Tickets and information are available at the booth outside of the visitor center.

From the visitor center, start the hike by heading straight (west) across the North Lawn to the service road leading over the lake at the far end of the garden. On the other side of the bridge, pine trees grow on the left and buckeye trees grow on the right. Take the service road to the left (south). A smidgen ahead, hop on the path at the right that runs parallel to the road. In the lake is Spider Island, thick with alders, birch, and serviceberry trees. On the right, the Skokie River runs along the bottom of a shallow ravine; also on the right are a brick wall and 1,600 tree plantings intended to block noise and pollution from I-94. Extending from Spider Island to the serpentine-shaped bridge that leads to Evening Island is the Sensory Garden, which hosts plants and trees that produce an array of colors, sounds, fragrances, and textures.

Just ahead on the left, take the gravel trail to Evening Island. In gardening circles, the design of this 5-acre island is called the New American garden style and is inspired by landscapes such as the meadow and the Midwestern prairie. As you climb the hill in the center of the island, watch how the placement of trees nicely frames the views of the nearby shoreline and prairie. Near the top of the hill, a circle of large stones provides a great place to relax. The square metal tower, or carillon, contains 48 bronze bells that weigh between 24 pounds and 2.5 tons (check in at the visitor center for information on regular carillon concerts). The bridges on the north side of the island provide a connection with the main gardens and complete the outline of a section of the lake called the Great Basin.

Back on the outer path, pass a few burr-oak trees and several purple-martin houses attached to poles as you head into the 15-acre prairie. Entering the prairie,

Chicago Botanic Garden Hike

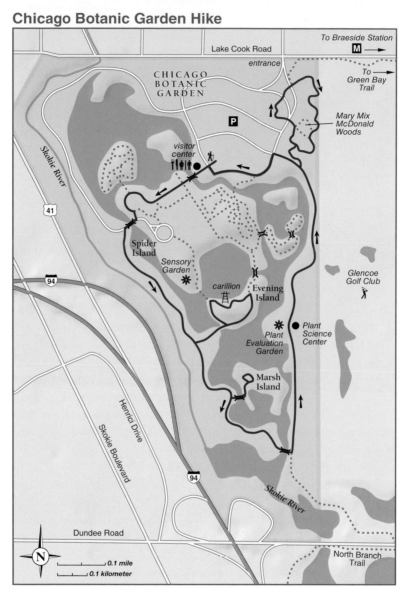

take the gravel trail left (east), and stay left at the next couple of junctions before crossing a bridge for a quick tour of Marsh Island. Botanic Garden staff maintains that Marsh Island (actually a wet prairie) is the best location on the grounds for spotting water birds and songbirds. Coming off Marsh Island, stay left (south) as you pass a section of hilly prairie on the right—the dry, rocky soil is the reason that the grass is shorter at the top of the hill compared to the sides and bottom. After the small hills, take your pick of following the paved road, the dirt path, or the paved path, all of which lead to the bridge. On the way to the bridge, you'll pass compass plants (tall yellow flowers) and more burr oaks.

The bridge divides the Botanic Garden lake on the left and the Skokie River on the right. On the other side of the bridge, turn left (north) on the paved road and pass the plant-production area, which grows 420,000 plants annually. Next on the right is the Shade Evaluation Garden, followed by the new Plant Science Center, which is topped off with roof gardens that you can tour. On the left are the Sun Evaluation Garden and a footbridge that will take you back out to Evening Island. After you pass a stand of downy hawthorn trees next to the road, three more islands come into view, each carefully landscaped and pruned in traditional Japanese styles. A low zigzag bridge connects the first and second islands. Off in the distance, between the second and third islands, a waterfall tumbles some 45 feet over granite boulders. The inaccessible third island contains smaller trees that are intended to present the optical illusion that the island is far off in the distance.

Finish the hike with a brief stroll through the Mary Mix McDonald Woods, the only location at the Botanic Garden where the soil is undisturbed. Enter the oak woodland on the right (north) before the road curves to the left. Stay to the left on the path as you pass over a series of footbridges spanning intermittent streams and several boardwalks. Along this path, a steady progression of signs identifies plants and animals of the area and describes the basic concepts of woodland restoration in northeastern Illinois; because this trail crosses the park road, watch for traffic, especially on weekends. In a number of spots, you'll see that the Botanic Garden is engaged in a serious fencing campaign to keep deer out of the area.

When finished with the hike through the McDonald Woods, continue ahead (northwest) along the paved road to the parking lots ahead. Or if you wish to return to the visitor center or explore more of the interior gardens, take the service road left (south) to the visitor center.

NEARBY ACTIVITIES

At the southern edge of the Chicago Botanic Garden, visitors can connect with the recently extended 33.5-mile **North Branch Trail.** One of the great urban pathways of Chicagoland, the North Branch Trail runs along the North Branch of the Chicago River south from the Botanic Garden all the way to West Foster Avenue and North Pulaski Road. The forest preserve recently launched a bike-sharing system with bikes available at the Botanic Garden and south along the North Branch Trail at Tower Road, Old Orchard Road, and Devon Avenue. Just to the south of the Botanic Garden along the North Branch Trail are the **Skokie Lagoons,** a great place to walk, run, bike, and paddle. For an interactive map of the route, go to map.fpdcc.com and type "North Branch Trail" in the search box to the left.

Another nearby opportunity for walking and bicycling is the **Green Bay Trail/ Robert McClory Bike Path,** which runs 36 miles from Kenilworth in Cook County north to Wisconsin. From the Botanic Garden, take the new trail that runs east along Lake Cook Road for 0.7 mile to reach the Green Bay Trail.

• •

GPS TRAILHEAD COORDINATES N42° 08.958' W87° 47.342'

DIRECTIONS From the northern intersection of I-90 and I-94, drive 13 miles north on I-94 West. Continue forward to take Exit 29 for US 41 North/Waukegan. Drive 0.7 mile; then take the exit for Lake Cook Road. Turn right (east) onto Lake Cook Road, and drive 0.6 mile. Turn right into the entrance of the Botanic Garden, and follow the signs to the parking areas.

PUBLIC TRANSPORTATION Save yourself the steep parking fee and take **Metra** instead. The Union Pacific/North Line stops within a mile of the Botanic Garden. From the Brae-side Station, head west for 0.7 mile on the newly built trail along Lake Cook Road to the garden entrance. On Sundays during the warmer months, take Metra to the Glencoe Station and then take the Garden Trolley to the Botanic Garden (for trains arriving and departing 9:30 a.m.–5 p.m. at the Glencoe Station).

BICYCLE Three long multiuse trails run into or near the Botanic Garden. To the east is **Green Bay Trail,** to the west is the southern terminus of the **Skokie Valley Bikeway,** and coming from the south is the ever-popular **North Branch Trail,** which brings you right into the garden's grounds. See the Active Transportation Alliance's *Chicagoland Bicycle Map* ($8; activetransreg.org/shop) for more information about connecting to these trails.

A turtle quartet strikes a pose.   *Photo: Jim Miner*

SITUATED AMONG THE rolling hills of far northwest Cook County, Crabtree Nature Center is a place that invites you to linger while admiring wild-flowers, spotting waterfowl, and relishing the rapid shifts from prairie to woodland to wetland.

DESCRIPTION

The Cook County Forest Preserve District added an attractive parcel to its holdings in the mid-1960s when it bought a country estate and adjoining farmlands and transformed these into the Crabtree Nature Center. Over the years, the county restored the prairie and the scattered plots of woodland that once adorned this 1,100-acre plot. This hike takes place in the western side of the preserve, notable for its varied landscape: prairie, savanna, woodland, ponds, marshes, and a lake are all packed into a small area. Another attraction here is the exhibit building, which offers a collection of handmade displays, as well as some live-animal exhibits.

From the parking lot, follow the paved path to the back of the nature center. At the trail board, stay to the right (northeast) as the trail skirts the edge of Sulky Pond

DISTANCE & CONFIGURATION: 2.5 miles, 2 connected loops

DIFFICULTY: Easy

SCENERY: Ponds, marshes, lake, woodland, prairie, and plenty of birdlife

EXPOSURE: The prairie is exposed, while the rest of the hike is mostly shaded.

TRAIL TRAFFIC: Minimal

TRAIL SURFACE: Wood chips, dirt, mowed grass

HIKING TIME: 1.5 hours

DRIVING DISTANCE: 34 miles from Millennium Park

ACCESS: 8 a.m.–5 p.m., March–October; 8 a.m.–4 p.m., November–February; open daily

except Friday, Thanksgiving Day, Christmas Day, and New Years' Day; no fees or permits

MAPS: Available at exhibit building; USGS *Streamwood, IL*

FACILITIES: Exhibit building, restrooms, water

WHEELCHAIR ACCESS: None

CONTACT: 847-381-6592, fpdcc.com/nature-centers/crabtree-nature-center

LOCATION: 3 Stover Road, Barrington Hills, IL 60010

COMMENTS: Dogs are prohibited at Crabtree, as is picnicking. The exhibit building is open daily, 9 a.m.–5 p.m., March–October, and 9 a.m.–4 p.m., November–February; closed Fridays year-round.

(formerly a sulky track sunken in the ground). The oaks hanging out over the water, the lightly wooded island, and the geese and ducks make this pond an enjoyable spot.

Continue the hike by turning right (northeast) on the Phantom Prairie Trail. An amusing sign at the beginning of this trail stirs some interest with a warning that this prairie is "not for the meek" because of the harsh winter wind and a lack of shade during the summer. Initially, this trail runs between a woodland on the left and a vast cattail marsh dotted with black willows on the right. Then it winds through a grassy scrubland with goldenrod, staghorn sumac, and cherry trees before crossing an intermittent stream and finally emerging in a rolling tallgrass prairie. After brushing against stands of maple and white oak, the trail runs through an area rife with rattlesnake master, a member of the parsley family (round heads dense with little flowers), which at one time was thought to cure rattlesnake bites.

Keep watch at the edges of the prairie for raptors—either perched or soaring. Higher up, you're likely to see (and occasionally hear) a progression of airplanes on the flight path to O'Hare Airport. After passing several small sections of wet prairie, look for honey locust trees on the right. These trees are unmistakable due to their clusters of thorns—up to 8 inches long—growing from the bark. Turn right (west) when you reach the Burr Edge Trail.

On the Burr Edge Trail, you'll start to make your way around Bulrush Pond, which is fringed with pasture rose and walnut and hickory trees wrapped in vines, and enormous weeping willows. Along with plenty of waterfowl, the pond is home to muskrats, kingfishers, and, according to park staff, a 40-pound snapping turtle.

Several silver maples border the trail on the way to a grassy area interrupted with stands of black willow and walnut. After catching a few more fleeting views of the pond through stands of willows, you'll see clusters of cattails, and box elder trees.

Crabtree Nature Center Hike

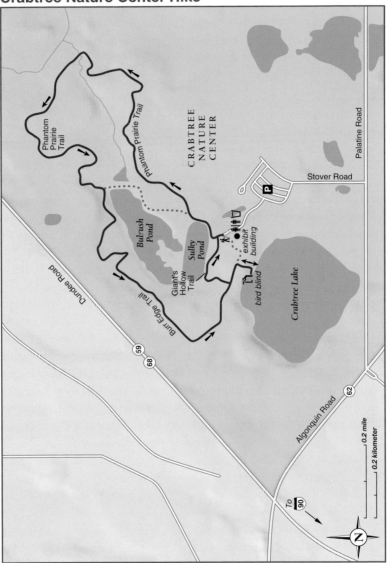

Leaving the pond, the trail enters a prairie dominated with big bluestem grass and prairie dock and dotted with quaking aspen. From the prairie, the trail runs alongside a split-rail fence through a woodland with specimens of maple, pine, shagbark hickory, and burr oak. For now, continue past the Giants Hollow Trail on the left while you pay a visit to the bird blind on Crabtree Lake (a short stroll ahead—turn right [south]). Inside the little blind, handy hand-painted signs identify the lake's ducks and geese in flight and at rest. After visiting the lake, turn back around and head back to the Giants Hollow Trail. Turn right (north) on the Giants Hollow Trail, and you'll return to Sulky Pond and then pass through a savanna with sprawling oaks on your way back to the exhibit building.

NEARBY ACTIVITIES

To the west of Crabtree Nature Center are a couple of hiking opportunities within other Cook County forest preserves. A few miles south of Crabtree and south of I-90, **Poplar Creek Forest Preserve** offers a large expanse of woods, prairies, savannas, and wetlands. From the parking lot at Poplar Creek, follow the trail to the lake and along the top of the dike. After the dike, keep straight ahead until you reach a major trail junction. Hanging a right at the junction takes you on a longer hike through mostly grassland and eventually back to the park road. Heading to the left takes you on a shorter hike through woodland and marsh and back to the lake. From Crabtree, take a right on East Palatine Road, which soon turns into IL 62, and turn left on New Sutton Road (IL 59). Follow New Sutton Road until you reach Shoe Factory Road Prairie parking lot, 0.6 mile south of Shoe Factory Road, on the right.

Northwest of Crabtree, trails can also be found among the lakes, grasslands, woods, and marshes at **Spring Creek Valley Forest Preserve.** In the southern section of the preserve, 2.4 miles of established trails are accessible from the Beverly Lake Parking Area. Starting from the shore of Beverly Lake, the loop begins after a half mile of hiking. Follow the entire loop, or shorten the hike via connector trails. Bring a smartphone or GPS unit, because these trails can be confusing. To reach Beverly Lake, follow the directions to Poplar Creek Forest Preserve (see previous paragraph). As you're heading south on New Sutton Road and before crossing I-90, turn right on West Higgins Road/ IL 72. The parking area is 2.1 miles ahead on the right.

· ·

GPS TRAILHEAD COORDINATES N42° 06.867' W88° 09.696'

DIRECTIONS From the intersection of I-90 and I-290, head west on I-90 for 11 miles. Exit north (right) on Barrington Road, drive 3 miles, and then turn left onto West Palatine Road. Follow Palatine Road for 1 mile before turning right on Stover Road, following the signs for Crabtree Nature Center. Take Stover Road for 0.3 mile before reaching the parking area. From the parking lot, look for signs to the exhibit building.

Thickly forested Deer Grove affords hikers plenty of solitude.   *Photo: Elizabeth Vera*

THE ROLLING LANDSCAPE at Deer Grove is blanketed with thick groves of oak, hickory, and maple. Mixed in with the dense forest are ravines, marshes, ponds, and the occasional stream straddled by picturesque old limestone bridges.

DESCRIPTION

In 1916, Cook County started acquiring land to create one of the nation's first networks of county forest preserves. The county's first parcel—500 acres that is now part of Deer Grove—was prized for its wooded ravines, winding streams, and countless marshes and ponds. Over the years, as the size of Deer Grove nearly quadrupled, the preserve was split into two sections. The west section of the preserve, the destination for this hike, encompasses a larger, more heavily forested area, while the east section offers more open space and fewer trails (for more about the east section, see Nearby Activities, page 31).

DISTANCE & CONFIGURATION: 5.6-mile loop

DIFFICULTY: Easy

SCENERY: Rolling woodland, ravines, streams, and wetland

EXPOSURE: Shaded

TRAIL TRAFFIC: Minimal but generally busier on weekends

TRAIL SURFACE: Old pavement, dirt, some gravel

HIKING TIME: 2 hours

DRIVING DISTANCE: 29 miles from Millennium Park

ACCESS: Daily, 6:30 a.m.–sunset; no fees or permits

MAPS: Forest Preserves of Cook County offers a map on its website: fpdcc.com/preserves-and -trails/maps; USGS *Lake Zurich, IL*

FACILITIES: Picnic areas; restrooms in the preserve's eastern section across Quentin Road

WHEELCHAIR ACCESS: None

CONTACT: 800-870-3666, fpdcc.com/deer-grove

LOCATION: Palatine, IL 60067

COMMENTS: Dogs must be leashed. If you're visiting after a rain, plan on getting some mud on your shoes. During summer, bring mosquito repellent. In winter, Deer Grove is popular with cross-country skiers.

While Deer Grove claims some of the best hiking in Cook County, the charm of this place has not always been guaranteed. In recent years, sections of the preserve have been plagued by illegal bicycle trails crisscrossing the forest and eroding hillsides.

Start the hike on the Orange Trail, which follows an old, crumbling, narrow paved road. At 0.2 mile, turn right (northwest) on the Purple Trail, and then quickly turn left (west) on the Yellow Trail. While hiking, keep an eye peeled for buckthorn, an invasive shrub that has been the source of many headaches for the volunteers and county employees who maintain Deer Grove and other natural areas in the region. Since it was imported from Europe in the early 20th century for use on the lawns of lakefront mansions, buckthorn has spread widely throughout Chicagoland. Requiring constant vigilance to keep it under control, buckthorn grows quickly to a height of 20 feet, taking over wooded areas while blocking sunlight for all underlying plants (the oval-shaped leaves are 1–2.5 inches long with fine, wavy-toothed edges).

As you approach a large marshy pond on the right, the trail crosses a bridge spanning a small ravine. At just over 2 miles into the hike, turn left (north) on the Orange Trail, a former park road. As this paved trail dips and rises, you'll pass a parking area on the right. At 2.6 miles into the hike, turn right (southeast) on the Black Trail. This wide and fairly flat trail runs through a pleasant oak forest before meeting up again with the Yellow Trail. After turning left (east) on the Yellow Trail, you'll descend a gradual hill, and then cross a park road and pass a parking area on the left. On the other side of the park road, the trail accompanies a paved bicycle trail for a bit and crosses a stream. Stay on the Yellow Trail as the paved path cuts right and crosses Quentin Road, providing access to the east section of Deer Grove.

As the trail arcs toward Lake Cook Road, the woods are dense and the landscape remains flat; if rain has fallen recently, get ready to encounter some mud. To return

Deer Grove Loop

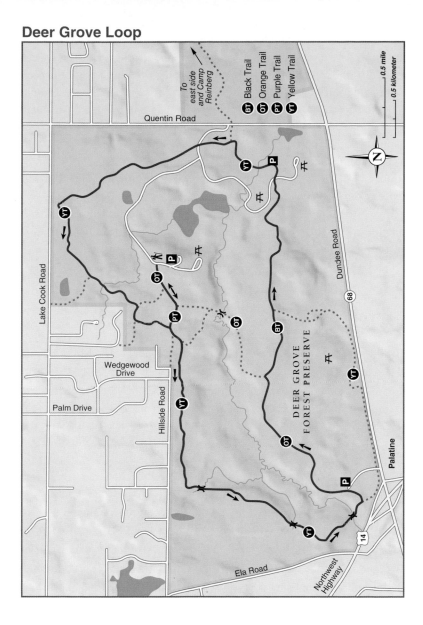

to the parking lot, turn left (east) on the Purple Trail and then turn left (northeast) again on the Orange Trail.

NEARBY ACTIVITIES

On the other side of Quentin Road, the east section of Deer Grove contains wooded areas, marshes, and an ample amount of gently rolling open space, as well as restrooms and water. This section contains recently restored wetlands and prairie, including 23 wetlands restored by disabling drain tiles that drained former farm fields. There are a few miles of dirt trails and a 2.5-mile loop of smooth pavement. Park at the picnic area 1 mile east of Quentin Road on Dundee Road or at the Camp Reinberg lot on the east side of Quentin Road, just south of the main entrance for the west side of Deer Grove. You can also walk across Quentin Road on the paved connector trail that accompanies this hike near the main entrance.

Camp Reinberg is one of the newer campgrounds opened in recent years in Cook County. Options are available for tent and RV camping, and there are cabins of varying sizes. The facility also offers gear rental, beginner camping classes, and family programs. For people in the northern suburbs without time to travel to more-far-flung spots, Camp Reinberg offers an enticing option for introducing their families and friends to the outdoors.

• •

GPS TRAILHEAD COORDINATES N42° 08.854' W88° 04.450'

DIRECTIONS From the intersection of I-90 and I-290, follow I-90 west for 2.2 miles. Exit at Roselle Road, and take a right (north), following Roselle Road for 3.2 miles. Turn right on West Palatine Road, and continue 0.8 mile. Turn left on North Quentin Road, and continue for 2.3 miles until you see the entrance to the preserve on the left. Follow the forest-preserve road for 0.2 mile until you come to the first right. Follow this unnamed road for 0.6 mile, and then park at the first parking spaces you see on the right, next to the map board.

PUBLIC TRANSPORTATION The Palatine **Metra** station on the Union Pacific/Northwest Line is less than 2 miles from Deer Grove, and you can follow a paved trail for much of the distance. From the station, head north on North Smith Street. Two blocks after crossing North Northwest Highway, take the Palatine Trail left and follow it for 1.4 miles to the junction of Dundee and Quentin Roads. Catch the Black Trail at the northwest corner of this intersection. Follow the Black Trail to the Yellow Trail, and turn right on the Yellow Trail to start the hike.

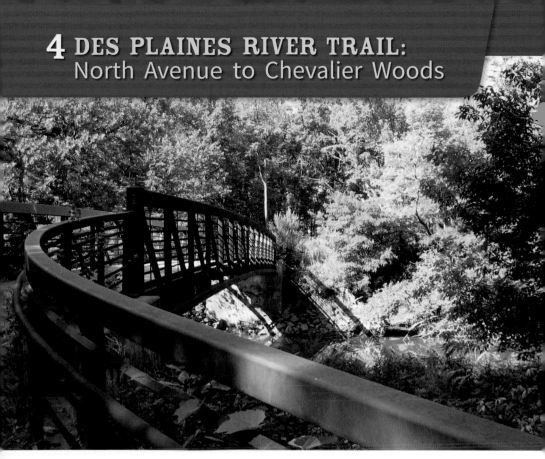

A picturesque footbridge over the Des Plaines River   *Photo: Ted Villaire*

NEARLY EVERY STEP of this trail closely traces the tree-covered banks of the Des Plaines River while wending its way north through a series of forest preserves in Cook County. As you follow a small bluff, you're treated to nearly continuous views of the river as it flows through bottomland woods sprinkled with big specimens of maple, cottonwood, and oak.

DESCRIPTION

Trails and rivers go with one another like peanut butter and chocolate. Walking alongside a slender body of water winding through the landscape encourages the mind to pleasantly wander. Despite its built-up surroundings and its sometimes-noisy atmosphere, the Des Plaines River is no exception when it comes to the palliative power of a river.

As with most riverside hikes, you should expect some mud on your shoes afterwards. At worst, brief sections of the trail will be under water—particularly if heavy rain has recently fallen. At best, puddles occur here and there, as do small patches of mud. While the mud certainly annoys, on the positive side, it probably keeps the

33

DISTANCE & CONFIGURATION: 11.4-mile out-and-back

DIFFICULTY: Moderate–strenuous

SCENERY: River, bottomland woods, marshland

EXPOSURE: Mostly shaded

TRAIL TRAFFIC: Somewhat busy

TRAIL SURFACE: Dirt, perhaps some mud

HIKING TIME: 4–5 hours

DRIVING DISTANCE: 20 miles from Millennium Park

ACCESS: Daily, sunrise–sunset; no fees or permits

MAPS: Forest Preserves of Cook County offers a map on its website: fpdcc.com/preserves -and-trails; USGS *River Forest, IL*

FACILITIES: Restrooms, picnic tables, water pump, and shelters

WHEELCHAIR ACCESS: None

CONTACT: 800-870-3666, fpdcc.com/preserves -and-trails/trail-descriptions/#des-plaines

LOCATION: River Grove, IL 60171 (trailhead)

COMMENTS: Dogs must be leashed. Plan on getting some mud on your shoes, especially after a rain. During summer, bring mosquito repellent. This is more of an urban hike, so expect plenty of other trail users and traffic sounds from nearby streets.

trail from getting busier than it already is. Also, keep in mind that human civilization regularly intrudes on this trail with traffic noise, and toward the end of the hike, you'll know you're getting very close to O'Hare Airport.

From its headwaters in southern Wisconsin, the Des Plaines River runs south for 133 miles, eventually meeting the Kankakee River to form the Illinois River, a tributary of the Mississippi River. Cook and Lake Counties, which possess the lion's share of the Des Plaines River, both have trails that run alongside the river for long stretches. In Cook County, the trail is 17 miles, and in Lake County the trail runs for a whopping 31.4 miles. Generally, the Lake County section (see Hike 27, page 136) is better developed, with more signage, better trail-surface drainage, and better access points. Agencies plan to revamp the northern section of the trail in Cook County soon, and we hope the south section won't be far behind.

This hike, which follows the Yellow Trail for nearly the entire route, starts at the very southern end of the Cook County portion of the trail. As you start hiking from the Sunset Bridge Meadow Parking Area on North Avenue, the trail immediately mounts a steel footbridge and then passes several spur trails diverge toward the parking lots to the right. (Throughout the hike, trails regularly branch to the right toward parking and picnic areas; ignore these, staying to the left on the Yellow Trail until you get to Catherine Chevalier Woods.)

You'll soon come upon bottomland woods—dense, lush, and intensely green in summer—that look like a fairytale forest landed in the midst of one of the most populated counties in the nation. Moisture-loving trees hang overhead while an understory of grasses, bushes, and saplings create a damp, shady atmosphere.

And what's a woodland like this without families of deer trotting about, munching on the understory, nearly oblivious to the humans in their midst? The absence of natural predators combined with an abundance of food have launched the local deer

Des Plaines River Trail: North Avenue to Chevalier Woods

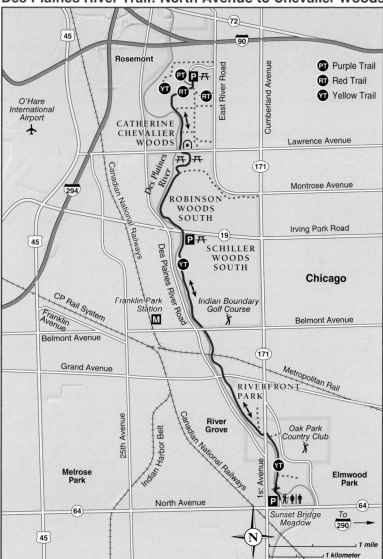

population into the stratosphere, resulting in some awful consequences. They often obliterate plant life in an area—and, tragically, traffic crashes can ensue when they wander onto local streets.

While the deer show surprising boldness, there's another mammal in your midst that is terribly shy, but you can still see its handiwork. After passing under First Avenue and then brushing against a couple of small ponds, look at the muddy bank on the left that seems to jut into the river. This is where you'll find nearly a dozen trees felled by beavers. Note the animals' careful engineering skills at work: all of the affected trees have fallen toward the water.

While progress has been made in cleaning up the Des Plaines River—there's far less odor and far more aquatic species that call it home—plenty of work still needs to be done. Commonly detected nasties in the water include mercury, arsenic, and phosphorus, not to mention coliform bacteria that enter the river when raw sewage gets released during heavy rains. As with other waterways close to the city, skin contact with the water is ill-advised.

Before reaching Grand Avenue, the next major cross street, you'll encounter diminutive Riverfront Park, which offers a water fountain, restrooms and picnic tables. Just ahead, after ducking under Grand Avenue through a cavelike underpass, you're greeted with another stretch of those fairytale bottomland woods thick with maple trees. As the trail swings closer to the river, the heaps of wood debris left by rising river water litter the sides of the trail and the banks of the river.

After passing beneath the Milwaukee District–West Line Metra tracks, you'll see a graveyard on the other side of the fence to the right that contains the final resting place of George "Baby Face" Nelson, the notorious Depression-era bank robber who was a partner of the equally notorious John Dillinger. Responsible for killing more FBI agents in the line of duty than any other person, Nelson (born Lester Joseph Gillis) was killed by the FBI during a shootout in Barrington in 1934.

Not long after passing under Belmont Avenue and then briefly walking alongside the Indian Boundary Golf Course, you'll enter open areas that feature the occasional towering specimen of oak, maple, and cottonwood, among others. Look for mayapple in shaded spots and thistle in the open areas. Soon you'll arrive at a good spot for a breather—a picnic area on Irving Park Road.

Continuing north, be extra-cautious while contending with the heavy traffic on Irving Park Road: traffic is going faster than the posted 45 mph speed limit, there's no traffic light or stop sign, and the curve in the road limits visibility. Fortunately, a plan is in the works to improve this trail crossing, making it safer and easier for hikers to navigate.

The sounds of jet engines on this stretch of the hike signal that one of the busiest airports in the world sits a short ways to the west. As you approach Lawrence Avenue, the next street north, you can practically wave to the pilots as they prepare for landing at O'Hare. Despite the airplane noise, the path between Irving and Lawrence welcomes you with another swath of attractive bottomland woods. Before arriving at a big grassy picnic area on Lawrence Avenue, you'll cross a sandy bottom creek on a stone bridge (the trail junction has a trailside box for making emergency calls). At the Lawrence Robinson Woods South Parking Area, stay right as the trail skirts the perimeter of the picnic area. Drop down to enter a tunnel that runs underneath Lawrence.

On the final stretch of trail before you reach the turnaround point at Catherine Chevalier Woods, look for kingfishers and woodpeckers in the bottomland woods littered with deadfall. After passing what looks like infrastructure for storm-sewer outflow on the left, follow the Orange Trail as it branches to the right (east). Pass a pleasant marshy area on the left, and then follow the purple trail to the left (north) toward the Chevalier Woods Parking Area, where you'll turn around and retrace your steps back to North Avenue.

NEARBY ACTIVITIES

About 1 mile east of the parking area on North Avenue, a few casual restaurants occupy a strip of storefronts. A couple of restaurants focus on Italian food. There's also a sushi restaurant, along with a Cuban place that offers a nice selection of hearty, affordable sandwiches. If you've been hiking on a hot day, cool off with one of their sweet and tasty mojitos.

· ·

GPS TRAILHEAD COORDINATES N41° 54.584' W87° 49.922'

DIRECTIONS From Chicago, follow I-290 west. Exit at IL 43/Harlem Avenue, and turn right (north). Drive for 2.5 miles, and then turn left (west) on North Avenue. In about 2 miles, after crossing the Des Plaines River, look for the red sign for the Sunset Bridge Meadow Parking Area, on the right. The trail starts toward the back of the parking area.

PUBLIC TRANSPORTATION **Metra**'s North Central Service line provides good access to this trail from the Belmont Avenue Station in Franklin Park. From the station, the trail is just a 0.6-mile walk. Walk south to Belmont, and then turn left (east). After you cross to the east side of the river, the trail access is on the left.

The **Chicago Transit Authority (CTA)** Cumberland Blue Line train station requires only a 0.5-mile walk to the north section of the trail (not covered on this hike). From the Cumberland Station, head south on the walkway over the I-90 off-ramp. At street level, head to the right (west). At the first opportunity, look for access to the next street south (to the left), Bryn Mawr Avenue. The first option is a driveway that turns into Delphia Avenue. Turn right (west) on Bryn Mawr. Cross North East River Road into Catherine Chevalier Woods, and follow the Yellow Trail. In a mile or so, you'll connect with the Yellow Trail route covered in this hike.

5 HUMBOLDT PARK LAGOON AND PRAIRIE RIVER LOOP

Humboldt Park's Tudor-style Cultural Center   *Photo: Ted Villaire*

THE PHRASE *URBAN OASIS* comes to mind when many Chicagoans think of Humboldt Park. For a concentrated dose of nature in the city, this park is a perfect destination. You'll take a trip around a scenic lagoon and a "prairie river" that offer striking views nearly every time you turn your head.

DESCRIPTION

For more than 100 years, people living in Humboldt Park's dense surrounding neighborhoods have escaped to this lovely park in search of respite from Chicago's concrete grid. In recent decades, the park and the lagoons have undergone dramatic improvements, making it one of the most alluring stars in Chicago's constellation of great parks. In addition to being perhaps the most charming city park away from the Loop and the lakefront, Humboldt Park is fascinating because it was part of movement that launched a whole new landscape design philosophy that transformed parks and gardens, and has since become accepted wisdom for landscape designers.

Humboldt Park emerged as an important spot in the history of landscape design thanks to the person who designed much of the park: Jens Jensen, the park's former superintendent, who went on to oversee many Chicago parks and then launched his own landscape architecture business. Jensen's pioneering work in Chicago's western parks, including the design of Columbus Park and the extensive redesign of

DISTANCE & CONFIGURATION: 1.7-mile loop

DIFFICULTY: Easy

SCENERY: Lagoons, prairie flowers, grassy parkland, statuary, boathouse, formal garden

EXPOSURE: Mostly open

TRAIL TRAFFIC: Busy

TRAIL SURFACE: Gravel, asphalt

HIKING TIME: 1.5 hours

DRIVING DISTANCE: 5 miles from Millennium Park

ACCESS: Daily, sunrise–sunset; no fees or permits

MAPS: A map is available at the website at right (click "Map & Facilities"); USGS *Chicago Loop, IL*

FACILITIES: Boathouse with a café, restrooms, benches, fishing piers, swimming pond, sports fields

WHEELCHAIR ACCESS: Mostly—a few spots aren't accessible, but easy alternative routes can be arranged.

CONTACT: 312-742-PLAY (7529), chicagoparkdistrict.com/parks-facilities /humboldt-park

LOCATION: 1301 N. Sacramento Ave., Chicago, IL 60622

COMMENTS: Because this is an urban park, you're bound to have lots of company from other people enjoying the scenery. Dogs must be leashed. Humboldt Park is safe, but as in any urban setting, you should keep an eye on your surroundings. To learn more about the park, go to chicagoparkdistrict.com/parks-facilities /humboldt-park-audio-tour for a free audio tour, which includes descriptions of the statues along the way.

Humboldt, Garfield, and Douglas Parks, was guided by his belief in the humanizing power of parks and his commitment to using indigenous plants and emphasizing the region's prairie heritage. Jensen also played a role in the creation of the Cook County Forest Preserve District, the Illinois State Parks system, and the Indiana Dunes State Park and National Lakeshore.

From the boathouse, you'll take a counterclockwise loop around the lagoon. But before you start, head up the boathouse steps for a great view of the sprawling lagoon. The boathouse, built during the 1920s in the Prairie style, has a series of graceful arches that frame the lagoon. Either before or after the walk, consider visiting the boathouse café, which offers outdoor seating overlooking the lagoon during the warmer months. Once you start the hike to the right of the boathouse, you'll immediately encounter a series of stone platforms among the swaths of lily pads and water grasses at the edge of the lagoon. Just 20 feet from the boathouse, the trail leads you to an island with prairie flowers such as goldenrod, asters, and bitterweed. On the island and elsewhere around on the edges of the lagoon, there's a steady supply of little nooks and places to sit and hide away among the rocks and plants.

More views of the water open up as you make your way around the lagoon. You'll pass a spot on the shore that is popular for feeding the geese and ducks that call the lagoon home. On the north side of the lagoon, closer to North Avenue, you'll see a series of newly planted gingko trees, a newly refurbished playground, and another big swath of prairie plants. Another small island also sits in this section of the lagoon. This one, laden with trees and surrounded by lily pads, is inaccessible.

Humboldt Park Lagoon and Prairie River Loop

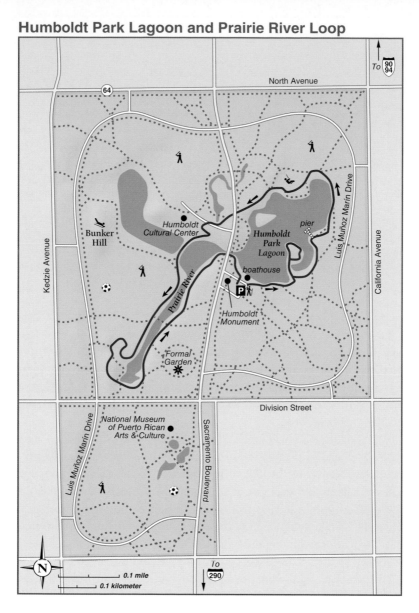

Keep straight ahead on the trail and cross North Sacramento Boulevard, or go under Sacramento by taking the trail to the left. Stay left (southwest) after crossing Sacramento and the park access road, and then turn right (west) once you reach the lagoon. To the left is a statue of the explorer Leif Erikson, which brought out some 5,000 Scandinavian Americans when it was dedicated in the park in 1901. The building to the right is the Humboldt Cultural Center; behind that is a pond with a swimming beach. In recent years, the local community successfully rallied to keep the beach open after the city threatened to close it as a cost-saving measure. The surrounding neighborhood, which has the same name as the park, is home to a mix of African Americans, whites, and Latinos (many of whom are Puerto Rican).

Now you'll explore what Jensen called the "prairie river," an extension of the lagoon made to look like a lovely stream flowing through the open prairie. Prairie flowers layer the banks, trees hang over the water, and tufts of marsh grass grow at the edge of the water. Elements like the prairie river make Humboldt Park stand out within Chicago's system of large parks, which are connected with a series of boulevards. Humboldt Park is the northernmost park in the chain. Initially designed by William Le Baron Jenney, Humboldt Park was built and opened in 1877. The boathouse, a formal garden, the prairie river, and extensive native plants were added by Jensen in following decades.

After passing the wind turbine and solar panels on the right that provide power for pumps that filter the water from the lagoon, be sure to step out on the bridge for nice views up and down the "river." To the west, you'll see a top-notch baseball field for kids built largely by the Chicago Cubs. Not so long ago, the lagoon and river were a lot less scenic because the river became filled in, invasive plants were taking over, and garbage was strewn in the lagoons. Then the river was dredged and the invasive plants were replaced with native wetlands plants, prairie grasses, and wildflowers. The illicit activity that often kept people away was pushed out. Now the park is a regional attraction—one of the city's jewels in a crown of impressive parks.

Eventually you'll reach a "prairie waterfall" over blocks of sandstone that looks as if it's a source of water for the river. After going around the end of the river and heading back toward the main lagoon, be sure step away from the river for moment to see the Formal Garden. Also designed by Jens Jensen, it's slightly recessed and edged with pergolas. You'll see roses, zinnias, butterfly weed, grapevines, and many other plant and flower species. Plans are now under way to begin restoring this treasured but neglected corner of the park.

Finish the walk by following the river under Sacramento and then back up to the boathouse. Before wrapping up your trip, on the west side of the boathouse parking lot, take a short visit to the statue of the park's namesake, Alexander Von Humboldt, a Prussian geographer, naturalist, explorer, and influential proponent of Romantic philosophy and science.

NEARBY ACTIVITIES

The park itself marks the western gateway of **Paseo Boricua,** the Puerto Rican culinary, cultural, and entertainment district. Just across Division Street from the prairie river is the **National Museum of Puerto Rican Arts & Culture** (3015 W. Division St.; 773-486-8345, nmprac.org). Located in the beautiful and historic Humboldt

Park Stables, the museum contains an art gallery and rotating exhibits focusing on Puerto Rican culture. It's open Tuesday–Friday, 10 a.m.–4 p.m., and Saturday, 10 a.m.–1 p.m.

Just a couple of blocks east of the park, try the *jibarito* sandwiches at **Papa's Cache Sabroso** (2517 W. Division St.; 773-862-8313, papascache.com). A jibarito is usually steak topped with lettuce, onion, tomato, cheese and garlicky mayo, and the "bread" is flattened fried green plantains.

If you're looking for another opportunity to stretch your legs, visit the **Bloomingdale Trail,** just two blocks north of the park on North Humboldt Avenue. The 2.7-mile elevated path, which occupies a former train line, has been wildly successful since its opening in 2015 and is one of the most exciting pieces of new infrastructure in the city of Chicago.

• •

GPS TRAILHEAD COORDINATES N41° 54.322' W87° 42.031'

DIRECTIONS Start the hike at the Humboldt Park Boathouse, on North Sacramento Boulevard between West Division Street and West North Avenue. Driving from the north, take I-90/I-94 to the California Avenue exit, and head south for 1.6 miles. At North Avenue, turn right (west). After 0.2 mile, turn left (south) on North Humboldt Boulevard, and look for the boathouse at the edge of the pond, on the left.

Driving from the south or west, take I-290 to the Sacramento Boulevard exit, and follow it north for 1.7 miles all the way to the boathouse, on the right.

PUBLIC TRANSPORTATION Humboldt Park is easily accessible using **CTA**'s 52 Kedzie/California bus, as well as the 72 North Avenue and 70 Division Street buses.

Jackson Park's tranquil Japanese garden   *Photo: Thomas Barrat/Shutterstock*

AT THE HEART of Jackson Park is a wooded island containing a serene Japanese garden and placid lagoons lined with cattails. Much of this quiet refuge is a remnant of one of the most important events in Chicago history: the World's Columbian Exposition of 1893.

DESCRIPTION

In preparation for Chicago's 1893 World's Columbian Exposition, a team of the nation's most significant architects and sculptors came to the grounds of Jackson Park to create the "White City," made largely of plaster buildings designed in a classical style. The city included sculptures, fountains, and some 200 buildings exhibiting art, machinery, animals, plants, food, and other items. The exposition was an absolute success: more than 27 million people attended this event, held to celebrate 400 years of post-Columbus civilization. After the exposition, the city converted the ground's 700 acres—from East 56th Street south to East 67th Street, and from the shoreline west to South Stony Island Drive—back to a city park.

While the exhibition was not meant to be permanent, one notable exception was the sprawling Palace of Fine Art, which was eventually converted to the Museum

DISTANCE & CONFIGURATION: 1.35-mile loop

DIFFICULTY: Easy

SCENERY: Lagoon, islands, Japanese garden, meadow, open parkland

EXPOSURE: Half shaded, half exposed

TRAIL TRAFFIC: Busy

TRAIL SURFACE: Pavement, dirt

HIKING TIME: 30–45 minutes

DRIVING DISTANCE: 8 miles from Millennium Park

ACCESS: Daily, 6 a.m.–9 p.m.; no fees or permits

MAPS: A map is available at the website below (click "Map & Facilities"); *USGS Jackson Park, IL*

FACILITIES: Drinking fountains, restrooms

WHEELCHAIR ACCESS: None

CONTACT: 312-742-PLAY (7529), chicagopark district.com/parks-facilities/jackson-park

LOCATION: Columbia Drive, Jackson Park, Chicago, IL 60637

COMMENTS: Dogs must be leashed. As in any urban area, be mindful of your surroundings. The Jackson Park Advisory Council offers a great website with extensive information about the park and the World's Columbian Exposition: hydepark.org/parks/jpac.html.

of Science and Industry. Two other attractions left over from the exposition are a lovely Japanese garden and the Wooded Island. The latter recently underwent an enormous habitat restoration that removed hundreds of invasive trees and acres of invasive plants. Underwater habitat was created around the edges of the island, and tens of thousands of native trees and plants were put in the ground. If you've ever seen the long-term results of big habitat-restoration projects like this, you know that it's bound to make the Wooded Island even more of a city treasure.

The hike starts on the west side of the parking lot, on the bridge overlooking a pool lapping at the back steps of the museum. This bridge is named after Clarence Darrow, a famous Chicago defense lawyer who was one of many featured speakers at the 1893 Exposition. On the other side of the bridge, looking south, is the East Lagoon, along with a wooded island and a sprinkling of other tiny islands. After crossing the Clarence Darrow Bridge, take a quick left to cross North Bridge.

Over the bridge, you'll see a new art piece that was added to the island at the same time the island was opened after the habitat-restoration project. The first public-art installation in the United States created by multimedia artist Yoko Ono, *Sky Landing* brings to mind to huge flower petals or flames emerging from a grassy clearing. Given that Ono is a native of Japan, it's fitting that her sculpture is situated just outside the entrance to the Garden of the Phoenix, a storybook Japanese garden on the shore of the lagoon. Built for the Columbian Exposition in 1893, the garden was virtually abandoned after World War II, then was rebuilt in 1981. While walking along the 0.15-mile winding gravel path, lined with red-granite blocks taken from Chicago's old streetcar tracks, you'll enjoy a pleasant waterfall, stone lanterns, and a little bridge arching over a rock-lined lily pond. The teahouse, added to the garden in 1981, is one of many places where you can have a seat and enjoy the view.

Jackson Park Loop

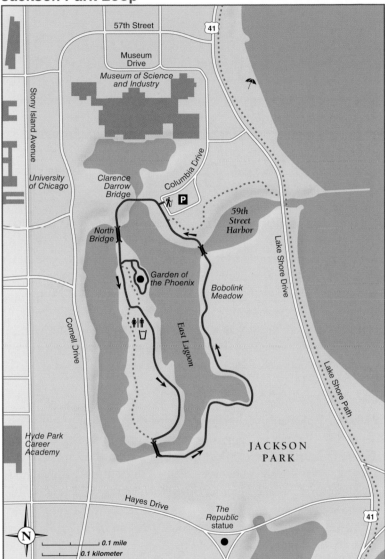

Continuing south on the island, take either route at the fork: both trails lead along the wooded banks for the lagoon and offer a series of overlooks of the lagoon. Even before the habitat-restoration project, this small island was a hot spot for birders; 250 bird species have been sighted here, while 55 species make nests here. One bird species that dwells in Jackson Park and the surrounding neighborhoods but is rarely seen elsewhere around Chicago is the monk parakeet—a green, talkative, medium-sized bird native to South America. Since the parakeets mysteriously appeared a few decades back, their origin has remained a matter of speculation: some say they were pets set free; others say they escaped from a crate at the airport.

At the southern tip of the island, cross the bridge and then cut left along the shoreline. First, however, you may want to take a short detour straight ahead to Hayes Drive and then left to South Richardson Drive to visit an impressive bronze statue called *The Republic,* a replica of the much larger statue that was built for the Columbian Exposition.

Continuing along the shore of the lagoon, you'll pass groves of weeping willows and a lagoon fringed with prairie plants. After 0.2 mile of hiking along the shore of the lagoon and past the soccer fields on the right, follow the boardwalk that starts at the limestone fishing platform. Stay left through the small parking lot to the beginning of the trail through Bobolink Meadow.

Largely ignored by human visitors, this meadow is alive with animals and plants: rabbits scurry across the trail, and songbirds serenade each other while perched on big bluestem, Indian grass, goldenrod, and other prairie plants. On your left, several side trails lead toward the trees drooping lazily over the water. Before the Columbian Exposition, this was a swampy marshland. Later it was used for athletic fields, and, surprisingly, from 1956 to 1971, it hosted an Army missile base. Since 1982, this plot has served as a nature preserve. Stay left as you pass through the gate, and head toward the bridge overlooking 100 or so boats moored in 59th Street Harbor. Continue along the shore of the lagoon, straight ahead to the parking lot.

NEARBY ACTIVITIES

While in Jackson Park, consider taking a short walk to **Promontory Point,** perhaps the best slice of open parkland in the city. From the parking lot where the hike starts, head toward the lake on the paved path that runs on the north side of the harbor. After passing a lawn-bowling green on the left, the path enters a tunnel under Lake Shore Drive. Emerging from the tunnel, you turn left and continue past the beach, arriving at Promontory Point 0.4 mile north of the tunnel. Known locally simply as The Point, the park occupies a small piece of land jutting into the lake and offers plenty of benches and big rocks from which to enjoy a great view of the downtown skyline.

Walking west of the parking lot where this hike starts, you'll encounter the southern edge of the **University of Chicago** campus and the **Midway Plaisance,** a mile-long strip of green space running east–west. During the Columbian Exposition, the Plaisance hosted amusement rides and a collection of re-created villages from around the world; today, it's open parkland with statuary and an ice rink operating in the winter. Starting at the east end of the Plaisance—closest to Jackson Park—you'll pass the large, round Perennial Flower Garden; a statue of Saint Wenceslas; the

Rockefeller Memorial Chapel (with dozens of outdoor statues of religious figures); another garden; and several university residence halls.

Architecture fans will enjoy the English Gothic style that characterizes many of the University of Chicago's buildings. To see more of the campus, turn right on South Woodlawn Avenue, just east of the Rockefeller Chapel. One block ahead, turn left on East 58th Street toward the center of campus. At the northeast corner of Woodlawn and 58th, don't miss Frank Lloyd Wright's **Robie House,** considered the most complete expression of the architect's Prairie School style. Call 773-834-1847 or go to flwright.org/visit/robiehouse for tour information.

For information about the **Museum of Science and Industry**'s hours and admission prices, call 773-684-1414 or visit msichicago.org.

• •

GPS TRAILHEAD COORDINATES N41° 47.298' W87° 34.915'

DIRECTIONS From South Lake Shore Drive, take the Science Drive exit, just south of the 57th Street exit and just north of the Hayes Drive exit. Immediately, you'll enter a parking area—stay left and park as far to the left as you can. Start the hike at the west edge of this parking area.

PUBLIC TRANSPORTATION Take the **South Shore Line** to the 59th Street Station. On East 59th Street, head 0.3 mile east (toward the lake), crossing South Stony Island Avenue and South Cornell Avenue, to the Clarence Darrow Bridge.

Lake Katherine's waterfall garden   *Photo: Tim Putala*

AS AN URBAN nature walk, this is one of the best in the area. Nestled alongside the Cal–Sag Channel, 136-acre Lake Katherine Nature Center features an attractive lake, an arboretum, a waterfall garden, an herb and conifer garden, and expansive views from atop a ridge in the eastern section of the preserve.

DESCRIPTION

In the 1980s, this patch of land was an eyesore, with mounds of debris and junk strewn amid piles of boulders and overgrown bushes. Then the city of Palos Heights decided to transform it into parkland. The result is a charming urban park, half of which is carefully landscaped and the other half of which is fairly wild.

Much of this hike runs alongside the Cal–Sag Channel, a 16-mile waterway between the Little Calumet River and the Sanitary and Ship Canal. Slow-moving barges frequently use this channel to transport cargo such as fuel oils, coke, and gasoline between the Mississippi River and Calumet Harbor, the largest harbor on the Great Lakes. The digging of the channel started in 1911 for the purpose of creating a feeder channel for the Illinois and Michigan Canal. It also diverted polluted water from Lake Michigan, keeping Chicago's drinking water safe and clean. In following years, after the channel was widened and dredged, it proved to be an important shipping route. Today, a 26-mile trail runs alongside the canal and through Lake Katherine (see Nearby Activities, page 51).

From the parking lot, head toward the buildings at the edge of the lake. The first building on the right is the E. G. Simpson Clubhouse, a remnant of a former gun club, now used for banquets. After passing the small pier and the Environmental Learning

DISTANCE & CONFIGURATION: 3.2 miles, 2 connected loops

DIFFICULTY: Moderate

SCENERY: Lake, canal, woodland, specialty gardens, human-made waterfalls

EXPOSURE: Mostly shaded

TRAIL TRAFFIC: Moderately busy

TRAIL SURFACE: Wood chips, dirt, gravel

HIKING TIME: 1.5 hours

DRIVING DISTANCE: 26 miles from Millennium Park

ACCESS: Park open daily, sunrise–sunset; nature center open weekdays, 9 a.m.–5 p.m., and Saturdays, 10 a.m.–4 p.m.; no fees or permits

MAPS: Available at Environmental Learning Center and the website below; USGS *Palos Park, IL*

FACILITIES: Benches, restrooms, Environmental Learning Center with exhibits, ice-skating rink in winter, canoe and kayak rentals

WHEELCHAIR ACCESS: None

CONTACT: 708-361-1873, lakekatherine.org

LOCATION: 7402 W. Lake Katherine Drive, Palos Heights, IL 60463

COMMENTS: Dogs must be leashed and picked up after

Center, which caters largely to school groups, you'll see a small herb garden with dozens of plants growing in raised beds. Next is a bird-and-butterfly garden hosting a variety of shrubs, flowers, grasses, and vines meant to attract the winged creatures.

Staying left on the wood-chip trail brings you past a cluster of conifer trees and a bench overlooking the canal. Farther along is an observation platform at the edge of the lake. Just ahead is the Children's Forest, which had its beginnings on Arbor Day in 1990 when some 500 children and their families planted trees and bushes on this several-acre plot. If you continue ahead, you'll start following with the Cal–Sag Trail, which quickly ducks under two bridges. Instead, stay left (south) alongside the lake, and soon you'll pass an arch from the front doorway of a former Palos Heights elementary school. Continuing around the of Lake Katherine's shoreline, the shoreline opens up, providing a view of the cattails, sedge grasses, and lily pads out in the water.

While conifers and cottonwood grow fairly thickly on the north side of the lake, the south side hosts about 70 different tree species, many of them identified with plaques. Along with more than a dozen crab apple trees, there are silver maples, burr oaks, gingkos, locust and green ash trees, American filberts, and swamp white oaks. As the trail winds around the lake, multiple benches are situated on the little pieces of land jutting into the lake. On the wooded island across from one of the promontories, look for the heron rookery made from two-by-fours.

At the clubhouse, cross over the trail that you started on, and then continue straight ahead to the waterfall garden, featuring a maze of rocks and trees built up on a little hill. At the top of the hill, lake water is pumped out among the stands of Norway spruce, quaking aspen, and staghorn sumac before tumbling over four short waterfalls and through several shallow intermediate pools. From the base of the falls, the water runs along a brook back to the lake. On the back side of the waterfall, dozens of shrubs, trees, and ground-cover plants grow in the small conifer garden. From the conifer garden, look for the paved road that runs next to the canal, and follow it right (east).

49

Lake Katherine Hike

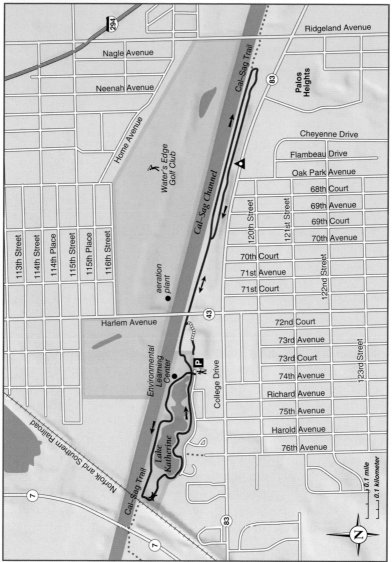

After you pass under the Harlem Avenue Bridge, you'll see a series of waterfalls flowing over concrete embankments on the opposite side of the canal. This is one of five SEPA (sidestream elevated pool aeration) stations along the canal and the Little Calumet River. The SEPA stations clean the water by cooling it and increasing its oxygen content, while also providing a pleasant recreation area for local residents. Beyond the bridge, look for the small side trail leading to a bench overlooking the SEPA station.

After the SEPA station, you'll pass a couple of junctions on the right. Soon a clearing provides a nice view of the wooded banks across the channel. As the trail turns right, a small side trail leads to a bench with a view of the Ridgeland Avenue Bridge. Continuing to the right, follow the arrow pointing to the trail heading into the woods. The trail occasionally becomes rugged and steep as it follows the rise and fall of a ridge running parallel to the canal on the right and IL 83 on the left.

Nearly halfway through the ridge hike, you'll encounter an overlook with a pavilion and benches. At one point, the trail drops down sharply before crossing an intermittent stream on a line of boulders. Continuing on, the trail grows wider and the surface becomes fuzzy with moss. Once you reach the open gravelly area, head back down to the trail on the side of the canal.

Just after passing under the bridge on the way back to the parking lot, take a left on the wide wood-chip trail. This trail leads to a boardwalk and a set of stairs and benches that winds through a wooded gully containing an intermittent stream. Following the stairs up the side of the gully brings you to the vegetable garden, complete with scarecrows and a variety of flowers and common vegetables. From the vegetable garden, continue to the left through the small prairie and back to the parking lot.

NEARBY ACTIVITIES

The eastern part of this hike follows part of the brand new 26-mile **Cal–Sag Trail,** which runs along the canal from IL 83 near Lemont to the Burnham Greenway near the Indiana border. The paved trail links four marinas, three golf courses, and six nature and forest preserves, including Lake Katherine and Palos–Sag Valley Forest Preserve to the west. Learn more at calsagtrail.org.

• •

GPS TRAILHEAD COORDINATES N41° 40.609' W87° 48.068'

DIRECTIONS From the intersection of I-55 and I-294, follow I-294 south for 5.6 miles. Take the US 12 East/US 20 East/95th Street exit, and continue ahead for 0.3 mile. Turn right on IL 43/Harlem Avenue. After 3.1 miles, turn right on 119th Street/West College Drive. After 0.4 mile, turn right on South 75th Street. Turn right on Lake Katherine Drive, and park just ahead.

PUBLIC TRANSPORTATION Take the **CTA** Orange Line to Midway Airport. At the Midway Station, take Pace Bus 386 to the corner of South Harlem Avenue and IL 83/West College Drive. The entrance to Lake Katherine is a quarter mile west on West College Drive.

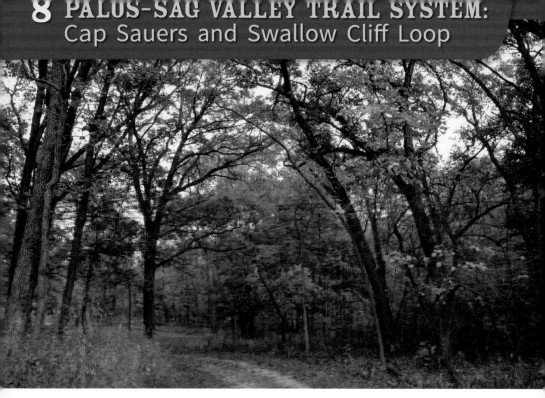

Autumn colors on the Yellow Trail *Photo: John Ruberry*

AS PART OF the larger Palos–Sag Valley Forest Preserve and Trail System, Cap Sauers Holding and Swallow Cliff Woods offer great hiking close to Chicago. The terrain is varied and sometimes dramatic, with bluffs and ravines, pristine oak savannas, and scenic stream crossings.

DESCRIPTION

In a county of more than 5 million people, the wild and isolated ambience of Cap Sauers Holding seems like an impossibility. Named after Charles Goodwin "Cap" Sauers, the first superintendent of the Cook County Forest Preserve District, this is the largest roadless tract in the county and the largest nature preserve in Illinois. One striking part of this hike features an 80- to 100-foot-high bluff known as Swallow Cliff, formed by torrents of meltwater as the most recent glacier retreated about 12,000 years ago. As the last glacier shrank, Lake Michigan swelled. The growing lake eventually released some of its meltwater by carving a couple of channels in the Palos area. One of these outlets sculpted the bluffs and the basin of the nearby Des Plaines River, and the other created Swallow Cliff and the Cal–Sag Channel, which flows just a quarter mile north of the cliff.

DISTANCE & CONFIGURATION: 3.8-mile loop

DIFFICULTY: Easy–moderate

SCENERY: Bluffs, rolling hills, streams, marshes, savannas, woods, deep ravines, and a toboggan run

EXPOSURE: Shady with some exposed stretches

TRAIL TRAFFIC: Minimal

TRAIL SURFACE: Crushed limestone and dirt

HIKING TIME: 2–3 hours

DRIVING DISTANCE: 25 miles from Millennium Park

ACCESS: Daily, 6:30 a.m.–sunset; no fees or permits

MAPS: Forest Preserves of Cook County offers interactive and PDF maps on its website: fpdcc.com/preserves-and-trails/trail-descriptions; USGS *Sag Bridge, IL*

FACILITIES: Water, restrooms, and picnic tables at the Teason's Woods picnic area

WHEELCHAIR ACCESS: None

CONTACT: 800-870-3666, fpdcc.com/preserves-and-trails

LOCATION: Palos Park, IL 60464

COMMENTS: Dogs must be leashed (prohibited in esker area). If you're hiking with children, be careful crossing 104th Avenue.

Swallow Cliff rises immediately south of the Teason's Woods parking lot, where the hike starts. Hop on the Yellow Trail, which runs along the back side of the parking area. Heading left (east, away from 104th Avenue) on the crushed-limestone trail at the base of Swallow Cliff, hikers will see trails going up the slope on the right. Those in the mood for exploring can find dramatic ravines and bluffs within this several-mile network of unmarked trails. Be warned, though, that some sections are not quite so beautiful. Despite the signs banning bicycles on these trails, damage from off-road biking is clearly a problem. Because this cluster of trails can be confusing, bring a map and compass, or carry a GPS unit.

While hiking along the base of Swallow Cliff, look for the points where steep ravines intersect the bluff. At 0.6 mile, cross a small bridge, and follow the first marked trail on the right after the bridge. From the trail, head over to the lengthy stone staircase to the right. At the top of the stairs, continue ahead on the Cream Trail. After passing a marsh on the left at 0.8 mile, turn right (west) on the Brown Trail at a T-intersection. As the terrain flattens, an attractive oak canopy develops overhead. At 1.2 miles into the hike, keep right on the Yellow Trail. A short distance ahead, keep straight as the Black Trail merges from the left. After the junction with the Black Trail, Horsetail Lake will be visible through the trees on the left.

On summer weekends, the first half of this hike from Swallow Cliff south to Horsetail Lake is active with runners, equestrians, bikers, hikers, and people using the lengthy stone staircase for an outdoor workout. If solitude is what you're after, visit this section during off-peak hours. Within the 1,520 acres of Cap Sauers, however, solitude is usually in abundant supply.

As you cross 104th Avenue into Cap Sauers Holding on the Yellow Trail, the terrain is flat and shrubby, offering little evidence of the farming that once took place in this section of the preserve. You'll remain on the Yellow Trail for the remainder

Palos–Sag Valley Trail System:
Cap Sauers and Swallow Cliff Loop

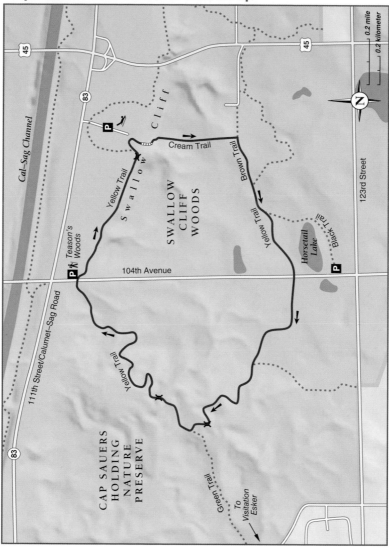

of the hike. At 2 miles into the hike, the trail drops down alongside a marsh and then continues through stunning oak savannas, sometimes thick with deadfall. At 2.7 miles, when you arrive at the junction with the Green Trail, keep right on the Yellow Trail. Turn right to hike through a semiopen area, over a shallow stream, and alongside a few ravines. While hiking this section of trail, keep an eye out for animal trails that cross the Yellow Trail. Look for mud near these trails to determine what creatures recently passed by. Coyotes, rabbits, and raccoons are common in Cap Sauers, as are deer; in fact, deer become nearly as common at dusk as squirrels in a city park. As traffic noise from 104th Avenue comes within earshot, the trail loses elevation and winds through wild rose bushes before reaching a grove of stately walnut and oak trees. At 104th Avenue, the Teason's Woods parking lot where you began is straight ahead.

If you're in the mood to extend the hike a couple of miles and you're interested in seeing an esker—a long mound left behind by glaciers—here are some directions. Be advised, though, that this esker is sometimes tricky to find, and the trail that leads to it is not always well defined. (*Note:* Dogs are not allowed in this area.)

Before the Yellow Trail turns northeast, take a left on the Green Trail. After hiking 0.4 mile beyond the junction, take the first side trail on the right, indicated with a marker. Right away, the trail passes over a hilltop and then through a labyrinth of dense shrubs. Turn right at a trail intersection at the edge of a savanna. Shortly after passing through a small, muddy ravine and alongside a marsh on the left, the trail starts to snake along the top of what is known as Visitation Esker. Sloping down 40–50 feet on each side of the trail, the esker looks like a perfectly shaped winding mound. Indeed, some geologists maintain that this landform—created by a subglacial stream—is one of the most well-defined examples of an esker in the state. On the sides of the esker, look for occasional remnants of controlled burnings: charred stumps and blackened tree trunks lying on the ground. These burnings clear out the invasive plant species and the understory, and, in turn, allow for open vistas of the rolling terrain sprinkled with oaks.

Nearly 1 mile into the esker path, the esker disappears, and the trail intersects another trail at the top of a bluff—this is your turnaround. Now retrace your steps to the Green Trail, and then return to the Yellow Trail, which you'll follow back to the Teason's Woods Parking Area.

• •

GPS TRAILHEAD COORDINATES N41° 41.052' W87° 52.164'

DIRECTIONS From I-55, take Exit 274. Follow IL 83/Kingery Highway south. At 4 miles, continue to follow IL 83 as it turns left and becomes 111th Street and then Calumet–Sag Road. After 3 more miles, turn right on 104th Avenue and park in the lot for Teason's Woods, immediately on the left.

Mushrooms grow wild in the wetlands. *Photo: Ted Villaire*

THE PALOS–SAG VALLEY Trail System is known for hills, wetlands, and many lakes and ponds. This hike has all of those in spades. Walk among stands of giant oak trees, enjoy big swaths of prairie plants and native flowers, and take in sweeping views of the surrounding landscape. Cranberry Slough, one of the few remaining peat bogs in northern Illinois, stands as one of the star attractions on this hike.

DESCRIPTION

More than anything, this hike serves as a testament to the total transformation that occurs in natural areas when you oust the invasive plants. Plucking out the invaders starts a process that allows native plants to thrive, rejuvenating the landscape and in turn creating more habitat for native insects and wildlife. Not so long ago, many trail sections on this hike were largely walled in by thick invasive species such as buckthorn, bush honeysuckle, and mustard garlic, which grew prolifically and choked out the native species. Hiking along here was often dark and a bit dreary, with very limited views of the surrounding landscape. But now, after decades of work by contractors and volunteers, the landscape has been revived, supporting many dozens of native plant species, more wildlife, and sweeping views.

DISTANCE & CONFIGURATION: 4.8-mile loop

DIFFICULTY: Moderate

SCENERY: Marshland, ponds, woods, savanna, prairie

EXPOSURE: A mix of shaded and open

TRAIL TRAFFIC: Minimal, with occasional cyclists

TRAIL SURFACE: Gravel, dirt

HIKING TIME: 3.5 hours

DRIVING DISTANCE: 21 miles from Millennium Park

ACCESS: Daily, sunrise–sunset; no fees or permits

MAPS: Forest Preserves of Cook County offers interactive and PDF maps on its website: fpdcc

.com/preserves-and-trails/trail-descriptions; USGS *Palos Park, IL*

FACILITIES: Restrooms, picnic tables, and shelter

WHEELCHAIR ACCESS: Erosion on parts of the trail would make this hike very difficult for wheelchair users.

CONTACT: 800-870-3666, pdcc.com/preserves -and-trails

LOCATION: Willow Springs, IL 60480

COMMENTS: Navigating this hike is easy—just follow the white butterfly icon on a gold square posted at all trail junctions. Dogs are prohibited on a segment of this hike that runs through the Cranberry Slough Illinois Nature Preserve, which starts when you turn left on the Yellow Trail at 0.7 mile and ends roughly where you cross 95th Street about 1.7 miles later.

You'll immediately start enjoying the benefits of the prairie-restoration efforts as you catch the trail heading south from the Country Lane Woods Parking Area. Attractive prairie unfolds on the left as the trail descends into a wetland. Soon, a small stream runs under the trail between a cattail pond on the right to a prairie marshland on the left. Throughout this hike, you'll encounter a network of streams connecting many of the ponds in the preserve. Another small cattail pond appears before you hang a left on the Yellow Trail at 0.7 mile into the hike. An emergency call box is located at this intersection.

After the turn, the gnarled limbs of stately oaks create a thick canopy overhead. The trail descends and wetlands again appear on both sides of the trail as you cross another creek. Passing the Brown Trail as it branches right to a parking area, the trail curves and climbs, and reaches a spot offering a commanding view of Cranberry Slough, one of only a handful of peat bogs in Illinois. (A *slough,* pronounced "slew," is a colloquial name for a shallow wetland or pond.) The landscape tilts down toward this majestic patch of open water, ringed by cattails and formed by an ice block stranded during the retreat of the glacier some 14,000 years ago. Growing beneath the oaks and black walnuts on the edges of the slough are plants including goldenrod, big bluestem prairie grass, white wild indigo, marsh blazing star, and tall bellflower (no cranberries, however). According to the forest preserve district, visitors can see pileated woodpeckers, eastern bluebirds, and tufted titmice, not to mention herons, egrets, ducks, gulls, and gadwalls lured by the open water.

As the trail curls around Cranberry Slough, you'll pass through open woodland and then embark on a lovely roller-coaster ride as the trail drops down and passes another cattail-fringed pond. The trail rises and then passes a marshy prairie area on

Palos–Sag Valley Trail System: Country Lane Loop

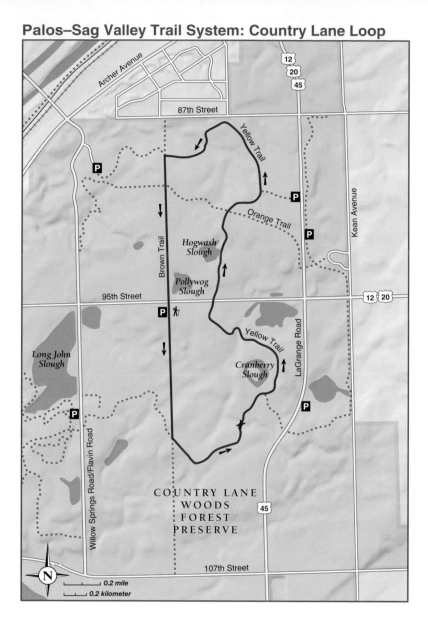

the left, then swoops down again alongside a picturesque wetlands prairie cradled within a ravine that is thick with goldenrod, cattails, and acres of attractive prairie plants. During the summer, clusters of cardinal flower create a blaze of red here and there. Rising quickly out of the ravine, the trail flattens, and towering specimens of oak and hickory take center stage. After you cross 95th Street, during the summer you'll see big swaths of orange jewelweed (small orange flowers on bushy plants 3–5 feet tall). If you happen to get a case of poison ivy, which, keep in mind, also grows abundantly on the edges of this trail, juice from jewelweed leaves and stems will provide relief, according to some Native Americans.

Another delightful pond, Hogwash Slough, soon appears beside the trail north of 95th Street. At first one might think the name of this slough is a remnant of the farming that once occurred in the area, but in this case, the name was simply was chosen for its whimsy (other ponds were named for their shape). Again, a small stream runs under the trail from the slough on the left to the grassy marshland on the right. Keep straight ahead at the trail junction, and soon you'll arrive in an open prairie thick with big bluestem prairie grass—and plenty of birds flitting about.

Another stream gurgles underneath the trail before you pass the Orange Trail, first branching right and then left. (You might consider adding a bit more mileage by taking the Orange Trail to the left to encounter yet another picturesque pond called Boomerang Slough.) On the final straightaway, the terrain takes on a more gentle character as you pass some swampy flooded areas on the sides of the trail, followed by swaths of bottomland woods featuring huge cottonwoods. Enjoy Pollywog Slough sprawling to the left just before you cross 95th Street and return to the parking lot where you started.

NEARBY ACTIVITIES

Outdoor explorers in the Chicago area are lucky to have the massive Palos–Sag Valley Trail System in their midst. With more than 14,000 acres of hilly woodland, rolling prairie, and scenic wetlands, it's the largest natural area in Cook County, containing many miles of multiuse trails. Two other great options in the trail system include the previous hike, **Cap Sauers and Swallow Cliff Loop,** and the **Little Red Schoolhouse** hike, which follows on page 61.

Not included in this book is an extensive network of about 50 miles of trails to the west. While these trails are scenic, rugged, and extensive, be warned that they can be heavily trafficked by mountain bikers. Especially on narrower trails, sharing space with a steady stream of bikers can be distracting. As someone who regularly hikes and rides the mountain bike trails at Palos, I can attest that the vast majority of riders at Palos are polite and safety-conscious, but unfortunately, as with all modes of transport, there are exceptions.

One of the most scenic spots within the mountain biking area is **Tomahawk Slough.** Fringed with cattails and waving stands of prairie grasses, it's easily one of the most scenic lakes in the Chicago region. Farther back from the water, a wall of big oaks surrounding the slough gives it an isolated, backwoods feel. Just a stone's throw from Tomahawk Slough is an attractive new campground at **Bullfrog Lake,** offering cabins, tent camping, RV sites, and gear rental (learn more at fpdcc.com/camping /camp-bullfrog-lake). The picnic tables on the small bluff above Bullfrog Lake provide a primo spot to enjoy the views of the surrounding woodland. Both Tomahawk Slough and Bullfrog Lake can accessed easily from several different parking areas on the west side of Wolf Road.

If you'd like to get your hands dirty helping out with the landscape restoration efforts at Palos, consider volunteering with the **Palos Restoration Project.** The group holds workdays at a dozen different sites and works every weekend of the year. Depending on the season, they cut and burn brush, pull weedy invasive plants like garlic mustard, or collect and distribute seed. For 25 years, this group has been working to increase biodiversity in the preserves, enhancing the variety of plants that in turn support a greater variety of insects, birds, and mammals. Learn more at restorepalos.com.

• •

GPS TRAILHEAD COORDINATES N41° 42.988' W87° 51.969'

DIRECTIONS Take I-55 to Exit 279A. Follow La Grange Road (US 12/20/45) south for 3.5 miles. Turn right (west) on 95th Street, and follow it 0.7 mile. Look for the Country Lane Woods Parking Area, on the left.

The trail carves a path through prairie grasses near Long John Slough. *Photo: Tim Putala*

WITH 2.5 MILES of laid-back hiking and plenty of engaging exhibits, Little Red Schoolhouse Nature Center is particularly appealing for kids and beginning hikers. The trails run next to Long John Slough and through oak forests and savannas, as well as the occasional prairie.

DESCRIPTION

When the first incarnation of the Little Red Schoolhouse opened its doors more than a century ago, it was a place where children from local farms learned the three Rs. Over time, as the Palos–Sag Valley Forest Preserve expanded, the school building was moved and eventually shut down. The schoolhouse, the accompanying nature center, and the grounds now serve as a place where adults and a new generation of kids can delve into the natural world—and receive a quick lesson on the history of rural education.

Along with a variety of taxidermy specimens, there are plenty of live animals hanging around in the nature center and on the grounds, including birds and a variety of local frogs and snakes. Mixed in with the exhibits are details about the old school, including photos and a diorama depicting life at the school when it was located just to the west along what is now the Black Oak Trail.

DISTANCE & CONFIGURATION: 2.5 miles, 3 loops

DIFFICULTY: Easy

SCENERY: Scenic lake, oak woods and savannas, rolling terrain

EXPOSURE: Mostly shaded

TRAIL TRAFFIC: Light–moderate

TRAIL SURFACE: Dirt with some gravel

HIKING TIME: 1.5–2 hours

DRIVING DISTANCE: 22 miles from Millennium Park

ACCESS: Grounds open daily, 8 a.m.–5 p.m., March–October, and 8 a.m.–4 p.m., November–February, Exhibit building opens 1 hour after the grounds open and is closed Fridays. Closed for major holidays.

MAPS: Available at exhibit building; USGS *Sag Bridge, IL*

FACILITIES: Water, restrooms, nature center with animal exhibits

WHEELCHAIR ACCESS: None

CONTACT: 800-870-3666, fpdcc.com/preserves -and-trails

LOCATION: Willow Springs, IL 60480

COMMENTS: No dogs allowed on trails. This hike includes the Farm Pond Trail, Black Oak Trail, and White Oak Trail. In addition to the trails, there's a historic schoolhouse, a nature center, and an outdoor play area with plenty of stuff that kids will enjoy.

Start the hike on the Farm Pond Trail, next to the nature center. From the nature center, the trail hugs the shore of Long John Slough, a 35-acre shallow lake fringed by cattails and oaks (a *slough,* pronounced "slew," is one of the names given to a lake formed by pieces of glaciers left behind during the retreat of the most recent ice sheets). During autumn and spring, the slough is a popular stop for migrating waterbirds. Between June and September, considerable sections of the slough are blanketed with lily pads and thousands of white water lilies in bloom.

At 0.2 mile, turn right (west) at the fork onto Black Oak Trail, which runs through a small restored prairie with grasses, sedges, and flowers. Passing beyond a gated fence, turn right (northwest) again at a second fork. Listen for bullfrogs along the marshy edge of the slough.

As the trail turns away from the slough at 0.5 mile, the woods become dense and quiet. The terrain flattens. Deadfall, charred stumps, and other indications of controlled burnings become plentiful. Appearing regularly are trailside benches and folksy signs showing the animals and plants found in the preserve. Watch for the trail's namesake black oaks, which possess jagged (as opposed to rounded) lobes on their leaves.

At 0.9 mile is a sign for the former site of the schoolhouse. First built in 1870, the school burned to the ground in the mid-1880s and was quickly rebuilt. At about that time, 68 children were enrolled at the school, but only a third showed up for class, particularly in the spring and fall, when they were most needed on their farms. Life in the area began to change in 1915, when the forest preserve started acquiring many of the local farms. School enrollment dwindled. As families moved, the location of the schoolhouse was no longer convenient for many students. Shifting

Palos–Sag Valley Trail System:
Little Red Schoolhouse Hike

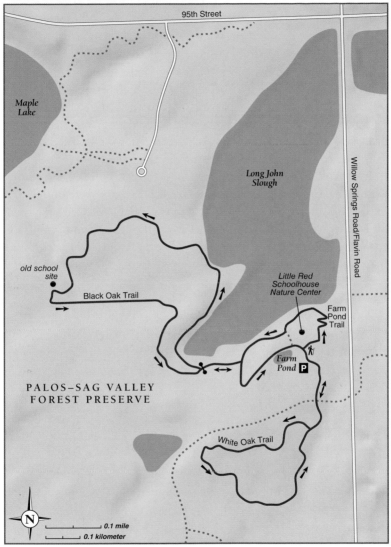

populations, combined with flooding problems at the site, prompted school officials to move the building in 1932. A local man using one mule and log rollers earned $75 for moving the wood structure three-quarters of a mile east to 104th Avenue. The forest preserve continued to expand, and the school was eventually closed; the last class graduated in 1948. In 1955, the school was moved to its present location and reopened as a nature center.

After passing the former school site, the trail shoots straight along what was at one time 99th Street. Beyond a marsh on the right at 1.2 miles is a short trail leading into a prairie. Finish the loop at 1.4 miles, and then head back through the gate, turning right (south) to regain the Farm Pond Trail. Be sure to check out the enormous cages containing the birds of prey.

Even on busy weekends when the Black Oak Trail and the exhibit buildings host a steady stream of visitors, you're still likely to find a quiet atmosphere on the White Oak Trail. Start the hike across the parking lot from the Little Red Schoolhouse. Just beyond a bench on the left overlooking a small pond, the trail crosses a multiuse path that runs through many sections of the 14,000-acre Palos–Sag Valley Forest Preserve. When you reach a fork at 0.2 mile, stay to the right (northeast) as the path leads through lightly rolling terrain. Watch for woodpeckers, flickers, and Eastern bluebirds within the canopy of oak leaves overhead. Joe's Pond, one of the many small bodies of water in the area left behind by glaciers, can be seen through the trees on the right at 0.6 mile. As the trail turns back toward the schoolhouse, you'll see a small ravine to the right. Lush with plants, this ravine is a favorite spot for deer during the summer. Complete the loop at 0.8 mile, and head back to the parking lot.

NEARBY ACTIVITIES

Up for more hiking? From the Little Red Schoolhouse, you can easily walk to Palos–Sag Valley's **Country Lane Loop** (see previous hike), which starts a half mile to the east. On the White Oak Trail, just take the Yellow Trail left (east). Also, a few miles south on Willow Springs Road, you can hook up with the **Cap Sauers and Swallow Cliff Loop** (see Hike 8, page 52).

· ·

GPS TRAILHEAD COORDINATES N41° 42.531' W87° 52.601'

DIRECTIONS Take I-55 to Exit 279A. Follow La Grange Road (US 12/45/20) south for 3.5 miles. Turn right (west) on 95th Street, and follow it 1.25 miles, turning left (south) on 104th Avenue (Flavin Road). The Little Red Schoolhouse Nature Center is on the right, a half mile south of 95th Street.

Boats rest in Chicago Harbor as skyscrapers rise in the distance.   *Photo: Photoluminate LLC/Shutterstock*

ENJOY STUNNING VIEWS of the downtown skyline as you hike along this strip of parkland that links the city and the lake. Pass Chicago landmarks such as Soldier Field, the Field Museum, and Buckingham Fountain on your way to the new Chicago Riverwalk.

DESCRIPTION

Chicago wouldn't be Chicago without the great expanse of Lake Michigan at its doorstep. The lakeshore not only offers urban dwellers refuge from the relentless concrete grid, but if you live in the city, it's probably the most accessible place to run, walk, cycle, or skate uninterrupted for miles. Indeed, for a great number of Chicagoans, a trip to the lake is synonymous with following this path as it snakes past harbors, museums, high rises, and acres of moored boats.

For those who prefer a less busy ramble on the Lakefront Trail, this south section is the place to go. This walk also offers a nice way to combine a shoreline stroll with a visit to one of the world-class museums along the way. The 31st Street Beach,

DISTANCE & CONFIGURATION: 5.2-mile point-to-point/10.4-mile out-and-back path along the shoreline of Lake Michigan

DIFFICULTY: Easy–moderate

SCENERY: Lakefront, parks, harbors, city skyline, a beach, the Chicago River, and various museums and attractions, including Northerly Island and easy side trips to North Michigan Avenue and Navy Pier

EXPOSURE: Open

TRAIL TRAFFIC: Heavy, especially on warm weekends

TRAIL SURFACE: Paved path. For much of this route on the Lakefront Trail, you can walk on the grass near the water or on the concrete revetments that protect the shoreline.

HIKING TIME: 3 hours

DRIVING DISTANCE: 4 miles from Millennium Park

ACCESS: Daily, sunrise–sunset. Pay parking is available at 31st Street Beach; for rates, see chicagoharbors.info/harbors/31st-street-harbor.

MAPS: Visit tinyurl.com/lakefronttrailmap for a PDF map; USGS *Jackson Park, IL,* and *Chicago Loop, IL*

FACILITIES: Snack shops, beach, bike rentals, benches, restrooms, and picnic tables; drinking fountains every mile or so; an assortment of restaurants and bars along the Riverwalk

WHEELCHAIR ACCESS: Yes

CONTACT: 312-742-7529, chicagoparkdistrict .com/parks-facilities/lakefront-trail

LOCATION: Lake Shore Drive between East 31st Street to the north and East 71st Street to the south, Chicago, IL

COMMENTS: Separate trails exist along much of this section for biking and walking/running— stick to the walking trail. Dogs must be leashed.

where this hike begins, hosts a playground, a beach, a beach house, restrooms, a snack shop, and a newly built harbor with room for 1,000 boats. North of the beach house, Burnham Park is fairly open and grassy, with plenty of new trees planted. In recent years, the city has relandscaped parts of the park and rerouted this and other sections of the south path.

Thanks to local advocacy efforts and the support of a private donor, the park district is building separate trails for people on foot and people on bikes along the entire 18 miles of the Lakefront Trail. Once that project is complete, trail users will get some welcome relief from congestion on the trail. Particularly on the north side, the congestion has been not only an inconvenience but a danger, sometimes causing horrible crashes between people biking and walking or running.

Until the trail-separation project is complete, some of the congestion can be avoided by walking close to the shoreline, either on the grass or on the new concrete revetments that protect the shoreline. Just before you reach McCormick Place, the world's largest convention center, you'll see a small bird sanctuary that occupies a fenced-in prairie. Nearby, several small sculptures and a garden are part of a memorial to Chicago firefighters and paramedics who died in the line of duty. The mammoth horizontal structure of McCormick Place looks more suited for a suburban office park. The waterfall that seems to tumble from its interior and the many limestone blocks scattered about are a halfhearted attempt to make the building fit into this crucial piece of urban lakefront.

South Lakefront Trail

McCormick Place is situated at the mouth of Burnham Harbor, which is well stocked with private boats in the warmer months. Across the harbor, you'll see Northerly Island; built in 1925, it was conceived by the park's namesake, Daniel Burnham. Burnham, an architect and urban planner, helped plan the 1893 World's Columbian Exposition in Chicago and is also known for his Plan of Chicago, a comprehensive design for the city. A private airport that operated on Northerly Island for 55 years was shut down in 2003, and now the property is a lovely nature preserve and a concert venue.

Coming up on the left is Soldier Field, a national landmark dedicated to Chicago's fallen servicemen. Built in 1922, the stadium received a controversial face-lift in 2003 when a glass-and-steel top section was added to the existing Neoclassical structure. Sandwiched between Chicago Harbor and Soldier Field are a sledding hill on the left and a harbor parking lot on the right. Just north of the Chicago Bears' home turf is the Field Museum, one of the most prominent natural-history museums in the world. This enormous marble structure, also designed by Daniel Burnham, houses a vast collection of exhibits on anthropology, zoology, botany, and geology. The main floor lobby contains the skeleton of the largest and most complete *Tyrannosaurus rex* ever found.

Continuing ahead through the museum campus, the trail gains a bit of elevation and then passes underneath East Solidarity Drive, which leads out to Adler Planetarium and Northerly Island. As the trail runs along the back side of the John G. Shedd Aquarium, you can see the paneled glass wall on the back of the oceanarium. Containing the world's largest indoor saltwater pool, the oceanarium is home to a family of beluga whales and a handful of dolphins.

As the path winds around the aquarium, you'll likely notice seagulls fishing from the long thin breakwater that protects Chicago Harbor. As you come out from behind the aquarium, instead of following the path up the hill and walking beside the traffic on North Lake Shore Drive, stay to the right and walk along the water. About halfway along this harbor walkway, you'll see the grand Buckingham Fountain in the midsection of Grant Park on the left. Passing the Chicago Yacht Club, continue alongside the shoreline as it bends right and then left, leading you alongside acres of moored boats and a large passenger ship.

Stay right (east) at the base of the ramp up the bridge that crosses the Chicago River. Follow the path as it swings left (west) alongside the Chicago River and then heads through an Art Deco–style passageway with scenes from Chicago history painted on tiled walls. At certain times along this stretch, you'll see a giant arc of water shooting across the river from the other side.

The Chicago Riverwalk, finished in 2016, is one of the most exciting infrastructure developments in downtown Chicago in recent years. Along with restaurants, bars, and kayak and bike rentals, there are loads of places to sit and admire the dramatic city skyline, the historic bridges, the constant boat traffic, and the persistently charming design of the Riverwalk itself.

You'll pass a couple of seasonal restaurants before arriving at the stretch of riverfront where tour boats dock. After you pass under the McCormick Bridgehouse & Chicago River Museum (bridgehousemuseum.org), the river curves south, and soon you'll pass a Vietnam War memorial. If the weather is warm, stop in for a glass of wine and a bite at the City Winery, and watch the crowds stroll by. Toward the end of the Riverwalk are an amphitheater, a floating garden, and a fountain that invites kids to play in it. At Lake Street, either turn around and start walking back to 31st Street, or catch public transit, a Divvy bike share, or a cab back to where you started.

NEARBY ACTIVITIES

If you have time, take a detour to **Northerly Island,** where you're likely to see migratory birds among the prairie and the wetlands, as well as the stellar views of the city and the lake. *Note:* Dogs are not allowed.

You could also combine this hike with visits to places you'll pass, like the **Field Museum** (312-922-9410, fieldmuseum.org), the **John G. Shedd Aquarium** (312-939-2438, sheddaquarium.org), and the **Adler Planetarium** (312-922-7827, adler planetarium.org).

If you're interested in heading farther north on the Lakefront Trail, the first thing you'll pass is **Navy Pier** (800-595-7437, navypier.org), the most popular tourist attraction in Chicago. While it often feels geared toward 12-year-olds with questionable taste, it does offer a nice place for an open-air stroll out onto the lake.

• •

GPS TRAILHEAD COORDINATES N41 50.269' W87° 36.429'

DIRECTIONS From South Lake Shore Drive, take the 31st Street exit. Turn east (toward the lake) on East 31st Street, and follow the driveway to the parking lot on the right. Alternatively, if you're approaching via I-90/I-94, exit on West 31st Street and head east (toward the lake). Proceed to the 31st Street Beach parking lot, 1.2 miles ahead.

PUBLIC TRANSPORTATION When you reach West Lake Street at the west end of the Riverwalk, head back to North Michigan Avenue. Catch the **CTA** 3, X3, or X4 bus heading south on North Michigan Avenue, and get off at the corner of South Martin Luther King Jr. Drive and East 31st Street. Head east for 0.5 mile to reach 31st Street Beach.

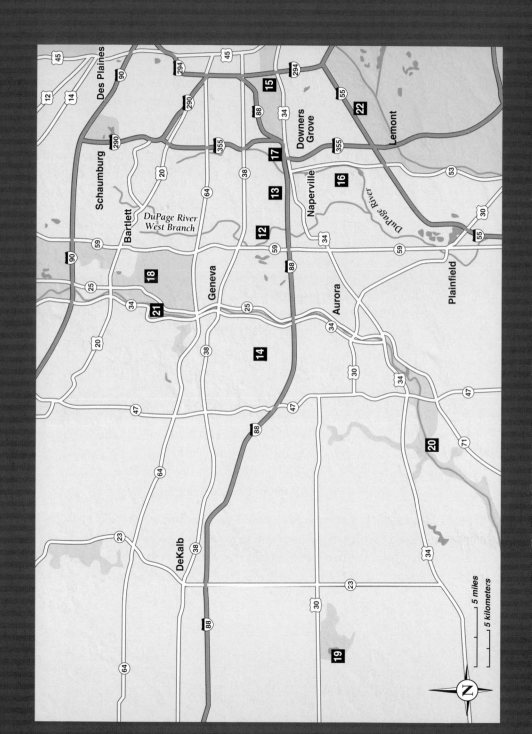

DuPAGE COUNTY AND DESTINATIONS WEST

Blackwell Forest Preserve encompasses both sweeping prairie and dense woodland.   *Photo: Ted Villaire*

THE MOST PRISTINE landscape at Blackwell Forest Preserve is in the vicinity of McKee Marsh, an expansive wetland cradled in prairie and savanna. As you hike the gently rolling terrain around the marsh, you're likely to see herons, egrets, bluebirds, and bobolinks. Other parts of this hike run through thick stands of oak, hickory, and elm and across rocky-bottomed Springbrook Creek. When finished, visitors may consider renting a canoe, climbing Mount Hoy, enjoying one of the park's great picnicking spots, or trying additional hiking options to the east and west.

DESCRIPTION

The gently rolling terrain at Blackwell Forest Preserve has two distinct personalities. The southern part of this hike brings you through groves of maple, elm, oak, cottonwood, and white pine, which grow close to the trail and sometimes give the impression that you're passing through a gateway. All this changes, though, after you cross Springbrook Creek: the landscape opens up and treats visitors to views of the prairie, savanna, and expansive McKee Marsh.

   The first thing you'll see when you start the hike is White Pine Pond on the right and the hill beyond it—a former landfill called Mount Hoy. We can only hope that the county official who decided to style a 150-foot pile of trash as a "mount" had his tongue lodged in his cheek; in any case, Mount Hoy is a local landmark and one of the highest points in DuPage County. While the off-gases do lend a hint of *eau de garbage*

DISTANCE & CONFIGURATION: 6.3-mile lollipop loop

DIFFICULTY: Easy–moderate

SCENERY: Prairie, savanna, wetland, woodland, stream, ponds

EXPOSURE: Mostly unshaded

TRAIL TRAFFIC: Light

TRAIL SURFACE: Multiuse crushed gravel

HIKING TIME: 2–3 hours

DRIVING DISTANCE: 32 miles from Millennium Park

ACCESS: Daily, 1 hour after sunrise–1 hour after sunset; no fees or permits

MAPS: Available at trail boards in the parking areas and the website below; USGS *Naperville, IL*

FACILITIES: Restrooms, picnic areas, boat launch, campground, sledding hill, archery range, concessions, access to regional rail-trails

WHEELCHAIR ACCESS: Yes

CONTACT: 630-933-7200, dupageforest.org /places-to-go/forest-preserves/blackwell

LOCATION: Main Drive at Butterfield Road, Warrenville, IL 60555

COMMENTS: Dogs must be on leash no longer than 10 feet. This hike can be easily lengthened or shortened. Blackwell offers canoe rentals, along with great picnicking spots on the shore of Silver Lake. Blackwell also hosts the only campground operated by DuPage County.

at the top, the 360-degree summit view is well worth the trip—on a clear day, look for Willis Tower (formerly Sears Tower) 30 miles to the east. In September, October, and into November, visitors to Mount Hoy may see sharp-shinned, broad-winged, and red-tailed hawks passing by as they migrate south.

Continuing north on the trail, you'll pass a stand of white pine and then the forest preserve's archery range. This also is where stately specimens of oak, hickory, and elm begin rising high all around the trail. Not long after you pass a short spur trail that leads to the shore of Springbrook Creek, you'll cross the narrow, rocky-bedded stream on a steel bridge. At the edge of the creek, large cottonwood trees soar skyward and maples hang lazily from the banks. In late summer, nearby sections of trail are decorated with 15-foot-tall, yellow-flowered compass plants.

Past the creek, the landscape dramatically transforms: now grassland, savanna, and marshes rule the terrain, and for the next several miles, you'll get little or no shade from the sprinkling of walnut, willow, and maple trees growing in the open grassland. Around twilight, you're likely to see deer browsing among the goldenrod, milkweed, aster, and other prairie plants along this stretch. Just before crossing Mack Road, the trail winds through an attractive grove of black locust trees with long, thin, crooked trunks.

Shortly after crossing Mack Road, the trail cuts through a cattail marsh where you'll likely see some red-winged blackbirds flitting about. At the junction, take the trail to the right (east). From here, you'll pass clusters of cottonwood trees and cut through another cattail marsh on the way into a gently rolling prairie. If you're hiking on a warm summer day, take a break at the shaded split-log bench on the right. As the trail curves left, it rises just enough to allow a better view of the patchwork of goldenrod, compass plants, sumac, Queen Anne's lace, and other prairie plants,

73

Blackwell Forest Preserve Hike

Roosevelt Road

Gary's Mill Road

Catbird Trail

Regional Trail

Nighthawk Trail

Purnell Road

Bobolink Trail

McKee Marsh

59

Regional Trail

Mack Road

Regional Trail

Egret Trail

West Branch DuPage River

Williams Road

Winfield Road

Silver Lake

Springbrook Creek

Mount Hoy (836')

archery area

White Pine Pond

Butterfield Road

Illinois Prairie Path

59

Batavia Road

56

N

0.2 mile

0.2 kilometer

which create swaths of yellow, scarlet, and creamy white that remain vibrant through much of the summer and early fall.

Before reaching a handful of trail junctions heading to the right, the trail winds through patches of hickory and oak woodland. On the west side of the loop, you'll likely hear some traffic sounds drifting over from IL 59 to the west. Continuing ahead on the main trail, a series of trailside observation decks offer views of McKee

Marsh. A pair of field glasses may help you spot bluebirds, great blue and black crowned night herons, blackbirds, white egrets, various raptors, cormorants, and other birds that are known to visit the marsh; in late summer and fall, when the marsh is dry, the activity may slow down.

The first observation deck is near where the bones of a woolly mammoth were found in a clay deposit in 1977. The 13,000-year-old bones, which are on display at Fullersburg Forest Preserve (see Hike 15), nearly 15 miles to the east, belong to the largest woolly mammoth ever found in the Great Lakes region. Pass two more observation spots before completing the loop around McKee Marsh. Turn right (south) at the junction to follow the trail back to the parking lot.

NEARBY ACTIVITIES

A few miles west in Batavia, the grounds of **Fermi National Accelerator Laboratory (Fermilab)** offer several miles of hiking through prairie and woodland (see fermilab naturalareas.org for more information). Just to the east of Blackwell is **Herrick Lake Forest Preserve,** which hosts more than 6 miles of hiking around Herrick Lake and through woodland, prairie, and wetland. Both of these destinations can be accessed on bicycle trails from Blackwell. If you drive to Fermilab, turn right (west) on Butterfield Road, and then turn right (north) on Batavia Road after crossing the West Branch DuPage River; look for trail signs on the right after you pass Wilson Hall, Fermilab's main building. The entrance to Herrick Lake Forest Preserve is 1.5 miles east of Blackwell on Butterfield Road.

• •

GPS TRAILHEAD COORDINATES N41° 49.690' W88° 10.590'

DIRECTIONS From the intersection of I-355 and I-88, take I-88 West for 5.7 miles; then exit right (north) onto Winfield Road. In 1.5 miles, turn left on IL 56/Butterfield Road. After 0.5 mile, turn right into Blackwell Forest Preserve, and park in the first lot on the right. The trailhead is just across the park road, at the south edge of White Pine Pond; look for the sign pointing to McKee Marsh.

PUBLIC TRANSPORTATION You can catch this hike 2.3 miles from the Winfield Station on **Metra**'s Union Pacific/West Line; consider taking your bike aboard so that you can ride for the last couple of miles on low-traffic roads. From the Winfield Station, head south on Winfield Road, and then turn right on Gary Mills Road. The trailhead for the Nighthawk Trail is on the left after you cross IL 28; this trail connects with the loop around McKee Marsh. Another option is to get off at the Wheaton Station and take the Aurora Branch of the Illinois Prairie Path to the preserve.

A view of Rice Lake at Danada Forest Preserve   *Photo: Corey Seeman (cseeman/Flickr)*

NESTLED IN AN unlikely spot between subdivisions and I-88, Danada Forest Preserve offers terrific hiking through wide-open prairies and gently sloping savannas. Once a training ground for top racehorses, Danada still caters to equestrians with an array of programs.

DESCRIPTION

Before DuPage County acquired this 753-acre forest preserve, the land hosted a farm and a racehorse-training facility owned by commodity trader Daniel Rice and his wife, Ada. After buying the property in 1929, they began growing wheat and corn and raising livestock. Over the years, they built a 19-room mansion, a greenhouse, an employee boarding house, a swimming pool, formal gardens, a 26-stall Kentucky-style horse barn, and a horse-exercise track. The Rices entered their first horse in the Kentucky Derby in 1949. Fourteen years later, their horse Lucky Debonair won the Derby with the third-fastest time in the history of the race; the following year, their horse Abdicator took second place. The Rices sold their racehorse interests in the early 1970s for an estimated $5 million.

Once the county bought Danada in 1980, it was reborn as a hiking and biking destination, as well as a place for beginning and intermediate equestrians to learn

DISTANCE & CONFIGURATION: 5 miles, 2 loops

DIFFICULTY: Easy

SCENERY: Savannas, prairies, marshes, and a lake

EXPOSURE: Mostly open with some shade

TRAIL TRAFFIC: Light

TRAIL SURFACE: Dirt and crushed limestone

HIKING TIME: 2–3 hours for both loops

DRIVING DISTANCE: 28 miles from Millennium Park

ACCESS: Daily, 1 hour after sunrise–1 hour after sunset; no fees or permits

MAPS: Available at trail board at edge of parking lot and the website below; USGS *Wheaton, IL*

FACILITIES: Water, restrooms, equestrian center

WHEELCHAIR ACCESS: None

CONTACT: 630-933-7200, dupageforest.org /places-to-go/forest-preserves/danada

LOCATION: Naperville Road, Wheaton, IL 60189

COMMENTS: Dogs must be on leash no longer than 10 feet. To learn about programs offered by the Danada Equestrian Center, call 630-668-6012 or visit danada.info.

horse care and riding. Today, the Danada Equestrian Center offers an assortment of classes, lectures, trail and sleigh rides, and even a summer riding camp for kids.

Start the shorter 1.25-mile section of this hike on the wide gravel path known as the Regional Trail. Pick it up to the right (northeast) of the mansion, and head east past the main barn and past trail marker 15. At marker 16, take a narrow trail on the right, which leads into a beautiful lightly rolling savanna known as Parson's Grove. To hike the perimeter of the grove, stay to the right at the next four trail intersections. Once in the savanna, it's difficult to miss the birds chattering continuously among the tall grasses and the abundant oaks. As the trail proceeds, the savanna undergoes subtle changes in the concentration of oaks and the varieties of grasses. On some trail surfaces, you may notice coyote scat, which is recognizable by the fur it contains—a remnant of the coyotes' prey. (Coyotes are fond of marking trails and trail intersections with their droppings.)

The narrow path meets again with the Regional Trail 0.7 mile into the hike, at marker 17. Turn right and continue straight ahead, beyond the map board and the two-track intersection, for an expansive view of Rice Lake and the surrounding suburban development. Also visible is the continuation of the Regional Trail, which runs a mile along the shore of the lake to the intersection of Butterfield Road and Leask Lane. To the left is a trail leading up a small hill that provides an even better view of the prairie and the 40-acre artificial lake. After taking in the view, head back along the Regional Trail for 0.4 mile to the trailhead.

The longer 3.75-mile section of this hike begins by following the Regional Trail through the tunnel under Naperville Road, west of the parking lot. As you come out of the tunnel, the DuPage County Forest Preserve District Headquarters is on the left. Also on the left is Heroes' Grove, a planting of 9 burr oaks and 11 white oaks dedicated to American heroism demonstrated on 9/11. After passing

Danada Forest Preserve Hike

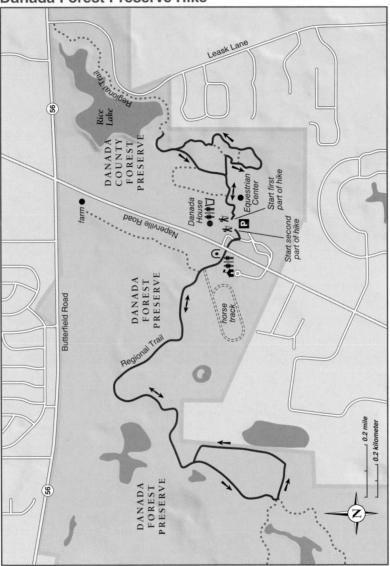

a gravel service road, the trail runs by horseracing starting gates and the beginning of the horse-exercise track. After the gates, another gravel service road on the right leads a half mile north to a small, 1950s-style model farm that operates in the northeastern section of the preserve.

As the trail enters Danada's wide-open prairie, hikers may want to refer to a sign along the way that will help them identify common prairie grasses such as goldenrod, big bluestem, compass plant, and Indian grass. This flat, grassy landscape draws in the birds, particularly swallows, goldfinches, and sparrows. Also common is the brown-headed cowbird, a member of the blackbird family known as a "brood parasite" because the female lays its eggs in the nests of the other birds, often to the detriment of the host's young.

At 1.2 miles from the parking lot, a marshy area appears on the right. Just after the mileage board, take the fork to the right. Clusters of trees and shrubs start to interrupt the grassy prairie just before reaching an intersection at 1.7 miles. At the intersection, stay left. Finish the loop at 2.3 miles and turn right, heading back the way you came. Follow the Regional Trail 0.9 mile back through the savanna and prairie. After you pass through the tunnel, the parking lot is straight ahead.

NEARBY ACTIVITIES

For those who want more of the open vistas seen on the this hike, continue beyond the final loop to **Herrick Lake Forest Preserve,** which offers several miles of hiking.

• •

GPS TRAILHEAD COORDINATES N41° 49.141' W88° 06.499'

DIRECTIONS From the intersection of I-88 and I-294, take I-88 West for 6.5 miles. Take the I-355 North exit toward the Northwest suburbs, and immediately use the left lane to follow the signs for IL 56/Butterfield Road. Turn left (west) on Butterfield Road and, in 4 miles, turn right (north) on South Naperville Road—the preserve is actually south of this intersection, but you can't turn left here, so look for a side street where you can turn around. Back at the intersection with Butterfield Road, drive south on Naperville Road for 0.9 mile, get into the far-left lane, and turn left at the sign for Danada into the parking lot.

PUBLIC TRANSPORTATION Take your bike on **Metra**'s Union Pacific/West Line to the Wheaton Station. From here, it's about a 5-mile ride on bike trails to Danada: Take the Prairie Path west as it runs beside the train tracks. Where the Prairie Path forks, take the Aurora Branch left. At Butterfield Road, turn left and continue to Herrick Lake Forest Preserve. From Herrick Lake, follow the Regional Trail into Danada.

Dick Young's interpretive platforms make for great bird-watching.   *Photo: Ralph Miner*

AS ONE OF the best birding spots in Kane County, Dick Young Forest Preserve possesses a great mix of wetlands, prairie, and woodland. In addition to this hike around Nelson Lake, you can add 6 or so miles to the hike by hitting some of the trails that run through the enormous prairie in the western half of the preserve.

DESCRIPTION

Dick Young Forest Preserve dishes up lots of good bird-watching. Woodpeckers, blue jays, white-breasted nuthatches, black-capped chickadees, cardinals, red-winged blackbirds, ring-necked pheasants, dark-eyed juncos, and various kinds of finches and sparrows often appear here. White pelicans come to the preserve for a few weeks around the beginning of April, sometimes gathering in flocks of 250 birds. Other birds less frequently seen in the area—such as the American bittern, Wilson's phalarope, black tern, sandhill crane, and Northern harrier hawk—also love the marshy thickets and open water in the park.

Start from the parking area beside the old concrete grain silo, a structure that gives you a good idea what the land was used for not so long ago. In just a few moments of hiking along the crushed-gravel trail, big, reedy Nelson Lake comes into view. You'll immediately notice that the lake sits in a depression, caused by the immense weight

DISTANCE & CONFIGURATION: 3.6-mile loop with a couple of smaller loops

DIFFICULTY: Easy

SCENERY: Lake, marsh, streams, prairie, woodland

EXPOSURE: Mostly open

TRAIL TRAFFIC: Moderate

TRAIL SURFACE: Mowed grass, crushed gravel

HIKING TIME: 1.5 hours

DRIVING DISTANCE: 45 miles from Millennium Park

ACCESS: Daily, sunrise–sunset; no fees or permits

WHEELCHAIR ACCESS: Only the first 100 yards leading to the first lookout platform

MAPS: Available at the website below; USGS *Chicago Loop, IL*

FACILITIES: Restrooms, picnic shelter, benches, observation decks

CONTACT: 630-232-5980, kaneforest.com /ForestPreserveView.aspx?ID=14

LOCATION: 2S326 Nelson Lake Road, Batavia, IL 60510

COMMENTS: Dogs must be leashed and cleaned up after. Bring binoculars to see the abundant birdlife around the lake and in the marshy areas, and to get a better view of the oodles of muskrat huts sprinkled throughout the lake if you visit during the colder months.

of glacial ice sitting on it some 10,000 years ago. In fall and winter, you'll see dozens of muskrat lodges, built with mounds of sticks and mud, pushing up from the water.

Commanding views of the lake unfold as you mount the metal viewing platform at the T in the trail. After taking in the splendor of this protected natural area, head to the right along a mowed grass trail, which is elevated about 20–30 feet above the lake. Down by the shore, big swaths of sedge grasses and a sprawling cattail marsh push out toward the open water; above you, big gnarled oaks and scraggly hickory trees reach across the trail; and to the right of the trail, prairie grass sways in the breeze.

At the next trail junction (Junction 5), take a left and you'll drop down alongside the marsh, where, for the next half mile or so, the trail threads its way between marsh-land on the left and Nelson Lake Road on the right. At about 0.8 mile into the hike, the trail changes course, curving left, and you pass the sign announcing that you're entering an Illinois Nature Preserve. At 1 mile, consider a stroll along the short trail heading left, which takes you to an observation spot out into the marsh. At different points around the lake, you can keep an eye on your progress with glimpses of the old grain silo in the parking area.

At 1.3 miles into the hike, the trail curves right, enters a wooded area, and then arrives at Junction 4—stay left here as you follow a trail that divides an attractive savanna on the left and the sprawling prairie on the right. At 1.6 miles, follow another junction left to a second metal viewing platform with more sweeping views of the 40-acre lake. Returning to the main trail, forge straight ahead, with the lake on the left; while this trail is clearly well used, it's not well marked. This narrower trail offers fine views of the lake from an open and grassy bank.

By now, this enchanting landscape undoubtedly has helped pry you from the day's—if not the week's—troubles. This is especially true on this section of the hike,

81

Dick Young Forest Preserve Hike

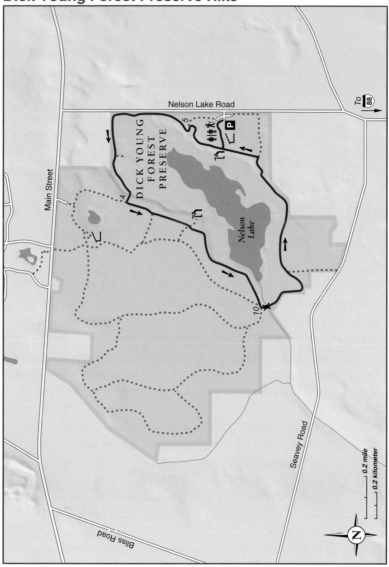

which imparts a surprisingly quiet, peaceful atmosphere despite the glimpses of housing developments in the distance. Another appealing feature of this section of the hike is the enormous prairie, which has benefited from one of the most extensive restoration efforts in the entire region. Prairie-flower aficionados will find shooting star, echinacea, rattlesnake master, liatris, compass plant, and many others.

The obvious beauty of this local treasure is what prompted local naturalist Dick Young to start working with others to preserve it. In addition to his efforts to expand parks, nature preserves, trails, and open spaces in Kane and Kendall Counties, he was also the author of the guidebook *Kane County Wild Plants and Natural Areas.* Young, who has another forest preserve in Kendall County named after him, died in 2011 at the age of 86.

At 2.3 miles, you'll arrive at a footbridge straddling a scenic little stream called Lake Run that feeds Nelson Lake. The benches flanking the bridge offer the perfect spot to relax, enjoy the view, and break out the sandwiches. A wooden post here announces that you've reached Junction 10. After crossing the bridge, you'll walk alongside a stretch of farmland before the trail again takes a short drop to the shore of the lake, where you'll see more big patches of cattails and sedge grasses growing.

One of the most charming features of this lake is how it changes with the seasons. In early summer, the lake is covered with a dense tangle of aquatic plants, including duckweed, hornwort, coontail, and great bladderwort. In mid-July, the lake is blanketed with white water lilies. And in fall and winter, you can expect to see the surface peppered with muskrat lodges.

For this final stretch of the hike, you'll cross another small stream that flows under the trail. Enjoy the final glimpses of the lake as you keep an eye peeled for the old grain silo that will guide you back to the parking area.

NEARBY ACTIVITIES

A few miles east of the preserve, the town of **Batavia** offers a pleasant Riverwalk as well as the Fox River Trail, which runs for 38 miles along the river between Algonquin to the north and Oswego to the south. Restaurants, shops, and bars are plentiful downtown, which is chock-full of beautiful historic limestone buildings. The **Batavia Depot Museum** (155 Houston St.; 630-406-5274, bataviahistoricalsociety.org) features exhibits on local history, including a small exhibit on Mary Todd Lincoln's stay at a local sanitarium. Also in downtown Batavia, **Water Street Studios** (160 S. Water St.; 630-761-9977, waterstreetstudios.org) has frequent exhibits featuring artists in the Fox River Valley area.

• •

GPS TRAILHEAD COORDINATES N41° 50.048' W88° 22.226'

DIRECTIONS From the intersection of I-355 and I-88, take I-88 West for 12.5 miles. Shortly after crossing the Fox River, exit right (north) onto Orchard Road. After 0.4 mile, turn left at the first traffic light onto Orchard Gateway Boulevard; then make an immediate right on Deerpath Road, which becomes Nelson Lake Road. The parking area is less than 2 miles ahead on the left.

Bridge over Salt Creek   *Photo: Tim Putala*

YOU MAY BE surprised to find this much natural beauty just 20 miles from the Loop. Nearly this entire hike accompanies Salt Creek as it meanders next to a bluff and winds around a couple of islands on its way to the historic watermill at the south tip of the park.

DESCRIPTION

Nestled against the communities of Hinsdale, La Grange, and Oak Brook, the 222 acres of Fullersburg Woods Forest Preserve have been a popular spot since they opened to the public in 1920. While visitors have always been drawn to the creek and its environs, more recently the historic mill and Nature Education Center have served as added attractions. When you pick up a map at the door of the Nature Education Center, be sure to duck inside to see the 13,000-year-old woolly mammoth skeleton, which was uncovered in 1977 at Blackwell Forest Preserve, about 15 miles west of Fullersburg (see Hike 12). The accompanying signs describe how researchers determined the animal's gender and age at death, and why researchers disagree about whether the mammoth was killed by humans. Kids will also enjoy a few mounted animal specimens, interactive displays, and the spotting scopes pointed toward Salt Creek.

To start the hike, look for the crushed-gravel trail on the north side of the Nature Education Center. After you pass a wide point in the creek, continue straight ahead over the bridge that leads to a part-time island, and head left (west). During the short stroll around the island, you'll pass a picnic shelter and a dried pond bed on the right.

DISTANCE & CONFIGURATION: 3.25-mile loop

DIFFICULTY: Easy

SCENERY: Salt Creek, woodland, marshes, islands, footbridges, and a mill that is now a museum

EXPOSURE: More exposed than shaded

TRAIL TRAFFIC: Generally moderate, sometimes heavy

TRAIL SURFACE: Crushed gravel

HIKING TIME: 2 hours, including a visit to Graue Mill and Museum

DRIVING DISTANCE: 21 miles from Millennium Park

ACCESS: Trails open daily, 1 hour after sunrise–1 hour after sunset; Nature Education Center open daily, 9 a.m.–5 p.m.,

except major holidays. Trail access is free, but Graue Mill and Museum charges admission; call 630-655-2090 or visit grauemill.org for more information.

MAPS: Available outside the Nature Education Center and at the website below; USGS *Hinsdale, IL*

FACILITIES: Nature Education Center, restrooms, water, benches, numerous log picnic shelters along the trail

WHEELCHAIR ACCESS: Yes

CONTACT: 630-850-8110, dupageforest.org /fullersburg-woods-nature-education-center

LOCATION: 3609 Spring Road, Oak Brook, IL 60523

COMMENTS: Dogs must be on leash no longer than 10 feet

Crossing the bridge again, turn right (west), passing a water pump and restrooms on the left. Here, the trail meanders beside an attractive stretch of Salt Creek: Trees hang lazily over the water; on the opposite bank, a small bluff rises above the creek. Just ahead, the trail passes an impressive stone picnic shelter with benches and a fireplace. Many of the preserve's picnic shelters, as well as the log Nature Education Center and Graue Mill, were built or restored by the Civilian Conservation Corps, which had a camp here in the 1930s. Beyond the large boulders on the left, stay to the right at the next five trail junctions.

After crossing Salt Creek again, you'll pass a trail heading left into the Paul Butler Nature Area. If you wish to add an extra mile or so to your hike, take this narrow footpath as it follows the creek upstream to a small dam. When you reach the pond beyond the dam, I suggest turning around and heading back to the main trail—the remainder of this trail can be flooded in spots and is noisy due to traffic on 31st Street.

Continuing on the main trail, the path curves left, away from Salt Creek, and then rises up a small hill. As the path returns to the side of the creek, look for the trail you just hiked on the other side of the creek. On the left, you'll soon pass the other end of the trail for the Paul Butler Nature Area. Not long after the landscape drops down to creek level, you'll pass over a couple of small streams; the first is intermittent, and the second seems to runs year-round. As you pass the island you hiked earlier, you'll start to see the backyards of houses on the left. At 1.9 miles into the hike, a picturesque log bridge leads over Salt Creek to the Nature Education Center.

After the bridge, the path runs straight south as the creek slowly curves to the right. When you meet back up with the creek, the water grows wider until you reach the dam, which is flanked by brick Graue Mill and its giant waterwheel. For

Fullersburg Woods Forest Preserve Loop

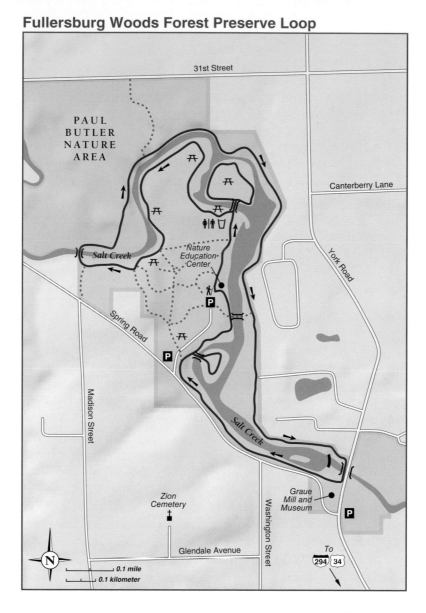

anyone with an interest in local history and water mills, the mill is well worth a visit: cross Salt Creek on the York Road footpath, and head over to the front door of the mill, which faces the Graue House. The owner of the mill, Frederick Graue, once lived here with his family.

For a small admission fee, you can hear a 20-minute presentation in which a white-aproned miller explains the 15,000-year-old practice of grinding grain and how it was done here. After Fredrick Graue built the mill in 1852, three generations of his family operated the mill until 1912, and it continued as a working mill until 1929. At the end of the presentation, the miller grinds a half bucket of cornmeal using the mill's original millstones, which are made from a type of quartz, known as buhrstone, imported from France.

In the basement, you'll learn that the mill was also a stop on the Underground Railroad. Along with other local stops in Plainfield, Aurora, Sugar Grove, Joliet, and Hinsdale, the Graue Mill was a part of the clandestine network of places where escaped slaves could rest and be fed on their way to Chicago, from which they could travel across the Great Lakes to Canada. On the second and third floors of the mill is a collection of artifacts from the period of 1850–1890, including room settings, farm implements, and a re-created general store.

From the mill, the path runs back to the Nature Education Center between the dam's backwater and Spring Road. Along the way, you'll pass a sign explaining that Salt Creek got its name when a farmer's wagon was stuck in the creek while hauling a barrel of salt. He left the wagon overnight and returned the next morning to find the salt had dissolved. Farther ahead, follow the trail branching right (east); then take the short bridge to the right (south) for a short loop around this little piece of land—sometimes an island—that sticks out into the water. Crossing back over the bridge, continue to the right until you see the parking lot on the left.

NEARBY ACTIVITIES

If you'd like to see more of Salt Creek, head over to **Bemis Woods Forest Preserve,** 1 mile directly east of Fullersburg Woods. Bemis Woods offers several miles of multi-purpose trails and the western end of the Salt Creek bicycle path. This paved path runs for 6.6 miles east, ending at the doorstep of the world-renowned **Brookfield Zoo.** To reach Bemis Woods, turn left (southeast) on Spring Road as you're leaving Fullersburg Woods. After passing Graue Mill, turn left (south) on York Road; then turn left (east) on Ogden Avenue, and drive 1.2 miles. The driveway for Bemis Woods will be on your left; the bicycle trail starts on the right, just before the sledding hill.

GPS TRAILHEAD COORDINATES N41° 49.582' W87° 55.948'

DIRECTIONS From the intersection of I-88 and I-294, head south on I-294 for 3.2 miles. Exit west onto Ogden Avenue (US 34/Walter Payton Memorial Highway) and, in 0.4 mile, turn right (north) on York Road. In 0.6 mile, turn left on Spring Road at the sign for Graue Mill. In another 0.5 mile, turn right and follow the road a short distance to the parking lot. The Fullersburg Woods Nature Education Center is at the north end of the lot.

16 GREENE VALLEY FOREST PRESERVE LOOP

A view of Anderson Creek through the oaks   *Photo: Corey Seeman (cseeman/Flickr)*

AT GREENE VALLEY Forest Preserve, you'll find groves of stately oaks, quiet twisting streams, and wide-open swaths of grassland—very likely with a red-tailed hawk or two nearby, waiting for their prey.

DESCRIPTION

In 1835, two years before Chicago was incorporated as a city, the first members of the Greene family settled on land that's now part of the Greene Valley Forest Preserve. As was the case with many other early residents of DuPage County, wheat fields and dairy cows were the Greenes' bread and butter. In 1969, the county bought a portion of the family's land, added it to existing holdings, and transformed it into a forest preserve. Some of the family's original structures, including a house built in 1841, remain on the corner of Greene and Hobson Roads.

Though knowing the human history gives you a better sense of this place, it's not the star attraction here. Instead, what grabs you are spacious prairies, sprawling floodplains, and dappled savannas. These attractions seem especially precious because they're surrounded by houses and streets humming with activity.

DISTANCE & CONFIGURATION: 4-mile loop

DIFFICULTY: Easy

SCENERY: Woodland, oak savannas, grassland, stream crossings, and forested floodplain

EXPOSURE: Mostly exposed

TRAIL TRAFFIC: Heavy at peak times on weekends, lighter during the week. Consider hiking one of the spurs if you're looking for more solitude.

TRAIL SURFACE: Crushed limestone

HIKING TIME: 1.5–2 hours

DRIVING DISTANCE: 26 miles from Millennium Park

ACCESS: Daily, 1 hour after sunrise–1 hour after sunset; no fees or permits

MAPS: Available at trailhead and the website below; USGS *Romeoville, IL*

FACILITIES: Restrooms, benches, water

WHEELCHAIR ACCESS: Yes

CONTACT: 630-933-7200, dupageforest.org /places-to-go/forest-preserves/greene-valley

LOCATION: Thunderbird Road, Naperville, IL 60565

COMMENTS: Dogs must be on leash no longer than 10 feet except in the preserve's off-leash areas. This is a multiuse trail, so watch for cyclists and give equestrians the right-of-way. Use caution when crossing the roads.

From the east side of the parking lot, take the trail heading left (north), which cuts through grassland toward an oak woodland. Skirting the edge of the woodland, you'll soon pass a connector trail on the right. Before crossing 79th Street at 0.7 mile, the trail dips and then rises as you pass over a branch of Anderson Creek, which runs through a culvert under the trail. On the other side of 79th Street, the shrubby savanna is replaced with open grassland, where you'll see encroaching housing developments and nearby power lines. The open space also allows you to scan the sky, the trees, and the edge of the grassland for red-tailed hawks and American kestrels, both of which are frequently sighted within the preserve. After another crossing of Anderson Creek, the trail swings right as it brushes against an oak woodland. Thanks to the long-term protection of this wooded area by its former owners, this tract serves as an important habitat to many birds, animals, and plants and provides an impressive display of wildflowers in the spring.

Leaving behind the oak woodland, the landscape starts to slump more noticeably toward the East Branch of the DuPage River. At 1.4 miles into the hike, take the trail junction to the left (east), and then cross Greene Road. On the other side of the road, turn left again, and head north through an area that is flat, wet, and generously sprinkled with poplar and sumac shrubs. As you approach 75th Street, stay to the right, passing a spur path that heads toward the Greene farm and the picnic shelters at the north end of the forest preserve. After the junction, the trail turns right and starts to run parallel to the East Branch of the DuPage River, which is 100–150 feet to the left through the stands of shrubs and the woods.

On the right side of this trail, you'll notice plenty of spots that have been cleared through controlled burnings, which remove invasive plant species and encourage native plant growth. As the trail moves farther away from the river, there's a junction

Greene Valley Forest Preserve Loop

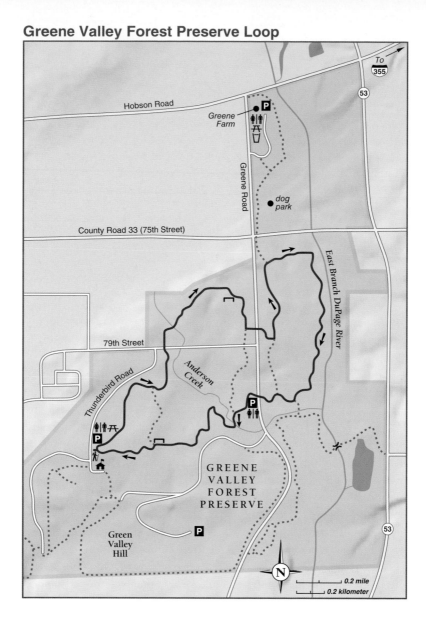

on the left. To take a peek at the East Branch of the DuPage, take this trail left and turn left again after crossing Anderson Creek. Continuing straight, you'll pass another trail junction on the right before crossing Greene Road.

On the other side of Greene Road, you'll see a parking lot and restrooms on the left. Beyond the parking lot, stay to the left (south) at the junction and follow the trail as it squiggles its way over Anderson Creek and through a mature oak woodland. Just south of here, you can't miss the 200-acre scenic overlook—at 980 feet above sea level, it's the second-highest spot in DuPage County. Used as a landfill from 1974 to 1996, the hill is now planted with native grasses and shrubs and offers limited recreation. On weekends May–October, 11 a.m.–6 p.m., visitors can drive to the top and hike a trail around the base of the hill.

As the landscape becomes more rolling, you'll pass a small ravine on the right and cross over a few drainage culverts. Soon you'll pass a connector trail on the right and then arrive back at the parking lot.

• •

GPS TRAILHEAD COORDINATES N41° 44.138' W88° 05.284'

DIRECTIONS From the junction of I-290 and I-88, bear left onto I-88 West and, in 7.6 miles, take Exit 131A onto I-355 South. In 4.5 miles, take Exit 17 right (southeast) onto 63rd Street, which quickly becomes Hobson Road. In 1.8 miles, turn left (south) on Greene Road. In 1.1 miles, turn right (west) on 79th Street and, in 0.5 mile, turn left (south) on Thunderbird Road. The parking lot is 0.6 mile ahead on your left.

The aptly named Big Rock   *Photo: Tim Putala*

TREE LOVERS COULD be busy for weeks exploring the hundreds of types of trees grouped according to geographical origin, species, and habitat. But trees are just part of the appeal of this place: the gently rolling terrain offers plenty of scenic beauty in the way of native woodlands, savannas, streams, marshes, and ponds.

DESCRIPTION

Occupying 1,700 acres of rolling wooded terrain and bisected by the East Branch of the DuPage River, the Morton Arboretum will captivate anyone with even a slight interest in woody vegetation. Joy Morton, founder of the Morton Salt Company, established the arboretum on his country estate in 1922. Morton's arboreal interests were passed down to him from his father, Julius Sterling Morton, who served as US Secretary of Agriculture under President Grover Cleveland and founded Arbor Day.

Joy Morton's plan was to gather trees and shrubs from around the world that could live in the climate of northern Illinois. Today, the arboretum boasts some 3,400 varieties of plants and trees, many organized according to botanical groups

DISTANCE & CONFIGURATION: 5 miles, 2 connected loops

DIFFICULTY: Easy

SCENERY: Rolling hills, dense woods, oak savannas, and prairie

EXPOSURE: Mostly covered

TRAIL TRAFFIC: Light–moderate

TRAIL SURFACE: Wood chips, dirt

HIKING TIME: 2.5 hours

DRIVING DISTANCE: 35 miles from Millennium Park

ACCESS: Grounds open daily, 7 a.m.–sunset; visitor-center hours vary seasonally (check the website for details). Admission: $15 adults ages 18–64, $13 seniors age 65+, $10 kids ages 2–17 ($10, $9, and $7, respectively, on Wednesdays).

MAPS: Available at the entrance gate and the website below; USGS *Wheaton, IL*

FACILITIES: Restrooms, benches, picnic tables, water, visitor center, café, gift shop

CONTACT: 630-968-0074, mortonarb.org

WHEELCHAIR ACCESS: None

LOCATION: 4100 IL 53, Lisle, IL 60532

COMMENTS: For information about classes and guided tours, inquire at the visitor center. Runners are asked to use the roads rather than the trails. Dogs allowed only on designated days; check the website for details.

and geographical origins. Mixed in with this extraordinary collection of trees and shrubs are a variety of gardens highlighting herbs, native plants, and hedges.

Most of this hike follows the outer edge of the Main Trail, a series of four connected loops numbered from west to east, on the arboretum's East Side. Facing the Big Rock Visitor Station, look for Main Trail Loop 3 to the left, heading west across the park road from the shelter. Passing a picnic spot, the trail enters rolling, open terrain, with the occasional bluebird house attached to a post. At 0.5 mile into the hike, where the woodland gives way to shrubby trees and more open space, you'll cross a wooden footbridge spanning a small ravine.

Up ahead, as the trail crosses the park road, a sign indicates Appalachian plants in this area. Gradually descending a gentle hill, the trail is accompanied by a small stream on the right. Soon you'll pass a collection of maples and then cross a service road before entering a collection of azaleas, rhododendrons, and other types of ornamental shrubs. The trail quickly rises to a small stone platform with a couple of benches. Behind the bench on the right is an Eastern redbud tree, which produces masses of pink flowers in early spring; behind the other bench is another flowering tree, the wild black cherry.

From the benches, take the trail to the left past plantings of locust, honeysuckle, and viburnum trees. As the trail enters an area with plants from Korea, look for trees common in Asia—such as mock orange and koyama spruce—that are marked on the side of the trail. After you pass a grouping of large hedges, Crowley Marsh appears on the right, soon followed by a connector trail on the left. As the trail curls around Burr Reed Marsh, you'll mount a short boardwalk and a viewing platform that offers an ideal spot from which to look for birds during migratory months.

Morton Arboretum: East Hike

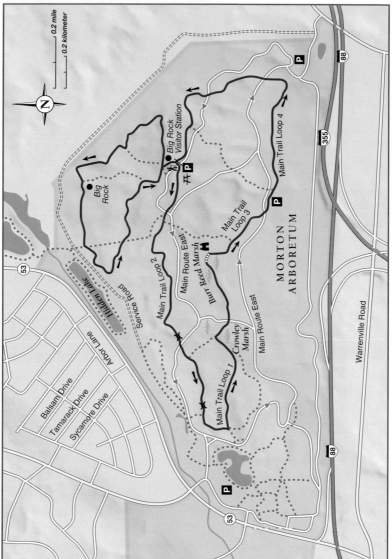

Passing a small pond and another connector trail, keep straight ahead as you enter a savanna and woodland area containing 43 types of oaks from around the world. Among these you'll find the six main types of oaks that grow in the Chicago region: white, swamp white, burr, black, red, and Northern pin. After leaving the oaks, cross the park road and then pass a parking area. Keep straight ahead at the next junction alongside a winding creekbed.

Here, the trail straightens and starts to rise gradually as it cuts through a fairly dense woodland. The stands of shrubs and abundant deadfall seem to draw in the critters. On one of my visits to this corner of the arboretum a couple of days after a snowfall, the hiking trail was crisscrossed with countless animal trails, some apparently used by more than one type of animal. Raccoons, mice, squirrels, rabbits, chipmunks, and deer all left behind their imprints.

As you cross the road again, the landscape regains its rolling quality. Here, the trail skirts a wooded hillside above a picturesque ravine sprinkled with fallen trees. Continuing straight ahead brings you back to the Big Rock Visitor Station.

For a quick introduction to the types of environments within this section of the arboretum, follow the short paved path bordering the back side of the visitor station, and peruse the informational signs along the way.

Find the beginning of the Big Rock section of the hike next to the shelter. Fifty yards ahead, turn right (northeast) and then quickly turn right again (north). After the second junction, the trail proceeds alongside a small stream on the right that has carved a shallow ravine. While the trail curves, dips, and rises through fairly dense woodland, keep an eye out for a few enormous white oaks. (Growing to 100 feet, the white oak—the Illinois state tree—has wide-spreading branches, leaves with rounded lobes, and ashy-gray bark that is plated and scaly.) After passing a junction on the left, the trail gradually descends toward a rock the size of a small car.

Weighing in at 12–14 tons, the Big Rock hitched a ride on a glacier many thousands of years ago from either northern Michigan or Canada. Geologists point to particular surface scratches on the rock and its position on the ground as possible evidence that farmers moved it out of an adjoining field about 100 years ago. (Up until the 1980s, the clearing west of the rock operated as a hay field.)

Passing a trail junction on the left, proceed straight ahead into the former hay field. After a quarter-mile hike through this restored prairie, the trail crosses a two-wheel track and then enters a savanna that is often alive with avian activity: look for woodpeckers, flickers, juncos, and cedar waxwings in the winter and a host of migrating species such as warblers, vireos, and scarlet tanagers in the spring and fall. Local birders say that the arboretum's variety of plants and berries makes it one of the better bird-watching spots in the area. After crossing a small bridge, the trail gradually turns left, then starts to rise into dense woods. Stay right at the next two trail junctions—turn south, then southeast—on your way back to the Big Rock Visitor Station.

NEARBY ACTIVITIES

If you have kids along, be sure to take them to the arboretum's **Children's Garden**, near the visitor center. You may also want to explore some additional hiking trails near the visitor center, including a short trail around Meadow Lake, as well as trails featuring conifers, citrus trees, cherry trees, and trees that grow in northern Illinois.

There are 6 more miles of hiking trails on the arboretum's West Side, including trails along the DuPage River and a trail looping around a small lake. These trails will take you through a groves of pine, birch, hemlock, and nut trees. You'll also find plenty of flowering trees and a collection of trees that grow in Europe, as well as meadows, prairies, and streams. You can access the West Side near the visitor center by passing through a tunnel under IL 53.

• •

GPS TRAILHEAD COORDINATES N41° 49.118' W88 02.795'

DIRECTIONS The arboretum is just north of the junction of I-88 and I-355 in Lisle. From westbound I-88, exit right (north) onto IL 53; the arboretum's East Side entrance is just 0.6 mile ahead on the right. Or, from eastbound I-88, follow the signs onto I-355 South, and exit right (west) onto US 34/Ogden Avenue. In 1.2 miles, bear right at the exit, and turn right (south) onto IL 53/Lincoln Avenue at the end of the ramp. In 0.2 mile, turn left on Burlington Avenue; then take the second left onto Main Street. In 0.3 mile, turn left again on Southport Avenue, and then take the next right onto northbound IL 53; the arboretum's East Side entrance is 0.8 mile ahead on the right. After paying at the gate and receiving a map, follow Main Route East Side for 2.5 miles until you reach the parking area for the Big Rock Visitor Station, on your right.

PUBLIC TRANSPORTATION The arboretum is 1.5 miles from the Lisle Station on **Metra**'s BNSF Railway Line. From the north side of the station, head left (west) on Burlington Avenue; then turn right (north) on IL 53/Lincoln Avenue. The entrance to the arboretum is on the right after you pass under I-88. Use care when biking along busy IL 53. *Note:* Walking isn't recommended, as there's no sidewalk along IL 53 north of Warrenville Road, so book a cab or ride share in advance.

18 PRATT'S WAYNE LOOP

The ponds at Pratt's Wayne Woods started out as gravel pits.   *Photo: Dahai Zang*

AS THE LARGEST forest preserve in DuPage County, Pratt's Wayne Woods has no shortage of marshes, ponds, and prairies to explore. The western section of the preserve hosts sprawling open spaces, interrupted now and then with picturesque wetlands and groves of elm and cottonwood.

DESCRIPTION

Located in the far northwestern corner of DuPage County, this 3,432-acre forest preserve was pieced together with the help of an assortment of landowners. Some grew corn and grain here, some mined gravel, while others used the setting for a hunting and fishing club. After the preserve got its start in 1965 with the donation of 170 acres by the state of Illinois, a couple of the parcels were sold to the county by George Pratt, a local township supervisor and county forest preserve commissioner. The preserve is named after both Pratt and the nearby community of Wayne.

The hike begins by circling tree-fringed ponds on the northwest side of Pickerel Lake. Find the trailhead by heading right (west) along the lakeshore and looking for the crushed-gravel path at the far edge of the last parking lot. Once on the trail, you'll pass the east end of Catfish Pond on the right and then pass a paved wheelchair-accessible trail on the left that leads to one of two fishing piers on Pickerel Lake. After the trail to the pier, follow the next trail left, which brings you to the shoreline of Beaver Slough. Many banks of the slough are reinforced with stacks of limestone

DISTANCE & CONFIGURATION: 6-mile loop

DIFFICULTY: Easy–moderate

SCENERY: Ponds, lakes, prairies, savannas, marshes, and woodland

EXPOSURE: Mostly exposed

TRAIL TRAFFIC: Mostly light; moderate on the Prairie Path section

TRAIL SURFACE: Crushed gravel, mowed grass

HIKING TIME: 2.5–3 hours

DRIVING DISTANCE: 37 miles from Millennium Park

ACCESS: Daily, 1 hour after sunrise–1 hour after sunset; no fees or permits

MAPS: Available in the parking lot and at the website below; USGS *Geneva, IL,* and *West Chicago, IL*

FACILITIES: Restrooms, water, picnic tables and shelter, fishing piers

WHEELCHAIR ACCESS: None on main route

CONTACT: 630-933-7200, dupageforest .com/places-to-go/forest-preserves/pratts -wayne-woods

LOCATION: 6N179 Powis Road, West Chicago, IL 60185 (West Entrance)

COMMENTS: Dogs must be on leash no longer than 10 feet except in the preserve's off-leash areas. Although Army Trail Road is not terribly busy, use caution while hiking a short segment along the road. Also proceed with great care through the equestrian area if horses are present.

that sometimes serve as steps leading to the water's edge. All three of these ponds, as well as Pickerel Lake, were gravel pits about 50 years ago.

Keep straight ahead at the connector trail on the right that divides Beaver Slough and Horsetail Pond. At 0.3 mile, the trail takes a sharp right onto the metal bridge spanning the west end of Horsetail Pond, then passes a pleasant picnic area and connector trail dividing Horsetail and Catfish Ponds on the right. Just beyond the connector trail, turn left on the two-track. Be sure to take the trail to the right of the sign for Pratt's Wayne Woods—don't take the fainter trail to the left of the sign.

Leaving the woods behind, the trail enters a wide-open savanna bordered by groves of oak. Follow the next junction left (west), and you'll begin to see dozens of obstacles for horse jumping—everything from small logs to wooden fences to giant tree trunks stacked 5 feet high. The 100-year-old Wayne-DuPage Hunt Club organizes equestrian events here during the warmer months.

After you hike 0.7 mile through the horse-jumping area, the trail veers right through the trees and then turns left before passing through a gate (you may have to duck under a cable stretched across the gate). At 1.5 miles into the hike, turn left (southeast) onto a lovely slice of rail-trail known as the Illinois Prairie Path; this section—called the Elgin Spur—runs for about 15 miles between the towns of Wheaton and Elgin. Once you're on the path, keep to the right.

For the first 0.3 mile on the Prairie Path, the route shoots straight as an arrow behind a few houses, alongside dense woods, and next to a sizable cattail marsh. Soon the cattails on the left give way to open water, much of it covered in algae. Wooden railings mark the spot where Brewster Creek passes under the path. After the creek, open water comes and goes on the left, and eventually shrubs rise up on each side of the trail.

Pratt's Wayne Loop

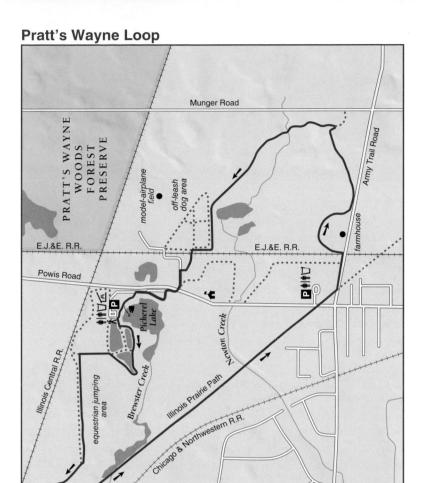

To the left, over the wooden railings at the Norton Creek crossing, is a wide, treeless swath of marshland and wet prairie. Farther along, thick woods and a dense, leafy canopy turn the trail into a shadowy tunnel. You'll pass an elementary school on the right and then cross Powis Road before arriving at Army Trail Road at 3.4 miles into the hike. Here, you'll find a portable restroom, a water pump, a bench, and a map board showing the entire 55-mile route of the Prairie Path. The hike continues less than 100 yards to the left (east) along Army Trail Road; then you take the first mowed path on the left, just after the train tracks.

Following the mowed path as it enters grassland and then swings around the back side of the farmhouse on the right, you'll encounter wet prairies, stands of shrubs, and occasional savannas. After returning to Army Trail Road for a short sweep, the trail heads back into the grassland, takes a dip, and then rises to meet a trail on the right that heads to Munger Road. Turning left (north) at the fork takes you through a grove of smaller trees and next to a wetland on the left. Keeping left (north) at another spur trail, you'll cut through a grove of elm, cottonwood, and cherry trees on your way to a high spot with the best view so far of this sprawling open space. Except for the big cluster of homes off to the east, you can see for nearly a mile in every direction.

As you approach the 23-acre off-leash dog area, you'll pass a cattail-fringed pond with open water on the left. For the next 0.3 mile, the trail follows the dog fence straight ahead and then to the right. At 5.5 miles into the hike, use caution as you cross the train tracks. On the other side of the tracks, you'll see the horse-trailer parking lot as you approach the park road. Take a left on the park road; then cross Powis Road into the forest preserve's main entrance. Stay to the left, heading toward Pickerel Lake, and follow the lakeshore 0.15 mile back to the parking lot.

NEARBY ACTIVITIES

Those interested in exploring more of the Illinois Prairie Path either on foot or on a bicycle can connect to the **Fox River Trail,** about 5 miles north of Army Trail Road in Elgin. To the south, the **Great Western Trail** is about 4 miles away, and downtown **Wheaton** is about 9 miles away. The **Active Transportation Alliance**'s *Chicagoland Bicycle Map* ($8; activetransreg.org/shop) is indispensable for getting around on the region's bikeways and rail-trails.

• •

GPS TRAILHEAD COORDINATES N41° 58.017' W88° 14.621'

DIRECTIONS From the junction of I-90 and I-290 in Chicago, head north and then west on I-90 for 7.9 miles. Exit left (south) onto IL 59/Sutton Road, and drive 6.7 miles. Turn right (west) on Stearns Road, and proceed 1.7 miles. Turn left (south) on Powis Road and, in 1 mile, turn right to enter Pratt's Wayne Woods Forest Preserve. Park in the first lot on the left.

The mowed-grass path makes its way into the forest.   *Photo: Ryan Afflerbaugh*

FOR A MAN-MADE artifact, Shabbona Lake is strikingly beautiful and varied. As you make your way around the lake, you'll encounter grasslands, hills, streams, marshes, dense woodlands, ponds—and the lake itself is in view for nearly the entire hike.

DESCRIPTION

It's hard to believe that nearly all of Shabbona Lake State Recreation Area was rolling farmland just 30 years ago. Since then, small forests were expanded, grasslands were established, and a 319-acre lake was created in the center of the park. If it weren't for the earthen dam and spillway on the south end of the lake and the occasional dead tree jutting out of the water, one would readily assume that the lake has been cradled in this landscape since northern Illinois emerged from the deep freeze.

The park is named for Shabbona, a Potawatomi chief who rode across northern Illinois to warn white settlers of impending Indian raids during the Black Hawk War of 1832. Black Hawk, chief of the Sac Nation, waged war to protest white encroachment on native lands; Shabbona originally shared Black Hawk's stance against the US, but he later came to believe that resistance was useless and became an ally to local settlers. Shabbona is buried about 35 miles southeast of the park in the town of Morris, but his wife and several children are buried near the park.

DISTANCE & CONFIGURATION: 4.9-mile loop

DIFFICULTY: Moderate

SCENERY: Lake, prairies, woods, marshes, streams, hills, and a man-made earthen dam

EXPOSURE: Mostly exposed

TRAIL TRAFFIC: Light

SURFACE: Mowed grass, dirt

HIKING TIME: 3 hours

DRIVING DISTANCE: 72 miles from Millennium Park

ACCESS: Daily, April–October, 6 a.m.–10 p.m.; November–January, 8 a.m.–5 p.m.; February, 8 a.m.–6 p.m.; and March, 8 a.m.–8 p.m.; no fees or permits. The eastern section of this hike is closed for deer-hunting season in the fall; check with the park for exact dates.

MAPS: Available at the park office and the

website below; USGS *Shabbona Grove, IL,* and *Waterman, IL*

FACILITIES: Restrooms, water, picnic tables and shelters, playgrounds, fishing piers, boat launches; campground, camp store, boat rental, and restaurant open seasonally

WHEELCHAIR ACCESS: None

CONTACT: 815-824-2106, www.dnr.illinois.gov /parks/pages/shabbonalake.aspx

LOCATION: 100 Preserve Road, Shabbona, IL 60550 (North Entrance)

COMMENTS: Though this hike is technically more than 60 miles from Chicago, its natural beauty makes it worth the trip. Dogs must be leashed. For a number of years, the park has had trouble funding maintenance for the Tomahawk Trail on the east side of Shabbona Lake—if you see a sign indicating RESTRICTED ACCESS, keep in mind that the trail is open but may not be maintained.

For a counterclockwise hike around the lake, follow the sign pointing to the dam and the Tomahawk Trail from the east side of the Shabbona Grove Picnic Area; just beyond the sign, stay left as you merge with the snowmobile trail. At the next junction, near a grove of pine and sumac, stay to the right as the trail mounts the 0.5-mile-long earthen dam that was constructed in 1975 in order to create the lake. At the end of the dam, the trail passes over what looks like a big washbasin, which collects water and directs it down a 60-foot concrete spillway that slopes gradually into Indian Creek on the right. The creek meets up with the Fox River about 20 miles south.

After crossing the spillway, the trail rises and runs through an open area before coming to a junction with the Tomahawk Trail, where you'll turn left. As you pass into the hardwood forest, you'll see a little ravine on the left, which was cut by an intermittent stream that runs through a culvert under the trail. Just ahead, the trail passes a bench in a clearing at the edge of the lake. Several dead trees sticking out of the water offer evidence that this lake is younger than it looks.

Don't be alarmed when you see a red sign announcing that the rest of this trail is closed. While ongoing funding shortages prevent the park staff from maintaining this trail, the park still invites hikers to use the trail with the warning that they should be prepared to step over fallen branches and the occasional fallen tree. Beyond the sign, the trail passes over another drainage ditch and begins winding through a gently rolling landscape. Throughout the hike on this side of the lake, the trail alternates between hugging the shoreline and going inland for short stretches. After cutting through an area thick with shrubs, the trail moves closer to the lake and soon meets

Shabbona Lake State Recreation Area Loop

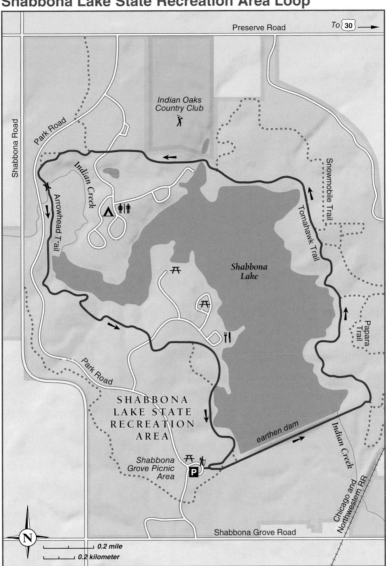

the Papara Trail. Stay on the Tomahawk Trail by turning left—watch your step, as this area can be especially muddy in the spring.

As the trail comes out into the grassland, it swings to the right, climbs a small hill, and then passes a trail branching to the right. From the top of the hill, the trail takes a steep 40-foot drop before it runs between a pond on the right and a finger of the lake on the left. For the next quarter mile, as you head toward the campground, the path runs parallel to the sometimes marshy shoreline.

Getting closer to the campground, keep straight ahead when the Tomahawk Trail merges with the snowmobile trail. Passing a marshy inlet of the lake on the left, you'll see the Indian Oaks Country Club on the right (north). At the campground, to the left (south), facilities include restrooms, water, a camp store, and a playground.

Keep straight ahead on the trail as it rises to a clearing and crosses the campground access road. After crossing the road, follow the sign for the Arrowhead Trail to the left. Turning left on the Arrowhead Trail, you'll suddenly enter a dense woodland. (These sudden transitions from grassland to dense woodland will happen regularly for the remainder of the hike.)

As the trail curves left, it begins a half-mile stretch running parallel to the main park road. Near where the trail crosses Indian Creek on a wooden footbridge, keep an eye out for signs of beavers: cone-shaped tree stumps with wood chips at the base. After continuing for a bit alongside Indian Creek, the trail rises to higher ground and then meets a short connector trail on the right that leads to the park road.

Soon the trail passes a wetland down below on the left, which is where Indian Creek enters Shabbona Lake. This marshy area is a great spot to look for waterfowl; some 30 species are said to drop in annually during their migrations. While walking the edge of this wetland, you can get closer to the water by using a few access points along the way.

Not long after crossing a park road again at 4.1 miles into the hike, you'll see the park's concession stand. The trail turns right before reaching the parking lot and soon runs near restrooms on the left. As you approach the lakeshore, a connector heads left toward the buildings you just passed. For the remainder of the hike, the trail mostly runs alongside the lake through open grassland. Stay to the right at the final junction near the grove of sumac and pine. From here, the parking lot is just ahead.

• •

GPS TRAILHEAD COORDINATES N41° 44.167' W88° 51.790'

DIRECTIONS From the junction of I-88 and I-290, bear left on I-88 West and, in 16.9 miles, take Exit 113 for Sugar Grove, 2.5 miles west of the Aurora tollbooth. Bear left at the exit onto IL 56/US 30, heading south and then west, for 25 miles. Then, 4.4 miles west of Waterman, turn left (south) on Indian Road and, 0.5 mile farther, turn right (west) on Preserve Road. The entrance to the park is 0.4 mile ahead on the left. Stay to the right on the main park road for 2.2 miles until you reach the Shabbona Grove Picnic Area, near the southern end of the park.

Colorful autumn foliage festoons the trail.   *Photo: Kymberly Janisch*

SILVER SPRINGS OFFERS a wealth of scenic pleasures. While hiking over ridges, through woodlands, and along Loon Lake and the Fox River, you will encounter a variety of trees, birds, and wildflowers.

DESCRIPTION

About 30 miles upstream from where the Fox River flows into the Illinois River, the Fox runs through a beautiful state park named for its sparkling water that seeps from the ground all year. Like many parks in the area, Silver Springs State Park was largely farmland before it was bought by the state in 1969. Now it's one of only a few refuges for hikers in Kendall County. While Silver Springs is a popular spot for walkers, it's also well liked by local hunters and anglers. Keep in mind that some of the lesser trails (see Nearby Activities) are closed for part of the season to accommodate hunters. The hike that follows, which is open all year, is neither the longest nor the most isolated hike in the park, but it is the most beautiful and varied.

Start in the northeast corner of the Loon Lake Parking Area, opposite the restrooms. From the sign indicating that the Silver Springs are 0.2 mile ahead, follow the wide mowed path west until you reach a junction, where you'll turn left (north). At the bottom of a short incline, a platform overlooks a gravelly spot where water seeps

DISTANCE & CONFIGURATION: 2.6-mile loop

DIFFICULTY: Moderate

SCENERY: Woods, ridges, lakes, wide river, and a natural spring

EXPOSURE: Mostly covered

TRAIL TRAFFIC: Light

TRAIL SURFACE: Mowed grass, dirt

HIKING TIME: 1–1.5 hours

DRIVING DISTANCE: 57.5 miles from Millennium Park

ACCESS: Daily, sunrise–sunset; no fees or permits

MAPS: Available at concession stand; USGS *Plano, IL*

FACILITIES: Restrooms, water, concession stand/bait shop, paddleboat rentals, and playground

WHEELCHAIR ACCESS: None

CONTACT: 630-553-6297, www.dnr.illinois.gov/parks/pages/silversprings.aspx

LOCATION: 13608 Fox Road, Yorkville, IL 60560

COMMENTS: Dogs must be leashed. Bring a fishing pole if you'd like to cast a line into the 2 man-made lakes near the parking lot. Only nonmotorized boats are allowed on the lakes, but motorized boats are allowed on the Fox River. Pick up a free wildflower checklist at the concession stand or park office—it's a great help to those interested in identifying the park's 130 flower types.

from the ground all year. As the water trickles out, it gathers in a small pool before flowing through patches of watercress and alongside a lush stream bank on its way to the Fox River. As you continue on the trail toward the river, look for orange jewel-weed flowers near the stream.

Before turning left (west) at the trail that runs parallel to the river, check out the rocky shoreline ahead. Depending on the water level, a small island or two may be visible within this wide, slow-moving waterway. As you follow the trail to the left alongside the riverbank, look high up in the trees at the water's edge for ospreys, a rare sight in Illinois. Brown on the top of their bodies and white underneath, these large hawks dine on fish they grab from the water. On two different occasions, I've seen ospreys on this stretch of the river, waiting for a meal to surface.

As the trail follows the river, you'll pass several short connector trails on the left. The first one leads back to the parking lot where you started, while the subsequent trails lead to Beaver Lake and beyond to Loon Lake, beside the parking lot. At both of these lakes, benches are on hand, offering pleasant spots to have a seat, eat lunch, and watch the water birds. After following the river for 0.5 mile, you'll pass through a metal gate and then cross the park road. Regain the trail just to the right of the restrooms. Moving away from the river, the trail winds through a mostly maple bottomland forest and skirts the edge of a small pond. Follow the arrow markers as you pass a few connector trails leading to nearby picnicking spots. You may want to have the park's wildflower checklist on hand in this area; it lists 130 flowers by color, habitat, frequency, and blooming season. Pick up the free checklist at the concession stand or at the park office.

After passing a playground on the right, the trail crosses the park road again at 1.1 miles into the hike. On the other side of the road, the trail brushes against a pond and then quickly starts to gain elevation on the way up Fox Ridge. Once you've

Silver Springs State Park Loop

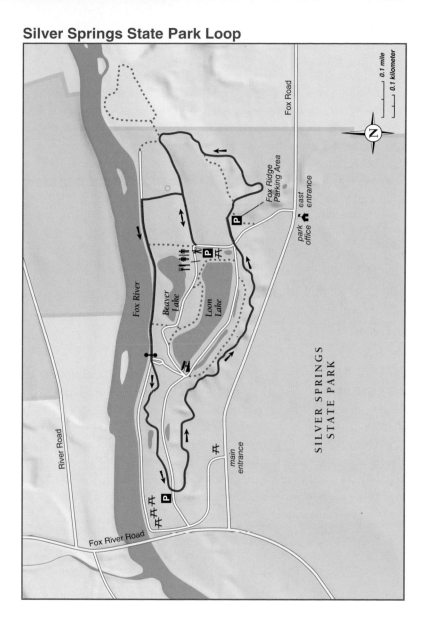

climbed for about 40 yards, keep walking straight ahead when the trail reaches a grassy open space next to a parking area with picnic tables and another playground. While following Fox Ridge for the next 0.7 mile, you'll notice that there are a couple of trails running parallel to and occasionally intersecting with one another. To follow the lower trail, stay to the left; for the higher one, stay right. There are plenty of confidence markers along the way for guidance on either, and you can look to Loon Lake on the left to reassure yourself of your location.

While following the ridge under a thick oak canopy, watch your step as the trail runs next to the small ravines. Once the trail descends the ridge, cross the park road at 1.8 miles into the hike. After passing the parking lot where you started the hike on the left, keep straight ahead for about 100 yards to pick up the rest of the trail in the back-right corner of the Fox Ridge Parking Area.

This final section of the hike can be a bit confusing—particularly if the park has changed the signage described here—but it's a relatively small section of the park, so it should be navigable without much trouble. Back on the trail, you'll first cross a small bridge, then follow an arrow to the right (east) at the trail junction. As you move up on the side of a ridge, the trail passes a wetland in the low spots on the right. Continue to follow the arrows at a few more trail junctions that will appear in the next half mile. Higher up on the ridge, you'll see several houses and an open field on the right. At 2.25 miles into the hike, follow the arrows through a hairpin turn to the left. Soon the trail reaches an open area, with power lines visible on the right. After crossing the open area, turn left at the sign for Silver Springs, and head back to the parking lot.

NEARBY ACTIVITIES

For more hiking at Silver Springs, consider the 1-mile-long **Duck Creek Trail,** the 2-mile-long **Beaver Dam Trail,** the 1-mile-long **Grasslands of the Fox Trail,** and the 6-mile-long **Prairie View Equestrian Trail.** The Duck Creek and Beaver Dam Trails are wooded and hilly; the Grasslands and Prairie View Trails are, as you might guess, flat and grassy. The Duck Creek, Beaver Dam, and Prairie View Trails are closed for part of the winter for hunting season; call the park office at 630-553-6297 for exact dates.

If you'd like to paddle on the park's lakes or the Fox River, **Yak Shack,** about 4.5 miles east of the park in Yorkville (301 E. Hydraulic Ave.; 630-479-8074, yakshack online.com), rents canoes and kayaks.

• •

GPS TRAILHEAD COORDINATES N41° 37.887' W88° 31.229'

DIRECTIONS From the junction of I-55 and I-355, follow I-55 southwest for 7.9 miles until you reach Exit 261, where you'll take IL 26 West for 15.8 miles. Turn right (north) on IL 47/North Bridge Street, and proceed 0.3 mile. Turn left (west) on West Fox Street, and follow it 2.9 miles. Turn right (north) on West Fox Road and, in 0.4 mile, veer left (west) to continue on this road. In 1 mile, with the Silver Springs State Park office on your left, turn right and drive 0.3 mile north to the Loon Lake Parking Area.

Fall color on the Fox River   *Photo: Jim Miner*

THIS HIKE LEADS you through two forest preserves divided by a scenic section of the Fox River dotted with wooded islands. While hiking through Tekakwitha Woods, visitors will enjoy the wooded ravines, bottomland forest, savanna, and riverbank. Across the river are more wooded riverbanks, as well as a lovely prairie, and the south end of a train line that takes visitors to a nearby trolley museum.

DESCRIPTION

From the early 1900s until 1990, what is now Tekakwitha Woods Forest Preserve was Villa Maria, a Roman Catholic retreat. The land was originally owned by Father Hugh McGuire, a Chicago parish priest who built a country home here (the house now serves as the administrative offices of the Kane County Forest Preserve District). Upon his death, Father McGuire left the property to the Sisters of Mercy. In 1990, when Kane County bought the retreat, the nuns requested that the new forest preserve be named in honor of the woman who would become the first Native American Catholic saint, who lived from 1656 to 1680 and was canonized by Pope Benedict XVI in 2012. After surviving a childhood bout with smallpox, Kateri Tekakwitha (pronounced "Tek-uh-WITH-uh"), a Mohawk from New York State, converted to Christianity at age 19 and spent the remaining five years of her life in prayer and

DISTANCE & CONFIGURATION: 2.2-mile lollipop loop; optional trails add 2 miles

DIFFICULTY: Easy

SCENERY: Fox River, wooded ravines, bottomland forest, savanna, prairie, river islands

EXPOSURE: Mostly shaded

TRAIL TRAFFIC: Light

TRAIL SURFACE: Dirt, pavement, and mowed grass

HIKING TIME: 1.5 hours

DRIVING DISTANCE: 41 miles from Millennium Park

ACCESS: Daily, sunrise–sunset; no fees or permits

MAPS: Available at the websites at right; USGS *Geneva, IL*

FACILITIES: Restrooms, picnic tables, and gazebo at Tekakwitha Woods Forest Preserve; picnic facilities, water, and restrooms at Jon J. Duerr Forest Preserve

WHEELCHAIR ACCESS: None

CONTACT: 630-232-5980, kaneforest.com/ForestPreserveView.aspx?ID=42 (Tekakwitha Woods), kaneforest.com/ForestPreserveView.aspx?ID=6 (Jon J. Duerr)

LOCATION: 35W071 Villa Maria Road, St. Charles, IL 60174 (Tekakwitha Woods)

COMMENTS: Dogs must be leashed and cleaned up after. Be aware that there are many more trails than shown on the map for Tekakwitha Woods—be sure to explore some of them.

contemplation at a Jesuit mission in Quebec. Along with St. Francis of Assisi, she is honored by the Catholic Church as a patron saint of the environment and ecology.

Either at the beginning or the end of the hike described, you should explore deep into Tekakwitha Woods. Because the paths are generally unmarked and resemble a bowl of spaghetti, it's not much help to describe particular trails. The forest preserve is small, and the ground mostly slopes down toward the Fox River, so there is little chance of getting lost. There are a couple of trailheads off the main park road at the edges of the prairie, as well one heading north from the parking area. As you make your way down toward the river while exploring these trails, you'll encounter plenty of oak and maple as well as hickory and walnut trees, and you'll see four of the five wooded islands in the river. As far as tree cover, some areas closer to the entrance to the preserve are open, while the canopy grows thicker as you get closer to the river.

The official hike begins just east of the parking area on the Fox River Trail, a 38-mile walking and biking path that runs through a number of parks on its route from Oswego north to Algonquin (from the bridge, South Elgin is 1.7 miles north and St. Charles is 4.6 miles south on the trail). From the parking area, turn left (north) and you'll descend the biggest hill on the entire trail. At the bottom of the bluff, you'll cross a 0.15-mile-long iron-and-wood bridge spanning the Fox River. The bridge, which offers lovely views upstream and down, connects with a small wooded island in the middle of the river. This section of the river is named Five Islands for a series of wooded islands along the river to the west. Beyond the islands, outside of your view, the river takes an abrupt hairpin turn on its way south to St. Charles.

On the other side of the bridge, now in Jon J. Duerr Forest Preserve, you follow the paved path to the left (west), and then take the wood-chip trail heading right (north). Along this trail sit a couple of small monuments marking the graves of two unknown

Tekakwitha–Fox River Hike

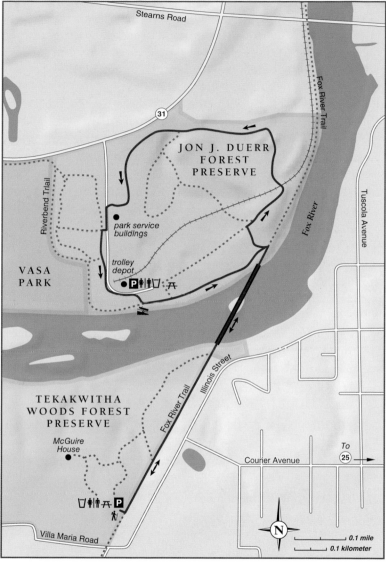

soldiers from General Winfield Scott's regiment who died of cholera during the Black Hawk War of 1832. (The preserve was called Blackhawk Forest Preserve until the summer of 2004, when it was renamed in honor of Jon J. Duerr, the former executive director of the Kane County Forest Preserve District.) Turn right (northeast) at the second monument for the soldiers, and head down a hill to cross the train tracks.

After you cross the train tracks, follow the paved park road that rises up the small hill and turns left. The road runs between an embankment on the right and mounds blanketed with sumac and cottonwood rising on the left. Shortly after passing a junction with a gravel road, the paved road curves left again and then arrives at several forest-preserve service buildings. At the service buildings, cross the main park road, and walk along a mowed grass trail that runs parallel to the park road.

Approaching the river, you'll pass the boarding platform for the Fox River Trolley (see Nearby Activities) and then head to the left side of the parking lot, where the paved trail parallels the river. (The trail on the right side of the parking lot—known as the Riverbend Trail—goes for about 7 miles, mostly along roads, to the Leroy Oaks Forest Preserve, where it connects with the Great Western Trail.) Continuing along the river to the left, you'll pass some pleasant picnicking spots before you get back on the bridge and return to the riverbank trail at Tekakwitha Woods.

NEARBY ACTIVITIES

If it's a summer weekend and you've got kids along, climb aboard a renovated electric intercity railway train for a 2-mile-long trip through Jon J. Duerr Forest Preserve and along the Fox River to the **Fox River Trolley Museum,** at 365 S. LaFox St. in South Elgin. (For museum hours and ride schedules, call 847-697-4676 or visit fox trolley.org.) The museum has 20 or so electric railway cars on display; the trolley follows the route of the Aurora, Elgin & Fox River Electric Company interurban rail line, which dates back to 1896.

• •

GPS TRAILHEAD COORDINATES N41° 57.851' W88° 18.071'

DIRECTIONS   From the junction of I-90 and I-290 in Chicago, head north and then west on I-90 for 7.9 miles. Exit left (south) onto IL 59/Sutton Road and, in 5 miles, turn right (west) on West Bartlett Road. In 3.2 miles, turn left (south) on IL 25. In 2.4 miles, turn right (west) on Courier Avenue, and proceed 0.6 mile. Turn left (southwest) on Illinois Street; then shortly veer right (west) onto Villa Maria Road and take another quick right to reach the Tekakwitha Woods Parking Area, on your right.

Alternate directions from the south: Exit I-88 onto IL 59, heading north. In 8.1 miles, turn left (west) on IL 64/North Avenue, and continue 5.3 miles. Then turn right (north) on IL 25, and proceed 2.6 miles. Turn left (west) on Pearson Drive, and then take a quick right (north) onto Weber Drive. In 0.8 mile, turn left on Villa Maria Road, and then jog immediately right to reach the Tekakwitha Woods Parking Area, on your right.

Footbridge over Sawmill Creek   *Photo: Mohamed Elashi*

THIS DIVERSE AND sometimes rugged landscape includes dense woods of oak and pine, a generous number of ponds and cattail marshes, a prairie, a small waterfall, and an overlook of the Des Plaines River.

DESCRIPTION

Waterfall Glen Forest Preserve surrounds Argonne National Laboratory, one of the U.S. Department of Energy's largest research facilities. Operated by the University of Chicago, Argonne and its previous incarnations have been involved in high-level national research over the years, including the top-secret Manhattan Project during World War II. The federal government gave the property surrounding Argonne

113

DISTANCE & CONFIGURATION: 9.6-mile loop, including a short side trip to a waterfall

DIFFICULTY: Moderate due to length

SCENERY: Rolling woodlands with ponds, marshes, and stream crossings

EXPOSURE: Shady with exposed stretches

TRAIL TRAFFIC: Busy, especially on warm weekends

TRAIL SURFACE: Hard-packed crushed limestone

HIKING TIME: 4–6 hours

DRIVING DISTANCE: 27 miles from Millennium Park

ACCESS: Daily, 1 hour after sunrise–1 hour after sunset; no fees or permits

MAPS: Available at the trailhead and the website below; USGS *Romeoville, IL* and *Sag Bridge, IL*

FACILITIES: Water, restrooms, a few scattered picnic tables, parking

WHEELCHAIR ACCESS: Yes

CONTACT: 630-933-7200, dupageforest.com /places-to-go/forest-preserves/waterfall-glen

LOCATION: Northgate Road, Lemont, IL 60439

COMMENTS: Dogs must be on leash no longer than 10 feet. Watch for cyclists, runners, and plenty of other people hiking during warmer weather at busy times of the week.

National Laboratory to DuPage County in 1971. As you hike, the only indications that you're circling this world-class science and engineering center are a fence or two and the occasional access road.

In the parking lot, look for the information board to find trail maps and the trailhead. Once you're on the trail, take the first left (south) for a clockwise hike through the forest preserve. For the first mile, you'll cross three roads—Northgate Road, Cass Avenue, and 91st Street—before you reach the serene 91st Street Marsh. The marsh, which is the size of a small lake, is surrounded by cattails, pines, and oaks. A bench offers a nice place to view the marsh; there's also a small pond behind you.

Continuing beyond the 91st Street Marsh, you'll pass under a canopy of oak and maple branches and soon reach a plantation of red, jack, and white pine. In the 1950s, Argonne planted these pines to protect the soil from erosion and to serve as a buffer against the surrounding community. Enjoy the aroma while you're here: northeastern Illinois is not known for its abundance of pine trees.

By now you'll have noticed the occasional side trail that branches off from the main trail. Some of these trails are dirt paths, and others are mowed-grass lanes; while a few of the mowed lanes show up on the park map, none of the dirt trails are indicated. Despite the lack of markers on most of these side trails, hikers are allowed to venture forth. Many of these trails offer short strolls to nearby destinations such as a pond, while other treks are longer. On summer weekends around midday, these side trails can provide the solitude that may be hard to find on the main trail. Given that the forest preserve occupies nearly 2,500 acres, you'll want to bring along a map, compass, and/or GPS unit if you go off the marked trail.

Shortly after crossing Bluff Road, you'll be rewarded with a picturesque waterfall bounded by scenic bluffs and ravines. Before you make your way to the waterfall,

Waterfall Glen Forest Preserve Loop

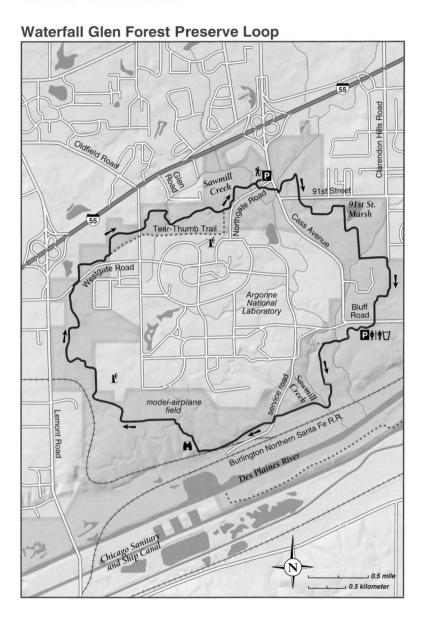

which is 3.5 miles into the hike, you'll find a parking lot, restrooms, and a water pump. Don't hesitate to top off your water bottle—other than the trailhead, this is the only spot along the trail with water. After traveling 0.2 mile beyond the parking lot, turn right (north) on the Rocky Glen Trail, which doubles as a gravel service road. A map board at this intersection shows your location. A hundred feet ahead on the Rocky Glen Trail, turn left to follow a 0.2-mile trail looking down at a ravine and Sawmill Creek. Situated at the bottom of a ravine, the 5-foot waterfall offers a fine spot for a picnic.

Surprisingly, Waterfall Glen Preserve is named not after this or any other waterfall, but a person: Seymour "Bud" Waterfall, who served as an early board president of the Forest Preserve District of DuPage County. Also interesting is that the waterfall is not natural but was built by the Civilian Conservation Corps in the 1930s with limestone from the preserve. During the late 19th century, there were three quarries in Waterfall Glen known for producing high-quality limestone. Waterfall Glen provided the limestone for one of the most famous structures in Chicago—the Water Tower, built in 1869 at Chicago and Michigan Avenues.

For a shortcut back to the main trail, take the first right up the hill as you head back the way you came. Back on the main trail, you'll get a nice view of the ravine and the 80-foot-high bluffs on the sides of which grow black and white oak, as well as bitternut and shagbark hickories.

At 0.5 mile ahead, you'll notice some railroad tracks before passing over Sawmill Creek. This section of the trail leads you through thick shrubs, as well as oak, pine, and maple. Near the electrical switching station, you'll pass through an area that was used as a plant nursery for Chicago parks. You'll see several concrete-and-stone building foundations from the early 1910s, remnants of when the nursery was in operation.

After passing the old foundations, keep an eye out for the overlook at the top of the bluff. This is where the trail takes a right turn, but a service road continues straight up a short hill to a picnic table and an information board. The spot offers a view of the Des Plaines River and the landscape on the other side of the river, which includes the small community of Lemont. Off to the right, outside of your view, is where limestone was quarried. Up ahead 0.3 mile on the main trail, you'll come to a 120-acre shortgrass prairie on the right. Among the many plants and animals inhabiting the prairie is a grass called poverty oats, which gives the area its name: Poverty Prairie. On your left is the 500-acre Poverty Savanna, which looks similar to the prairie except for the shrubs and the occasional oak tree.

If you're hiking on a summer weekend, you'll likely witness some takeoffs and landings at the model-aircraft field, just beyond Poverty Prairie; here, you'll also find restrooms and an information board. Crossing South Bluff Road, you'll pass a picnic table and then an idyllic pond likely to be occupied by a few mallard ducks. Just after the pond, you'll see the Kettle Hole Trail on the right.

Continue on the main trail as it meanders alongside Lemont Road, and watch for large, dramatic oaks with curving branches. After crossing Westgate Road and walking for 0.3 mile, you'll see Tear-Thumb Trail as it runs alongside the Argonne National Laboratory fence. Continuing on the main trail, you'll begin to catch glimpses of I-55 to the north. Following Tear-Thumb Marsh, plantations of pine, and a large wetlands area, you'll cross a footbridge over Sawmill Creek one last time on the way to the parking lot.

NEARBY ACTIVITIES

On the other side of the Des Plaines River is the **Palos–Sag Valley Trail System,** home to the largest network of trails in the Chicago area. Similar to Waterfall Glen, Palos has terrain that is woodsy and sometimes rugged. See the previous chapter for three hikes within this trail system (see Hikes 8–10, pages 52–64).

• •

GPS TRAILHEAD COORDINATES N41° 43.495' W87° 58.412'

DIRECTIONS Waterfall Glen Forest Preserve is bounded on the north by I-55 and on the south by the Des Plaines River. From the junction of I-55 and I-294, head southwest on I-55 for 4 miles; then take Exit 273A for Cass Avenue, heading south. In 0.2 mile, turn right (west) on Northgate Road at the entrance to Argonne National Laboratory. Less than 100 yards ahead, turn right at the signed entrance to Waterfall Glen Forest Preserve to reach the trailhead parking lot.

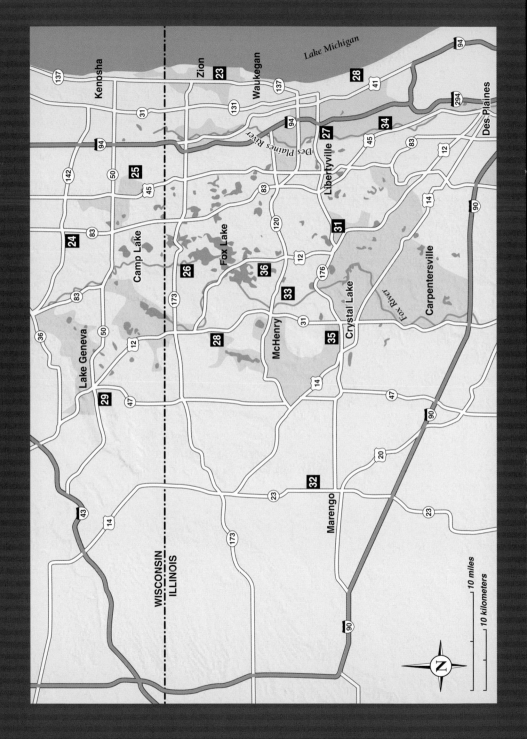

NORTH CHICAGOLAND AND WISCONSIN

The Dead River curves through marshland.   *Photo: Peter Gorman*

AFTER A RAMBLE along the shore of the Dead River, this trail brings you through some of the only sand dunes left in the state of Illinois. Halfway through the hike, take a break on a surprisingly quiet stretch of Lake Michigan beach.

DESCRIPTION

While it's true that Adeline Jay Geo-Karis Illinois Beach State Park contains one of the most popular beaches in the region, it's also true that visitors rarely seem to step away from the main beach and picnic area, leaving the trails and the out-of-the-way beach on this hike surprisingly quiet. The park, which was renamed in recent years to honor Adeline Jay Geo-Karis, a former Illinois state senator and Zion mayor, consists of two separate areas: the Northern Unit and Southern Unit. The Southern Unit, where this hike takes place, is the larger section, with more amenities, such as a campground, a store, and even a resort and conference center.

From the parking lot, with the restrooms behind you and the visitor center back to your right, look for the Dead River Trail, which heads right (southwest) near the far end of the lot. After you hike 0.2 mile through oak savanna, the trail meets up with the marshy waterway known as the Dead River. If you have the impression that this looks more like a long pond than a river, you're right—this river flows only during certain times of the year when the water levels rise. Most of the year, a sandbar blocks

DISTANCE & CONFIGURATION: 2.1-mile loop with a spur leading to the beach

DIFFICULTY: Easy

SCENERY: River, marshes, savanna, beach, dunes, Lake Michigan

EXPOSURE: Mostly exposed

TRAIL TRAFFIC: Light–moderate

TRAIL SURFACE: Dirt and sand

HIKING TIME: 1 hour

DRIVING DISTANCE: 47 miles from Millennium Park

ACCESS: Daily, sunrise–8 p.m.; no fees or permits

MAPS: Available at the website below; USGS *Zion, IL*

FACILITIES: Restrooms, water, campground/camp store, hotel, nature preserve

WHEELCHAIR ACCESS: None

CONTACT: 847-662-4811, www.dnr.illinois.gov/parks/pages/adelinejaygeo-karisillinoisbeach.aspx

LOCATION: Zion, IL 60099

COMMENTS: Dogs prohibited on the beach and in the nature preserve; must be leashed on trails

the mouth at Lake Michigan, thus keeping the water contained. Another 0.2 mile ahead is a platform overlooking the river and the expansive wetland. Some geologists have said the once-sluggish Chicago River looked much like the Dead River in pre-settlement times.

While the water here may be at a standstill, the environment certainly is not. During the spring, summer, and into fall, the trail hosts a variety of wildflowers, including milkweeds, shooting stars, and gentians. You're likely to see some waterbirds on the lake, and if you're visiting during the winter after snow has fallen, you might see a network of animal tracks on the ice.

Shortly after passing a kitchen stove–sized boulder in the middle of the stream, the trail turns east toward Lake Michigan, and the scenery starts to change. At 0.7 mile, turn right (southeast) at the junction. Leaving the wooded stream bank and oak savanna, you'll enter a washboard landscape made of sand. Because the prevailing winds blow the sand out to the lake, these are low dunes with gentle slopes. Each line of dunes was a previous shoreline for Lake Michigan during the past few thousand years. Here and there, the dunes are topped with scrawny oak trees that struggle to gather nutrients from the sandy ground. In all, an impressive 650 species of plants have been identified in the Southern Unit of the park. Some of the low creeping plants to look for among the dunes are the bearberry, with small paddle-shaped leaves and little egg-shaped white flowers, and the Waukegan juniper, an evergreen with whitish berries that turn purple in the winter.

The lake will come into view near the junction at 1.2 miles into the hike. Continue straight ahead (east) to a stretch of beach where you're likely to encounter few people, even on hot summer days. (*Note:* Pets are prohibited on the beach, so if your dog has joined you on this hike, skip to the next paragraph.) For a short beach stroll, walk 0.2 mile to the right to see the sandbar at the mouth of the Dead River. In addition to the natural scenery, you'll see some heavy industry: 1.5 miles to the south is

Adeline Jay Geo–Karis Illinois Beach State Park: Dead River Loop

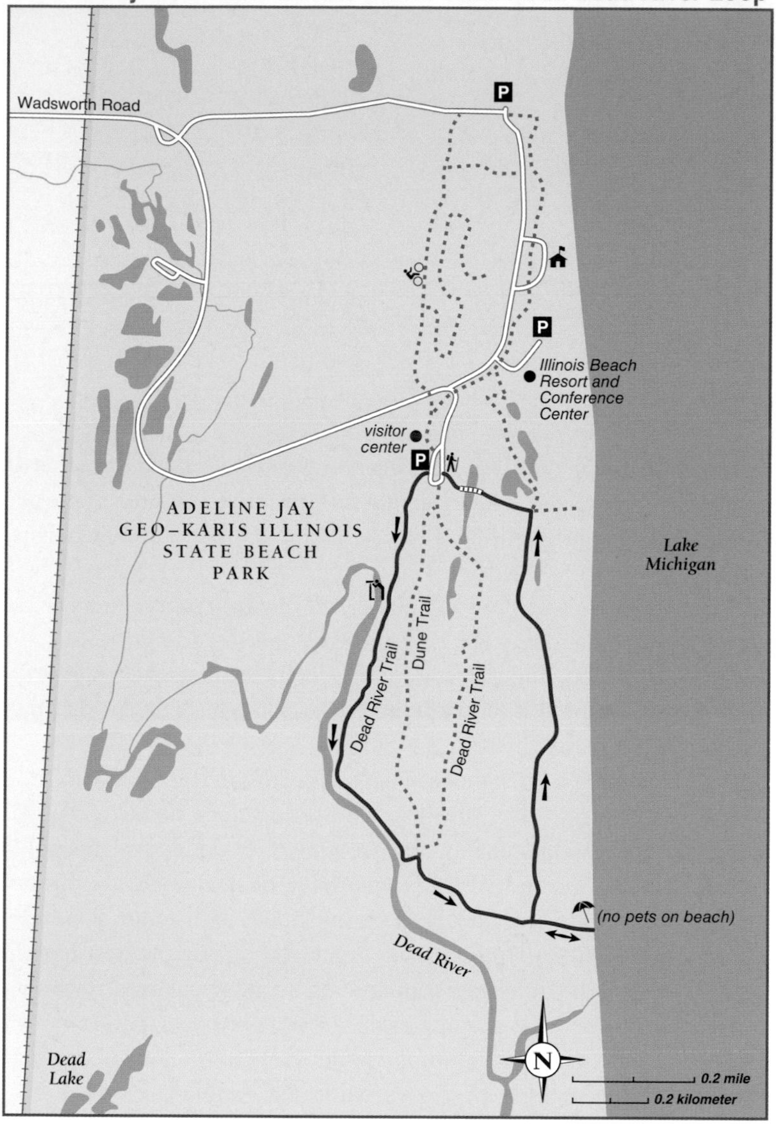

Wadsworth Road

Illinois Beach
Resort and
Conference
Center

visitor
center

ADELINE JAY
GEO–KARIS ILLINOIS
STATE BEACH
PARK

Dead River Trail

Dune Trail

Dead River Trail

Lake
Michigan

(no pets on beach)

Dead River

Dead
Lake

N

0.2 mile
0.2 kilometer

a coal-fired generating plant, and 2.5 miles to the north is the decommissioned Zion nuclear power plant, which once provided electricity for much of the Chicago area. Dedicated beach ramblers can follow the beach north 0.7 mile to catch the trail back to the parking lot.

To continue on the hiking route, head back up to the main trail and head north—right if you took the beach detour, left if you didn't. As you walk parallel to the lake, you'll see water between the swells of sand. At the base of the mounds, look for miniature blowouts where the wind has scoured away the plants and created hollow spots. As the trail bends inland, the oak trees grow larger and the landscape becomes blanketed in grasses typical of savannas and prairies. At 1.9 miles into the hike, turn left (northwest) at the junction, and then pass a large marsh on the right before following a boardwalk for 30 yards over a shallow dune pond. From the boardwalk, the parking lot is a short distance straight ahead.

NEARBY ACTIVITIES

If you're looking for a picnic area and a lively—sometimes crowded—stretch of beach, head back out on the main park road from the trailhead parking area, take a right, and continue past the Illinois Beach Resort on the right. North of the picnic area is the park's campground, offering 241 sites, many of which are fairly close to the beach.

Several more miles of hiking trails can be found in the Northern Unit of Adeline Jay Geo-Karis Illinois Beach State Park. To reach this section, leave the park the way you entered on Wadsworth Road. Just after the train tracks, turn right (north) on Sheridan Road. In 2.4 miles, turn right (east) on 17th Street, staying to the left at the forks in the road once you enter the park. About 1.3 miles farther, look for trails branching north and west from the parking loop/turnaround at the end of the road; several paths head east to the beach from here as well.

• •

GPS TRAILHEAD COORDINATES N42° 25.287′ W87° 48.507′

DIRECTIONS From the junction of I-90 and I-94 on Chicago's North Side, bear right (north) on I-94. In 35 miles, exit right (east) onto IL 132/Grand Avenue. In 3.5 miles, turn left (north) on IL 131/Green Bay Road; then proceed another 4 miles, turn right (east) on West Wadsworth Road, and follow it 3.1 miles into the park. Where the road forks, turn right, heading south and then east. In 1.1 miles, turn right at the NATURE PRESERVE sign into the parking lot.

PUBLIC TRANSPORTATION Take **Metra**'s Union Pacific/North Line to Zion. From the Zion Station, the trailhead is a 3-mile walk or bike ride, primarily along pathways. Head south on the path that runs on the west side of the train tracks. Turn left (east) on 29th Street, and then continue straight on the paved path where 29th Street ends and Deborah Avenue heads left (north). Follow the path as it snakes south along the beach; heads inland (west) past the campground, a large parking area, the park office, and the Illinois Beach Resort; and finally arrives back at the visitor center.

A pleasantly shaded pond view   *Photo: Jennifer Tomaloff*

HIKING AROUND WOLF LAKE, the centerpiece of this park, offers a pleasantly varied experience. The terrain on one side of the lake is flat or lightly rolling tree-speckled prairie, while the other side gives you dense woods, steep hills, and plunging ravines.

DESCRIPTION

In the early 1950s, the federal government determined that a jet-fighter base was needed to protect the Chicago and Milwaukee areas from enemy attack. Seventeen miles west of Kenosha, Wisconsin, a chunk of agricultural land spattered with woodlands was chosen for the site. The federal government spent $29 million toward acquiring land from 59 farm families and started development for an air base designed to house 5,000 airmen. Three days before the 2.4-mile-long runway was to be paved, the project was abandoned due to budget problems, possible air-space congestion, and concerns about the base being unnecessary.

In 1974, after much discussion and litigation, the state designated its first recreation area at the 4,515-acre air base that never was. The aborted base and subsequent park were named after Richard Bong, a World War II ace fighter pilot from the far reaches of northern Wisconsin. Bong, who was killed in 1945 while on a test flight in California, still holds the fighter-pilot record for shooting down 40 enemy planes.

At the beginning or end of the hike, stop in at the Molinaro Visitor Station to browse through an impressive collection of taxidermy specimens. Some of the more

DISTANCE & CONFIGURATION: 3.7-mile loop

DIFFICULTY: Moderate

SCENERY: Lake, woods, prairie, ponds, marshes, and hills

EXPOSURE: Partly shaded

TRAIL TRAFFIC: Light

TRAIL SURFACE: Mowed grass

HIKING TIME: 2.5 hours

DRIVING DISTANCE: 68 miles from Millennium Park

ACCESS: Daily, 6 a.m.–11 p.m. A parking sticker costs $8/car for visitors with Wisconsin license plates or $11 for those with out-of-state license plates (annual stickers cost $28/car in-state,

$38 out-of-state). When there's enough snow on the ground, expect to see cross-country skiers on this trail—don't walk in the ski tracks.

MAPS: Available at the entrance station and the website below; USGS *Paddock Lake, WI,* and *Union Grove, WI*

FACILITIES: Campground, picnic areas, beach, boat launch, restrooms, visitor center

WHEELCHAIR ACCESS: None

CONTACT: 262-878-5600, dnr.wi.gov/topic /parks/name/richardbong

LOCATION: 26313 Burlington Road, Kansasville, WI 53139

COMMENTS: Dogs must be on leash no longer than 8 feet. The 217-site campground is open all year.

striking examples are the northern goshawk, the snowy owl, and a dramatic portrayal of a coyote chasing a deer. For kids, there are bones, feathers, and pelts that can be picked up and examined.

Start the hike from the trailhead parking lot, just east of the Molinaro Visitor Station. Follow the blue and green arrows heading south to the boardwalk over the pond. After crossing the park road that leads to the Sunrise Campground, follow the Blue/ Green Trail to the left (northeast). For the next mile or so, you'll encounter a handful of trail junctions; some of these are horse trails, and others are connector trails to the campground. Fortunately, all of the intersections are well marked with arrows and the respective color of the trail painted around the top of the post. For now, keep an eye on the posts marked with blue and green.

As the trail curves away from the road, it heads down into a wooded area next to a small pond. The hill on the right serves as a sledding hill in the winter; campsites are located on the rise to the left. From the pond, the trail climbs a small hill, from which you'll see a grove of pine trees, a small prairie, and 150-acre Wolf Lake farther off. At the top of the next small hill, a junction of several trails comes together; follow the Blue/Green Trail on the left.

Hiking alongside the lake for 0.3 mile, you'll see stands of pussy willows on the lake side and groves of pine on the land side. Soon, you'll pass a hunter's blind at the edge of the lake on the right, followed by a little knoll with a bench at the top. After squeezing between WI 75 and the lake, the trail rises into a densely wooded area, then descends a steep hill under a canopy of gnarled oaks. At the bottom of the hill, the trail passes a pond connected to the lake. From here, head up another steep hill through a dense oak forest, and then enter a savanna area where a horse trail branches to the left.

Bong State Recreation Area Loop

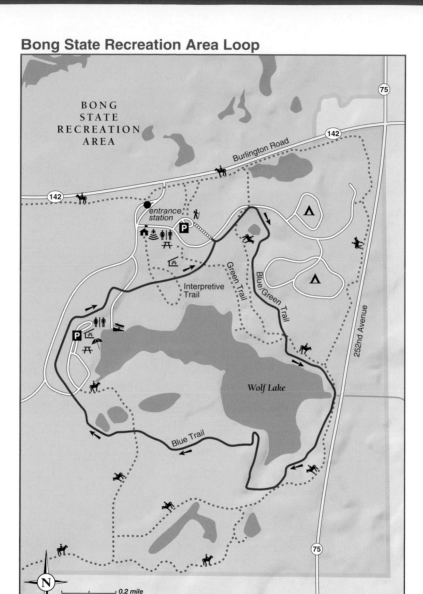

Soon the trail descends into a picturesque ravine with a small stream snaking through it. The piles of rocks on the sides of this ravine were likely moved here from the adjoining prairies by early farmers. Coming out of the woods, the trail takes a quick turn to the right as it enters a prairie, crosses a small stream, and then drops down to the lake through thick stands of poplars and oaks. The trail runs to a bench at the water's edge, and then swings back out into the prairie. While walking through this section of the prairie, you'll see a couple of small marshes, an intersection with a horse trail, another trail leading to a hunter's blind, and farther ahead, several ponds in a range of sizes. Small patches of trees grow here and there at the edge of the ponds.

Soon, the path comes to a large picnic area that includes pavilions, a 300-foot beach, a concession stand, restrooms, and a small fishing pier. Continue ahead with the park road and wide-open prairie on the left of the trail. On the right, the landscape drops down to a long thin strip of cattail marsh between the trail and the parking lot. When you reach the ball diamond, a set of stairs leads down to the parking lot on the right. Soon, the trail descends a bit and then crosses the driveway for the boat launch. The landscape becomes more rolling and conifers become more abundant as you approach the crushed-gravel Interpretive Trail that runs to the lake and loops back. Near the first intersection with the Interpretive Trail, a picnic area and restrooms are situated through the trees on the left. Turn left at the trail junction after the second intersection with the interpretive trail, and continue straight ahead until you cross the park road and the boardwalk over the pond to arrive back at the trailhead parking lot.

Note: This trail passes near one duck-hunting blind on the shore of the lake and in the vicinity of two others. The recreation area remains open to everyone during hunting season, and the park staff assures nonhunters that they may hike safely during this time, but if the idea makes you uncomfortable, then visit before or after designated hunting hours. Call 262-878-5600 for the schedule.

NEARBY ACTIVITIES

In **Burlington,** 8 miles northwest of the park on WI 142, you'll find a handful of restaurants. For more eating options, head 17 miles east on WI 142 to **Kenosha.**

Bong State Recreation Area offers 12 miles of mountain biking trails north of WI 142 that are also open for hiking. On these trails, you'll encounter prairies, woodlands, wetlands, and an artificial ridge made from topsoil, cleared for the airfield's runway. With a few exceptions, the terrain is mostly flat or moderately rolling.

• •

GPS TRAILHEAD COORDINATES N42° 38.052' W88° 07.444'

DIRECTIONS From the junction of I-90 and I-94 on Chicago's North Side, take I-94/I-41 north into Wisconsin. In 51.2 miles, take Exit 340 left (west) onto WI 142/Burlington Road. In 9.25 miles, turn left (south) into the park. From the entrance station, take the first left, passing the Molinaro Visitor Station. The next left is the trailhead parking lot.

Known for its trees, Bristol Woods also boasts brilliant seasonal wildflowers. *Photo: Stephen Gifford*

AT BRISTOL WOODS, hikers will enjoy the pleasantly rolling terrain covered in bottomland forest and oak woodland. Tree connoisseurs will enjoy the many oak specimens of considerable size, as well as a rare American Indian trail-marker tree.

DESCRIPTION

Once owned by a local parks commissioner, Bristol Woods offers visitors a pleasant stroll through nearly 200 acres of upland and lowland woods sprinkled with small marshes. The park came into existence in the 1970s when the county bought most of the property at a bargain price from Bob Pringle Sr., a onetime farmer who then served on the Kenosha County Parks Commission. Around the same time, the Pringle family also donated money toward the construction of a nature center, where you can see a collection of mounted birds and animals as well as habitat exhibits.

Starting the hike behind the Pringle Nature Center, you'll immediately come upon a tree with a strange crescent-shaped trunk. This 200-year-old oak is one of the last American Indian trail-marker trees in Kenosha County. While this tree is slightly different, most trail-marker trees were created by stripping a sapling of all its branches and then bending it to the ground in the direction of any number of important locations, such as camping or trading areas, sacred spots, or natural springs.

DISTANCE & CONFIGURATION: 2.6-mile balloon loop

DIFFICULTY: Easy

SCENERY: Oak and bottomland woods, marshes, pond, nature center, old town hall

EXPOSURE: Shaded

TRAIL TRAFFIC: Light

TRAIL SURFACE: Dirt, grass

HIKING TIME: 1 hour

DRIVING DISTANCE: 54.5 miles from Millennium Park

ACCESS: Daily, 7 a.m.–10 p.m.; no fees or permits

MAPS: Available at the Pringle Nature Center and the first website below; USGS *Paddock Lake, WI*

FACILITIES: Picnic tables, shelter, toilets, playground

WHEELCHAIR ACCESS: None

CONTACT: 262-857-1869, co.kenosha.wi.us /1660/bristol-woods-park; Pringle Nature Center, 262-857-8008, pringlenc.org

LOCATION: 9800 160th Ave., Bristol, WI 53104

COMMENTS: Dogs must be on leash no longer than 10 feet

Once a branch appeared on the top side in the middle of the bent trunk, this branch was allowed to grow skyward; the weight of the branch ensured that the trunk stayed bent. Later, the trunk beyond the lone vertical branch was removed.

Just ahead, at the T-junction on the edge of a small marsh, turn right (west). Turn right (north) again on the Red Trail (trails are marked with colored posts at nearly all junctions). Heading down a gradual incline, you'll pass by the little cattail pond in the open space in front of the nature center. Stay to the left as a grassy trail runs to the right toward the open area. The trail crosses an intermittent stream before it rises and runs through a small ravine filled with hickory, oak, and walnut trees. The terrain becomes more rolling as the trail swings left and then zigzags alongside the agricultural field on the right (keep an eye out for deer in the field). The trail eventually drops down a steep slope and heads through a small ravine strewn with deadfall.

After turning right (north) at the Green Trail, the path guides you along a raised bed with a crushed gravel surface. An attractive bottomland forest appears on the right and a steep hill rises up on the left. Stay to the right (north), and switch to the Blue Trail as it rises gradually toward the old town hall on County Road C. A sign in front of the white wood-frame building explains that it was built in 1870 and actively used for the next 100 years. As you backtrack along the blue trail, skip the first trail that heads toward the back of the town hall. Instead, take the second right (west), the Green Trail, which leads through a small clearing with a picnic table and then climbs before taking a couple of banked turns.

Passing the White Trail on the left, you'll see more agricultural land through the trees on the right. From here, the trail makes a long and gradual descent under a canopy of large, eye-catching oaks. Watch for downy woodpeckers gliding between the specimens of burr, red, white, and black oak. Heading away from the agricultural field, the trail starts to drop. You may notice that the sides of this trail, as well as other trails at Bristol Woods, contain a good number of rocks and modest-size

129

Bristol Woods Hike

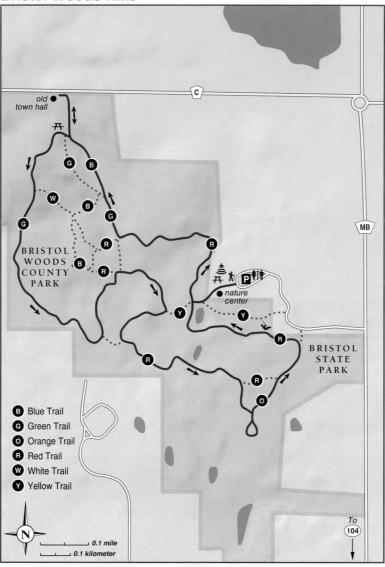

B Blue Trail
G Green Trail
O Orange Trail
R Red Trail
W White Trail
Y Yellow Trail

boulders. Dropped off by the last glacier, these rocks were usually removed by farmers so they wouldn't damage their plows. The abundance of rocks at Bristol Woods reveals that this area was never farmed; it was one of the few natural areas in the Chicago region to escape the plow. Just after the trail takes a sharp left turn at a large white oak, keep straight ahead on the Green Trail as you pass an unmarked trail on the right that connects with the Red Trail.

Arriving at a cluster of cottonwood and elm trees, turn right (east) on the Red Trail as it leads past a bench. After a few turns and a series of intermittent streams, you'll see a marker at a grouping of cedars, followed by another intermittent stream that runs through a small gully. After the junction with the Yellow Trail, you'll pass a couple of huge white oaks and then climb a bit before arriving at a bench situated under another cluster of cedars on a little hilltop. From the hill, walk down into a shallow ravine, and then cross an intermittent stream that has carved out a rocky trough. A short climb brings you to a junction with the unmarked connector trail on the right; nearby you'll see a wall from a foundation of a former barn.

After a stretch of bottomland forest thick with bushes, you'll encounter another junction with a connector trail, as well as a marsh behind the trees on the left. Following a dense section of trail that is almost tunnel-like, turn right (south) on the Orange Trail. Stay to the right, and you'll see more marshland through the trees on the right. Complete the loop and then head back to the Red Trail where you'll turn right (northeast).

Back on the Red Trail, look for a grove of apple trees that were once part of a nearby farm. After passing a trail on the right that goes toward the park road, the trail leads you into a little ravine containing a grove of quaking aspen. This final section of the trail brings you beside several monster-size oaks, some with knotty, arthritic-looking limbs. Turn right (east) on the Yellow Trail and then bear left back to the nature center.

NEARBY ACTIVITIES

West of Bristol Woods is **Silver Lake County Park,** which offers several miles of hilly trails running above the lake through groves of oak and sumac and pine plantations. Catch the beginning of the loop from the small parking area just inside the park entrance. Turning left on the park road at the entrance brings you to a lakeside picnic area. Taking the road to the right brings you through a number of picnic areas sprinkled throughout this pleasantly hilly park, which is open 7 a.m.–10 p.m. From Bristol Woods, take County Road MB left (north) to WI 50. Follow WI 50 left (west) for 6 miles to CR F/Silver Lake Road. Turn left (south) on Silver Lake Road, and the park entrance is nearly 2 miles ahead on the right.

• •

GPS TRAILHEAD COORDINATES N42° 31.972' W88° 00.370'

DIRECTIONS From the junction of I-90 and I-94 on Chicago's North Side, take I-94/I-41 north for 45.3 miles. Two miles into Wisconsin, take Exit 347 for WI 104/104th Street. Turn left (west) and proceed for 2.5 miles until you reach CR MB. Turn right (north) on CR MB, and proceed 0.4 mile. The entrance to Bristol Woods County Park is on the left.

The dirt trail meanders gently through the trees.   *Photo: Patricia Henschen*

CHAIN O' LAKES is full of natural treasures. The riches within the 6,023-acre park include expansive wetlands, gently rolling prairies, pleasant wooded areas, and a peaceful stretch of the Fox River—all accessed by a well-designed trail system.

DESCRIPTION

As the largest state park in northern Illinois, Chain O' Lakes State Park offers something for everyone. Along with prospects for camping, fishing, bicycling, and boating, there are picnic areas galore, playgrounds, boat and canoe rentals, and horse rentals for the trails in the western section of the park. With all this going on, it's no surprise that the park draws crowds—particularly boaters looking to access the series of 15 lakes connected by the Fox River and human-made channels. Despite the busy atmosphere in the summer months, plenty of tranquil hiking is readily found once you get away from the boat launch and the picnic areas.

The trails in the eastern section of the park are laid out in four connected loops running north and south. The two southern loops, hitting some of the busier sections of the park, brush up against Grass Lake and run through dense, hilly woods. The two northern loops are notable for hilltop views, quiet prairies, and a brief rendezvous with the Fox River.

While there are numerous places to start this hike, I recommend dropping in at the section near the park office—the office is easy to find and provides sweeping views

DISTANCE & CONFIGURATION: 7 miles, 4 connected loops	**ACCESS:** January–April, 8 a.m.–sunset; May–October, 6 a.m.–9 p.m.; park is closed for hunting during November and December; no fees or permits
DIFFICULTY: Easy	
SCENERY: Hills, prairies, wetlands, and woods, with sections along Grass Lake and the Fox River	**MAPS:** Available at the entrance station and the website below; USGS *Fox Lake, IL*
EXPOSURE: Northern 2 loops are mostly exposed; southern 2 loops are mostly shaded	**FACILITIES:** Water, restrooms, camping, picnic areas, concession stand, boat launch, and boat rental
TRAIL TRAFFIC: Heavier near boat launch and picnic areas; lighter elsewhere	**WHEELCHAIR ACCESS:** 3 northern loops
TRAIL SURFACE: Southernmost loop is mowed grass and dirt; other 3 loops are multiuse trails with a crushed-gravel surface	**CONTACT:** 847-587-5512, www.dnr.illinois.gov /parks/pages/chainolakes.aspx
HIKING TIME: 3 hours	**LOCATION:** 8916 Wilmot Road, Spring Grove, IL 60081
DRIVING DISTANCE: 60 miles from Millennium Park	**COMMENTS:** Dogs must be leashed and picked up after

of the prairie, savanna, woods, wetland, and the Fox River in the distance. Once you find the trail on the east side of the parking lot, take it to the right for a counterclockwise hike, saving the majority of the secluded areas and the river for the last leg.

As you head to the right (south) from the parking lot on the Badger Trail, you'll see a rolling prairie on the left and a mixture of woods and savanna down the hill on the right. Soon, you'll have a nice view of the middle section of the park—open space dotted with marshes, ponds, and the occasional oak tree. At 0.7 mile, turn right (southwest) on the Sunset Trail, and cross the park road before entering Deer Path Picnic Area, one of many picnicking spots clumped into this section of the park. South of the picnic area is where the Cattail Trail branches right, connecting hikers with 5.5 miles of less-used trails in the western section of the park. Bird-watchers shouldn't miss the marsh halfway along the 0.8-mile Cattail Trail; for much of the year, it's an excellent spot for seeing sandhill cranes (Chain O' Lakes Park is one of the few nesting sites in the region for these enormous gray birds with red foreheads).

Continuing on the Sunset Trail, cross the park road and stay to the right (southwest) as you meet the other end of the Sunset loop at 1.3 miles. At 1.7 miles into the hike, just beyond the Oak Grove Picnic Area, look for a marker on the right (southwest) for Nature's Way Trail.

While Nature's Way Trail can be confusing because of its profusion of side trails leading to camping areas, the route is well marked and easily followed. Nature's Way Trail quickly brings you across the park road and into a thickly wooded area. Soon you'll be skirting a swampy pond on the right—look for great blue herons, sandhill cranes, and tree trunks chiseled by beavers.

After a sharp left turn at 1.9 miles, the trail brushes against a fenced-in field and then takes a sharp right turn before accompanying a park road through the Fox Den

Chain O' Lakes State Park Hike

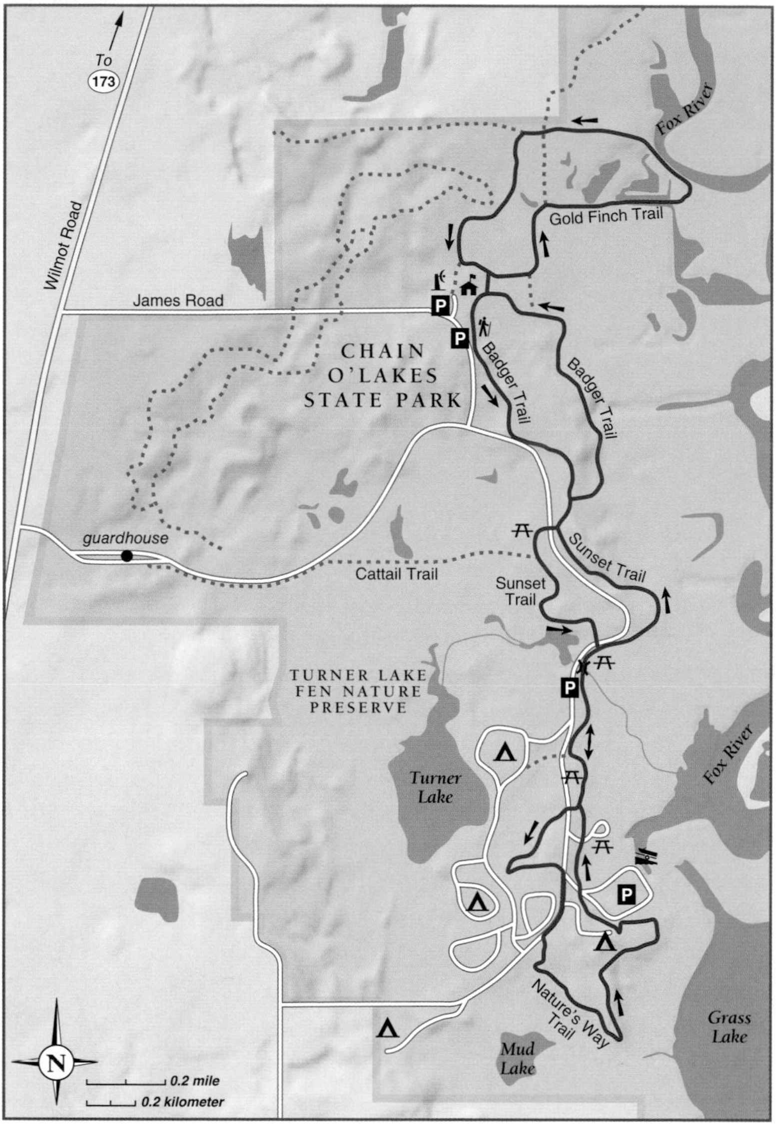

Camping Area. After 0.2 mile on the park road, follow the marker into the woods to the left (south). Immediately, there's a connector trail branching left that will trim 0.7 mile off this section of the hike. Ahead on the main trail, a grassy wetland known as a sedge meadow appears on the right. Soon, on the left, is another opportunity to shorten the hike via a brief connector path marked as the Black Cherry Shortcut Trail. Continuing on the main trail, hikers will encounter the occasional patches of open space, as well as thick woods with large specimens of shagbark hickory and oak.

At 2.7 miles, the trail takes a hairpin left turn at the tip of a little wooded peninsula extending out into the sedge meadow. After the turn, you'll climb a hill and soon arrive at a bench with a fine view of Grass Lake, which is the third largest of the 15 connected lakes and is one of only 3 natural lakes among them. In the early 20th century, a series of channels was dug to link what is the largest concentration of lakes in the state.

Nearly 0.5 mile after the little peninsula, hikers will pass a side trail that branches right to the boat launch and concession stand. After passing the boat-launch parking lot and several side trails leading to camping areas, the trail crosses two park roads before returning to the Oak Grove Picnic Area.

Just beyond the North Pike Marsh Picnic Area, at 4 miles into the hike, take the Sunset Trail to the right. Intermittent marshy spots appear through the trees to the right (northwest). Stay to the right (northwest) at 4.5 miles when you reach the connection to the Badger Trail. Turn right again where there is a picnic table from which you can enjoy an expansive view of the grassy wetland. At 4.8 miles, the trail runs next to a swamp on the right, just before entering a tallgrass prairie fringed by oaks and conifers. Stay to the right at two successive trail junctions, which you'll encounter as you leave the Badger Trail and begin Gold Finch Trail.

Starting on the Gold Finch Trail, perfect rows of planted pine trees grow on the right. By the time you arrive at a picnic table next to a small pond at 5.6 miles, the terrain has flattened considerably. After walking alongside a 0.2-mile-long cattail pond on the right, the trail arrives at an attractive slice of the Fox River. This is a good spot to scan the marshy shoreline for water birds while sitting on the bank, reviving tired feet with a bath in the river. Following the riverbank for 0.2 mile, the trail heads back into the woods and passes under a canopy of oaks. Winding through woods, savanna, and stands of shrubbery, you'll soon pass another picnic table by a pond. At 6.9 miles, pass a trail branching right to the park office. Stay to the right (south and then west) at the following two trail junctions as you complete the Gold Finch Loop and return to the Badger Loop. At 7 miles, the trail arrives back at the parking lot.

• •

GPS TRAILHEAD COORDINATES N42° 27.951' W88° 11.364'

DIRECTIONS From the junction of I-90 and I-94 on Chicago's North Side, bear right (north) on I-94 and, in 40.8 miles, exit left (west) onto IL 173/Rosecrans Road. In 13 miles, turn left (south) on Wilmot Road; in 1.7 miles, look for the sign for Chain O' Lakes State Park on your left. Stop at the guardhouse for a park map; then continue on the park road for 1 mile before turning left at the sign for the park office. Park in the first lot on the right.

Lily pad wetland at Old School Forest Preserve   *Photo: Evan Kane*

IF YOU LIKE RIPARIAN LANDSCAPES, you'll love the Des Plaines River Trail as it winds alongside tree-laden riverbanks, through dense bottomland woods, alongside ponds, and over footbridges spanning the river. There are also quiet oak savannas and many acres of tallgrass prairie thick with goldenrod, asters, and big bluestem prairie grass.

DESCRIPTION

Given all the development in the area surrounding the Des Plaines River, it may come as a surprise to see how much nature lines the river. Indeed, the many forest preserves that accompany the Des Plaines River in Lake and Cook Counties make up the longest greenway in the Chicagoland region. In addition to the aesthetic, recreational, and health benefits these greenways have for humans, ecologists will tell you these long, extended natural areas offer many advantages for local plants and animals, too.

In Lake County, no fewer than 10 forest preserves lie along a continuous path within the Des Plaines River Valley. Spanning nearly the entire length of Lake County, the northern section of the Des Plaines River Trail gives hikers an extended encounter with this attractive river and the surrounding (mostly wet) landscape. The following hike is just a small slice of this portion of the trail as it runs the entire north–south span of Lake County. (To the south in Cook County, the Des Plaines River Trail runs

DISTANCE & CONFIGURATION: 9.5-mile out-and-back

DIFFICULTY: Easy–moderate

SCENERY: Bottomland woods, Des Plaines River, ponds, lakes, marshes, prairies, savanna

EXPOSURE: One-third of the route is exposed; the rest is mostly shaded

TRAIL TRAFFIC: Moderate–busy

TRAIL SURFACE: Crushed gravel

HIKING TIME: 3–4 hours

DRIVING DISTANCE: 38 miles from Millennium Park

ACCESS: Daily, 6:30 a.m.–sunset; no fees or permits

MAPS: On kiosks in the forest preserves at the hike's beginning and turnaround point (paper maps sometimes available at the kiosks);

interactive trail map for all Lake County forest preserves at maps.lakecountyil.gov/trailmap; USGS *Libertyville, IL*

FACILITIES: Old School Forest Preserve has water, restrooms, and picnicking areas; Independence Grove Forest Preserve offers boat and bike rentals, a swimming beach, ice-skating, a sledding hill, a visitor center, and a seasonal café

WHEELCHAIR ACCESS: Yes

CONTACT: 847-367-6640, lcfpd.org/old-school, lcfpd.org/ig, lcfpd.org/dprt

LOCATION: 28285 St. Mary's Road, Mettawa, IL 60048 (Old School Forest Preserve)

COMMENTS: Dogs must be leashed. Trail junctions are well marked, indicating access points and the Des Plaines River Trail heading north and south.

another 20 miles or so, although not continuously; see page 33 for a hike along a section of the Des Plaines River Trail in Cook County.)

Once you've located the Des Plaines River Trail on its way through the woods in the southwest corner of Old School Forest Preserve, take the trail toward St. Mary's Road. Once you emerge from the tunnel under the road, the trail enters a prairie landscape where you'll find plants such as goldenrod, heath, and sky-blue asters, and big bluestem prairie grass.

Note: Hikers will encounter five road crossings each way on this excursion. Thanks to careful planning, the trail runs under the busy roads. Occasionally, however, the rising river swallows up underpasses. The county posts signs during flooding, and you can simply cross the road at street level instead.

The prairie gradually slopes down in the direction you're traveling: toward the Des Plaines River. Even though development exists on both sides of this piece of pathway, it's off in the distance and doesn't feel cramped. Getting closer to the river, the path curls to the right and runs through a riverside savanna and across West Rockland Road. You'll pass near a housing development and through thick bottomland woods and brush against a pond before heading under IL 176 and the North Shore Bike Path. (The bike path runs along IL 176 for 7.5 miles between Mundelein and Lake Bluff.)

Continuing north, the trail winds through woodland dense with maple, hickory, and oak trees. After crossing one of the many handsome wood and steel pedestrian bridges along the trail, it enters an area with many marshy spots and a scattering of ponds—some ponds with open water and others covered in bright green algae and littered with dead logs. After crossing Oak Spring Road, you'll see Minear Lake over

137

Des Plaines River Trail: Old School to Independence Grove

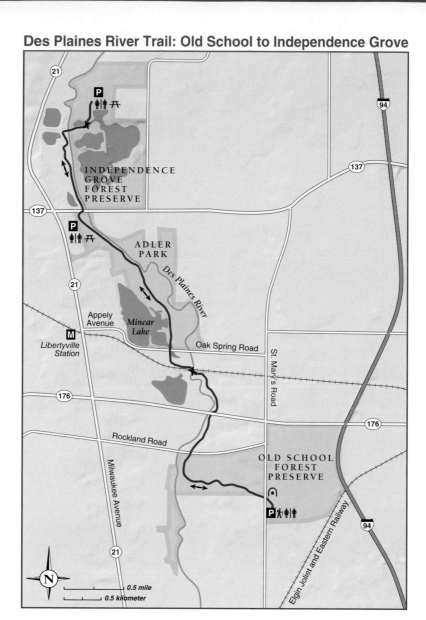

the embankment on the left. Minear Lake, like many of the lakes and ponds along the river, was created by a former gravel-mining operation. Soon you'll pass Adler Park, which is located up the bluff on the left. (The park has picnicking areas, water, restrooms, and a disc-golf course.) As you cross IL 137, you'll see an abundance of development along IL 21 to the west.

Entering Independence Grove Forest Preserve, the trail cuts through an attractive, gently rolling prairie and then passes a couple of ponds (also former gravel pits) on the left before crossing a pedestrian bridge into the main part of Independence Grove. In Independence Grove, you can turn around and head back to Old School Forest Preserve, or you can explore the 6 miles of trails that the circle the lake here. Or you may want to push ahead on the Des Plaines River Trail to see the sights farther upstream (see Nearby Attractions for details). First, though, you'll want to continue ahead a bit on the Des Plaines River Trail as it mounts a hill and allows an expansive view of the 1,110-acre preserve and the 115-acre lake at Independence Grove.

NEARBY ACTIVITIES

For a completely different set of views of the Des Plaines River, consider a paddling trip. Six canoe launches are located in the area, including launches at Oak Spring Road and at Independence Grove; go to lcfpd.org/paddling for more information on launch sites and rentals.

And if you're ready for more hiking along Des Plaines River Trail, you'll find more attractive prairie, savanna, and woodland along the trail north of Independence Grove. From Independence Grove, it's 2.5 miles north to IL 120.

Hiking south from the starting point at Old School Forest Preserve, you might consider following the Des Plaines River Trail for 2.4 miles to IL 60. From Old School, the path threads its way through patches of prairie and woodland before crossing Old School Road and then running through a savanna that sits beside railroad tracks. Passing under the tracks and crossing St. Mary's Road brings you to **MacArthur Woods**, an Illinois Nature Preserve with an attractive mix of woodland and savanna.

• •

GPS TRAILHEAD COORDINATES N42° 16.119' W87° 55.442'

DIRECTIONS From the junction of I-90 and I-94 on Chicago's North Side, follow I-94 north for 27.4 miles. Exit at IL 176/East Park Avenue, and turn left (west). After 0.8 mile, turn left (south) on St. Mary's Road. Look for the entrance to Old School Forest Preserve on the left. Follow the road to the right, and park in the first parking area. Look for the sign pointing to the Des Plaines River Trail at the far western edge of the parking area.

PUBLIC TRANSPORTATION **Metra**'s Milwaukee District/North Line stops in Libertyville less than 1 mile from the Des Plaines River Trail. The route from the train station to the trail runs along quiet streets and has paths and sidewalks along the way. Just north of where the train crosses IL 21/North Milwaukee Avenue, take Appley Avenue east. Turn left (east) on West Oak Spring Road. The trail crosses the road after you pass Minear Lake on the left.

Vistas of Lake Michigan abound on this hike.   *Photo: Ted Villaire*

THIS HIKE OFFERS a lot to enjoy in a compact area: deep wooded ravines, the historic grounds of Fort Sheridan, a sandy Lake Michigan shoreline, wetlands teeming with birds, open prairie, and to top it all off, another shoreline preserve a stone's throw to the south.

DESCRIPTION

Note: *Most of Fort Sheridan, including the area that contains the hike described, is closed for improvements until the summer of 2019. (The parade grounds and historic district at the southern end of the preserve remain open; the cemetery in the northwest corner remains open as well, but for now it's accessible only from Sheridan Road, on the west side of the preserve.) The improvements—which include woodlands restoration, replacement of aging boardwalks and bridges, new parking areas, and new turf and asphalt trail surfaces—are not expected to alter the hike route substantially; call the preserve or check lcfpd .org/preserves/improvement-projects for updates.*

While the suburbs of Chicago's North Shore generally aren't regarded as places rich in historical attractions, a few intriguing old landmarks do exist. One of these is Fort Sheridan, a U.S. Army base established in 1887 on the shore of Lake Michigan. The fort was originally built not to thwart foreign invaders but at the urging of North Shore businessmen so that troops could respond quickly to labor protests in Chicago and prevent the turmoil from spreading north of the city.

DISTANCE & CONFIGURATION: 1.7-mile loop

DIFFICULTY: Easy

SCENERY: Lake Michigan, sandy beach, prairie, marshes, ravines, streams, woodland

EXPOSURE: Mostly open

TRAIL TRAFFIC: Busy

TRAIL SURFACE: Mowed grass

HIKING TIME: 1 hour

DRIVING DISTANCE: 29 miles from Millennium Park

ACCESS: Daily, 6:30 a.m.–sunset; no fees or permits

MAPS: Interactive trail map at maps.lakecountyil .gov/trailmap; USGS *Highland Park, IL*

FACILITIES: Restrooms, picnic tables, and a "hawk's nest" play area for kids

WHEELCHAIR ACCESS: None on this hike; paved trails adjacent

CONTACT: 847-367-6640, lcfpd.org/fort-sheridan

LOCATION: Gilgare Lane, Lake Forest, IL 60045

COMMENTS: See Description for details about the current closures at Fort Sheridan. Also see Nearby Activities for an alternative hike just a mile south in Openlands Lakeshore Preserve.

Fort Sheridan was a busy place while it served as a training and administrative center from the Spanish American War through World War II, when more than 500,000 military men and women were processed at the fort. The centerpiece of the fort is a 227-foot-tall water tower, originally the tallest structure in the Chicago area. The long, squat row of buildings on each side of the tower served as troop barracks. The fort was shuttered in 1993, and the 100 or so attractive homes and administrative buildings were sold to private individuals. After the base closed, extensive environmental cleanup was needed before it could be transformed it into a residential development. A U.S. Army Reserve base continues to occupy some of the land, the majority of which is now privately owned.

This hike takes place on 250 acres that were once part of the fort but are now a county forest preserve. One of the geologic features on this stretch of shoreline is a series of ravines that run toward Lake Michigan. The V-shaped ravines, typically just a few hundred yards long, were carved 10,000–12,000 years ago by streams as they twisted from the higher, flat ground to the lower level of the lake. They provide a protected home for several endangered and threatened species. Most of the 30-odd ravines between Evanston and the Illinois–Wisconsin border are on private property, but here you can get close to a ravine on public land.

Start the hike from the midsection of the parking lot, and then immediately take a left (west) at the map board for a clockwise hike. Stay on the main trail as a couple of lesser trails merge with the main one (throughout this hike, stick to the main trail as smaller trails merge and branch). To the left, you can see some of the houses once occupied by officers at the fort. The houses were all built between 1889 and 1910; the earliest buildings were constructed of bricks molded and fired on site, using clay mined from lakefront bluffs. While you enjoy the open prairie dotted with flowers, you'll likely encounter oodles of red-winged blackbirds hanging out among the patches of cattails. After passing a junction with a signed trail that leads left to

Fort Sheridan Forest Preserve Hike

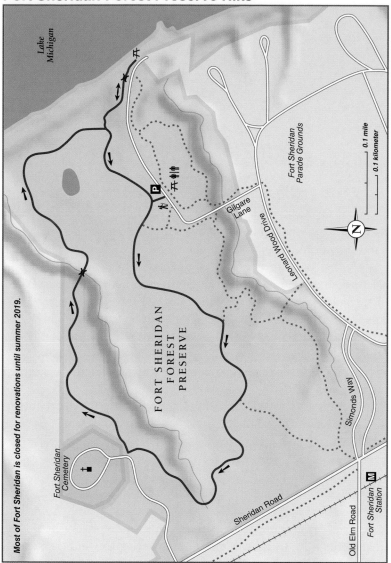

Sheridan Road, the main trail drops a bit before crossing a creek that may or may not have water depending on the wetness of the weather.

Cross another arm of the creek—this one with thickets of cattails and sedge grasses. Keep left on the main trail as another trail branches to the right. Traverse a small causeway with a pond on the left and the beginning of a ravine on the right. You'll hike alongside this ravine for the two-thirds of a mile on the way to Lake

Michigan. As the trail turns away from Sheridan Road, on the left you'll see the small military cemetery, in operation since 1890. Among the people buried here are nine Germans who died while in World War II POW camps in the Midwest, as well as four soldiers who served under General George Custer. A peek at the grounds reveals that nearly all of the tombstones are the same: squat white-marble slabs with rounded tops.

Leaving the cemetery behind, head through the prairie toward the grove of oaks that grows alongside the chain-link fence. As you mount the steel pedestrian bridge, you'll enjoy a bird's eye view of the 50-foot-deep wooded ravine. The rocky stream-bed at the bottom of the ravine was added to counter the effects of erosion.

As the big lake comes into view, you'll see that the prairie and savanna you've been walking through sit on a 75-foot bluff above Lake Michigan. The vistas are lovely thanks to the forest preserve's removal of invasive plants and trees that would be blocking your view. Stay alongside the bluff and you'll soon find a trail that leads down to the water. While crossing the asphalt access road, you can see the parking area where you started to the east.

Once you get down to the shoreline, take a break with lakeside picnic. After that, you can walk north along the length of the forest preserve. You may also walk to the south, but be warned that you're likely to encounter large pieces of concrete riprap that make for achingly slow and slightly treacherous travel. Note that swimming and wading are not allowed due to the possible presence of sharp metal and unexploded ordnance left over from the days when soldiers would practice their shooting. After you enjoy the shoreline, it's a short trip back up to the parking area.

NEARBY ACTIVITIES

The parade grounds and historic district in the southern part of the preserve are well worth a visit on their own. There's also a wonderful hiking alternative just a mile to the south within **Openlands Lakeshore Preserve.** In addition to strolling a sandy shoreline that's more than a mile long, you can walk along a paved trail at the top of a bluff, as well explore as a ravine trail. Scattered within the preserve is a collection of artwork inspired by the local natural world (don't miss the 30-by-50-foot mural in the ravine under Patten Road).

To reach Openlands from Fort Sheridan by foot or car, turn left on Leonard Wood Drive, and continue straight ahead as it turns into Whistler Road and then Patten Road. Just after the bridge over the ravine, the parking area is on the right. Enter the preserve on the trail at the left, or take the stairs into the ravine from the parking area. Visit openlands.org for more information, including trail maps.

Another attraction in the area is the **Robert McClory Bike Path,** which runs north from Fort Sheridan to the southern edge of Kenosha, Wisconsin. Running south from Fort Sheridan is the **Green Bay Trail.**

Jay Lovell's, a popular casual restaurant, is just a few blocks from the entrance to Fort Sheridan (766 Sheridan Road, Highwood; 847-780-3930, jaylovells.com). The Reuben sandwich makes for a nice way to top off a few miles of hiking. **Koya Sushi** is also very close by (508 W. Elm Road, Highland Park; 847-266-0891, koya -sushi.com), and you'll find a variety of eateries 1 mile south of the preserve in downtown Highwood.

• •

GPS TRAILHEAD COORDINATES N42° 13.367' W87° 48.734'

DIRECTIONS From the junction of I-90 and I-94 on Chicago's North Side, follow I-94 north for 13.2 miles. Exit on US 41/Skokie Highway, and continue for 5.9 miles. Turn right (east) on Old Elm Road. About 1.25 miles ahead, Old Elm Road turns into Simonds Way as you enter the grounds of Fort Sheridan. Turn left at Leonard Wood Drive, and then turn left again on Gilgare Lane, which takes you to the forest preserve's main parking area.

PUBLIC TRANSPORTATION **Metra**'s Union Pacific North train stops directly across Sheridan Road from Fort Sheridan. Grab the trail to enter the preserve on the northeast corner of Old Elm Road/Simonds Way and Sheridan Road. At the first junction, take the turf trail to the left, and you'll start the hike by going left at the next junction.

Please heed the signs posted along the route.   *Photo: Elaine Meszaros*

IT'S EASY TO SEE why so many wealthy Chicagoans built their opulent mansions on the shore of Geneva Lake during the late 19th and early 20th centuries. The views from the wooded bluffs along this silvery lake are fantastic. While enjoying the lake and the historic estates on this hike, you'll encounter flower gardens, carefully manicured lawns, boathouses, and charming little towns.

DESCRIPTION

In the early 1870s, after the Great Chicago Fire and the completion of a rail line connecting Lake Geneva with Chicago, estates began springing up on the shores of this Wisconsin lake. Many of the homes served as summer resorts for wealthy families with surnames such as Maytag and Wrigley. After the turn of the century, clubs, youth camps, and expensive subdivisions started squeezing in between the sprawling estates.

Given the upscale atmosphere at Geneva Lake, many people are surprised to learn that there's a public footpath circumnavigating the entire lake. (For the record: the lake proper is Geneva Lake, and the town is Lake Geneva.) While not all landowners

DISTANCE & CONFIGURATION: 10-mile point-to-point; car shuttle recommended

DIFFICULTY: Strenuous due to length and steep sections, including stairs; skip it in snowy or icy conditions

SCENERY: Geneva Lake, gorgeous historic mansions, bluffs, woodlands, public parks, and 3 pleasant lakeside villages

EXPOSURE: Mostly shaded

TRAIL TRAFFIC: Moderate but can get busy on summer weekends

TRAIL SURFACE: Grass, dirt, brick, gravel, stone, and concrete

HIKING TIME: 3–4 hours

DRIVING DISTANCE: 80 miles from Millennium Park

ACCESS: Daily, sunrise–sunset; no fees or permits

MAPS: No official map, but you can find

unofficial alternatives online; USGS *Walworth, WI,* and *Lake Geneva, WI*

WHEELCHAIR ACCESS: None

FACILITIES: Restrooms, water, benches, public parks, beaches, parking, and restaurants at towns along the way; no benches between Lake Geneva and Williams Bay

CONTACT: 800-345-1020, visitlakegeneva.com /lake-geneva-shore-path

LOCATION: 918 W. Main St., Lake Geneva, WI 53147 (Lake Geneva Public Library); 454 Lake St., Fontana-on-Geneva Lake, WI 53125 (Fontana Beach Public Parking Lot)

COMMENTS: Yes, this hike is farther than 60 miles from Chicago, but the breathtaking scenery makes it worthy of inclusion. No bicycles on the trail; dogs must be leashed and picked up after. Hiking in late fall, winter, and early spring will require navigating your way around the many docks that are stacked up in homeowners' yards.

have been happy with the path, they've been legally obligated to leave their gates open since a court decision in the 1970s granted the public right of passage. The decision was based on the fact that the pathway existed long before the homes and their owners did: indeed, before European settlers arrived in the area, the local Potawatomi Indians regularly used a narrow dirt trail along the entire shoreline of the lake. Frequently posted signs ask you to stay on the path. If you're hiking with a pet, please be considerate about cleaning up after it.

While walking through people's yards may feel strange at first, this feeling diminishes once you see the many attractive walkways installed by homeowners. Starting from Library Park, behind (west of) the Prairie-style public library, follow the sidewalk to the right. At the end of the park, the path turns to gravel and enters a yard. A sign just ahead identifies Maple Lawn, the oldest estate on the lake, dating from 1870. Next up are a number of newer homes, many with attractive flower bushes growing within carefully landscaped environments. After crossing a bridge over a rock-lined streambed and passing the lawns of Covenant Harbor Bible Camp, wooded bluffs start to rise along the shoreline.

Just ahead is Northwoodside, a green-trimmed Swiss-style mansion built in 1876 by the inventor of the paper milk-bottle cap. Between the estates on this section of the lake, the path runs through a number of brief wooded sections thick with weeping willows, sugar maples, and various oaks. *Note:* There are no public benches

Geneva Lake: North Shore Hike

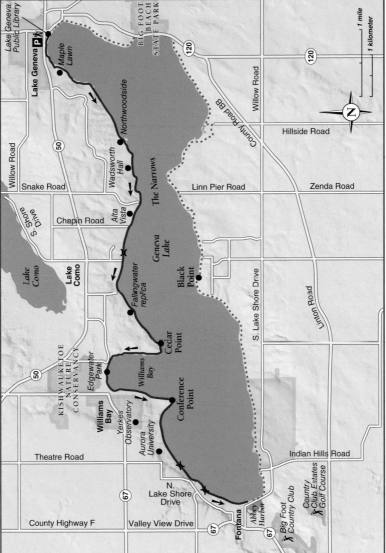

on the 7 miles between Lake Geneva and Williams Bay, so consider discreetly using logs or tree stumps in the wooded areas for your rest breaks.

At 2.5 miles into the hike, the path passes Wadsworth Hall, a stately redbrick mansion from 1905 with six fluted columns in front. Near the House in the Woods, a large tan home with green shutters, there's a stretch of woods where someone has installed little signs identifying nearly all of the trees that line the path. Just ahead, climb a set of stairs up the bluff past an elegant chalet-style home, and then follow the signs as the path heads down a steep, paved ramp with switchbacks. At the bottom of the ramp, the path cuts through a sandy beach. Not long after passing the narrowest section of the lake—appropriately called The Narrows—the path climbs a bluff leading to Alta Vista, a white-stucco mansion with a red-tile roof and a huge porch. Coming down from the bluff, the path flattens and then crosses a beautifully crafted iron footbridge with sides featuring ferns, flowers, and bluebirds. At 3.5 miles into the hike, the path crosses Chapin Road.

Beyond Chapin Road, the path runs next to a tight cluster of homes known as the Elgin Club. The closeness of the homes, the streetlamps, and the asphalt pathway makes this stretch feel like a city street. After passing a couple of private parks, you'll see a contemporary home that was designed to look like Frank Lloyd Wright's Fallingwater in Pennsylvania.

At 5.6 miles into the hike, on a promontory called Cedar Point, you'll climb a long flight of stairs up the bluff before taking in great views of Williams Bay. The dome of Yerkes Observatory (see Nearby Activities) is visible on the other side of the bay. The path descends as you get closer to the village of Williams Bay.

At 7 miles into the hike, across East Geneva Street from the boat launch in Edgewater Park, in Williams Bay, is one of the entrances to the Kishwauketoe Nature Conservancy, which offers nearly 4 miles of trails through a marsh and bottomland. After traversing a couple of wooden footbridges and passing a statue of a Potawatomi woman, you'll brush against the main business strip in Williams Bay. A few restaurants are located just to the right on WI 50.

Continuing on the trail, you'll soon pass through the boatyard at Gage Marine, which operates Geneva Lake's tour boats—if boats are blocking your path, go around them and stay to the left. Past a handful of old youth camps, the wooded bluffs rise steeply on the right as you get closer to Conference Point. From Conference Point, the path continues at the bottom of the wooded slope as it passes a big boulder called Kissing Rock. A cluster of brown cottages signals your arrival at Aurora University at 8.7 miles. The chairs and concrete wall on the veranda provide a welcome place to take a break. After the university, you'll catch glimpses of houses perched high up on the bluff, followed by some pleasant wooded stretches and a number of attractive fieldstone footbridges.

This hike ends a couple of miles later in the village of Fontana, which has a public beach, a marina, and an assortment of restaurants, hotels, and shops; from here, the path continues around the southern shore of the lake. If you're not up to turning around and hiking back or circling the entire lake, you'll want to take two cars and park one at each end of the route. An even better option would be to ride back to Lake Geneva on a tour boat. The cruising season runs May–October; reservations are a must. Call 800-558-5911 or visit cruiselakegeneva.com for the latest schedules and pricing.

NEARBY ACTIVITIES

One of the birthplaces of American astronomy, **Yerkes Observatory,** on the outskirts of Williams Bay, has been operated by the University of Chicago since 1897. The sprawling grounds and beautiful observatory building are well worth a visit. For more information, including tour hours and admission prices, call 262-245-5555, ext. 832, or visit astro.uchicago.edu/yerkes.

• •

GPS TRAILHEAD COORDINATES
N42° 32.913' W88° 34.340' (Fontana Beach Public Parking Lot)
N42° 35.501' W88° 26.238' (Lake Geneva Public Library)

DIRECTIONS For this hike, I recommend first leaving a car in Fontana and then proceeding to the start of the hike in Lake Geneva. From the junction of I-90 and I-94 on Chicago's North Side, bear right (north) on I-94 and, in 40.8 miles, exit left (west) onto IL 173/Rosecrans Road. In 19.1 miles, veer right at the four-way intersection onto Broadway Road and, 0.7 mile farther, make another right onto Keystone Road, heading north. In 1 mile, shortly after you enter Wisconsin, turn left (west) on County Road B/Main Street in Genoa City. In 10.8 miles, turn right (north) to continue on CR B/Swamp Angel Road; then, in 0.7 mile, turn left (west) on CR B/CR BB. In 1.7 miles, turn right (north) onto Indian Hills Road and, in 0.9 mile, turn left onto South Lake Shore Drive in Fontana. Metered public parking is available 0.7 mile ahead just off South Lake Shore Drive, on your right behind Lake Geneva Marine (454 Lake St.), but I suggest looking for free side-street parking nearby. Once you find a parking spot, leave your shuttle vehicle there and then continue to Lake Geneva.

From the intersection of Fontana Boulevard and WI 67/Valley View Drive, about 5 blocks west of Fontana Beach and Abbey Marina, head north on WI 67 and, in 1.9 miles, turn right to continue east on WI 67/North Walworth Road. In 2.1 miles, continue straight (east) on East Geneva Street in Williams Bay; 1.3 miles farther, turn right at the T to continue east on WI 50. In 4.2 miles, look for the Lake Geneva Public Library on your right, at 918 W. Main St.; again, however, the most convenient parking spots are metered. Two free public lots are located several blocks east of the library (see cityoflakegeneva.com/parking for details), but if you'd rather park closer to the trailhead, turn left (north) onto Madison Street just before you reach the library to look for side-street parking. Then walk back to the library to start the hike.

Trees and tall grasses flank the trail.   *Photo: Corey Seeman (cseeman)/Flickr*

WHILE HIKING THE TRAILS of Glacial Park Conservation Area, you'll glide through open prairies, meander beside a lovely creek, and bound over hills that undulate like ocean waves. The star attraction, though, is a collection of curious mounds left by a receding glacier.

DESCRIPTION

For those with an interest in learning the ways in which glaciers sculpted the landscape in northeastern Illinois, Glacial Park is a geologic jewel. The most eye-catching landforms in the park are mounds, or *kames,* that formed when glacial meltwater deposited heaps of sand and gravel in depressions in the ice or at the edge of a glacier. The 100-foot-high Camelback Kame, which this hike passes over, is said to have formed at the edge of a glacier as it receded 15,500 years ago. The park's bog and marshes also offer a link to the area's geologic past. These wetlands began to take shape when large chunks of ice detached from a receding glacier. As ice melted, a pond formed in the depression, and eventually vegetation overtook the pond.

But it's not just the geologic heritage that lends appeal to this 2,800-acre park: its variety—as well as its beauty and tranquility—make it a splendid place to stretch your legs and get a concentrated dose of the natural world. Start the hike from the west side of the Wiedrich Barn parking lot. Taking the trail on the right (west), marked by the sign for the Deerpath, Coyote, and Nippersink Trails, you'll enter a rolling prairie

DISTANCE & CONFIGURATION: 5 miles, 2 connected loops with a brief out-and-back segment

DIFFICULTY: Easy

SCENERY: Savannas, prairies, a marsh, a bog, a creek, and expansive views from high spots

EXPOSURE: Mostly open

TRAIL TRAFFIC: Moderate

TRAIL SURFACE: Hard-packed dirt, mowed grass, and wood chips

HIKING TIME: 2.5–3 hours

DRIVING DISTANCE: 62 miles from Millennium Park

ACCESS: Daily, sunrise–sunset; no fees or permits required except for camping, exclusive use of picnic areas/shelters, and groups of 16 people or

more; see mccdistrict.org/rccms/permits for more information.

MAPS: Available on trail boards at the parking areas, at the Lost Valley Visitor Center, and at the website below; USGS *Richmond, IL*

FACILITIES: Picnic areas, restrooms, water, sledding hill, canoe launch, and exhibits showcasing the natural environment at Lost Valley Visitor Center

WHEELCHAIR ACCESS: None

CONTACT: 815-338-6223, mccdistrict.org /rccms/glacial-park

LOCATION: Harts Road at IL 32, Ringwood, IL 60072

COMMENTS: Dogs must be on leash no longer than 10 feet. Park opens to cross-country skiing in winter.

fringed by oaks. After passing a small amphitheater built into the hillside with large stone blocks, turn right (north) at the first intersection. At 0.25 mile into the hike, the trail leaves the prairie and enters an oak savanna where the landscape begins to rise and fall in various directions. At 0.4 mile, take in a great view of the prairie, marshland, and creek to the west.

After the overlook, the path runs beneath a canopy of gnarled oak limbs as it descends from the hilltop. Following a hairpin turn to the right, the path rises toward the Camelback Kame. Stay to the right (west) at the next two trail junctions, and then head down the hill, saving the hike up the kame for the return trip. Turn right again (north) at 0.8 mile into the hike after passing through the metal gate. From here, it's a straight walk to a small glacial kame alongside Valley Road.

While hiking along this trail, keep an eye out over the prairie for the northern harrier, a medium-sized hawk that's fascinating to watch as it hunts for its prey by cruising close to the ground above grasslands and marshes. Once you reach the small kame, you'll have a better view of two more kames on the other side of the road. Follow Valley Road left (west) as it crosses Nippersink Creek, and then turn left again (south) on the horse-and-snowmobile trail that heads back on the other side of the creek.

At the junction near the footbridge, keep straight ahead (south) as the path comes alongside this twisting section of the creek. Continue ahead on this pleasant streamside path until reaching the Keystone Road Landing, where you'll find an observation platform at the edge of the creek, as well as a picnic area, a canoe launch, and restrooms. The presence of many little feeder streams in the area accounts for the Nippersink's name, which means "place of small waters" in the Algonquian language. The wetlands on the other side of the Nippersink contain one of these feeder streams.

Glacial Park Loop

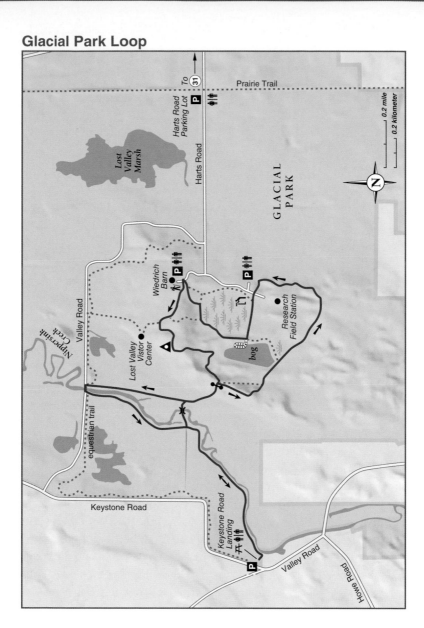

In the 1950s, local residents straightened sections of the Nippersink in order the drain the landscape better. They soon learned that faster moving water caused more erosion and increased the amount of silt swirling in the water. Animals that had previously used the slow-moving backwaters of the creek as nurseries for their young no longer could. Land downstream flooded. Today, Nippersink Creek flows in the path of its original meanders, thanks to a large-scale restoration project in recent years by McHenry County.

After visiting the landing at Keystone Road, retrace your steps to the footbridge you passed earlier. Cross the bridge and head right (south) toward the gate you passed through near the base of the Camelback Kame. At 3.3 miles, pass through the gate again, head up the hill, and turn right (south) to ascend the spine of the Camelback Kame, named for its gentle double hump. (Kames can be cone-shaped, like the ones by Valley Road, or they can be ridgelike, such as the Camelback.)

As you descend the kame, continue straight ahead at the next two trail junctions. Soon the trail leaves the prairie and enters a savanna. On the left, you'll see the park's research field station. At 4.3 miles into the hike, just before reaching the main parking lot, follow the trail left (west) as it runs through a picnic area. After crossing the park road, proceed straight ahead alongside a large marsh. First, however, you may want to take a short detour to an observation deck on the right.

When you cross the Deerpath Trail at 4.6 miles into the hike, continue ahead, following the sign for a bog boardwalk. The bog is dominated by leatherleaf, a shrub that keeps its leaves all year-round. Finishing the short boardwalk, follow the loop that brings you back up to the Deerpath Trail, where you'll turn left. After the trail takes a steep drop, keep straight ahead at the next junction, and then turn left (north) at another junction, heading up the hill and back to the Wiedrich Barn parking lot.

NEARBY ACTIVITIES

After entering the park on Harts Road, look for a parking lot for the **Prairie Trail,** a 25.9-mile multiuse path that stretches from the Wisconsin border south to Kane County. Once in Kane County, the Prairie Trail connects with a couple of other long trails: the **Fox River Trail** and the **Illinois Prairie Path.**

Either before or after your hike, be sure to visit the new **Lost Valley Visitor Center,** located north of the parking area where this hike starts. It has an interesting collection of exhibits and serves as a regional center for the study of natural resources. When snow reaches a depth of 5 inches in winter, the visitor center rents snowshoes. Open daily, April–October, 9 a.m.–5:30 p.m., until 4 p.m. November–March; 815-678-4532.

• •

GPS TRAILHEAD COORDINATES N42° 25.391' W88° 19.313'

DIRECTIONS From the junction of I-90 and I-94 on Chicago's North Side, bear right (north) on I-94 and, in 32.3 miles, exit left (west) on IL 120/West Belvidere Road. In 18 miles, turn right (north) on IL 31, and travel 6 miles farther. Then turn left (west) on Harts Road, and follow the signs for 1 mile until you reach the Wiedrich Barn.

153

Deer sightings are common at Lakewood Forest Preserve.   *Photo: Jeff Goldberg*

THIS QUIET HIKE takes you through a gently rolling oak forest dotted with cattail marshes and attractive lakes. After you're done, you may want to hike or go for a spin on the forest preserve's rapidly expanding bicycle/pedestrian trail.

DESCRIPTION

During much of the 1800s, Lakewood Forest Preserve was little more than a source of lumber and firewood for local farmers. After the Civil War, however, trees were cleared and small farms were built in the area. In 1937, some of these small farms were absorbed by a Chicago businessman named Malcolm Boyle, who assembled a country estate comprising livestock, orchards, gardens, and crops. Many of Boyle's efforts are still visible today, such as 16 major structures and the landscaping around the lakes. In 1961, Boyle's estate was transformed into a dairy farm that operated only a few years. Over the next 30 years, Lake County slowly acquired nearly 2,600 acres, making Lakewood the largest forest preserve in the county. Many of the former estate's buildings, including a couple of barns and a chicken coop, are still in use as offices, storage, and the museum.

DISTANCE & CONFIGURATION: 2.6-mile loop

DIFFICULTY: Easy

SCENERY: Oak forest, marshes, lakes, prairie, savanna

EXPOSURE: Mostly shaded

TRAIL TRAFFIC: Light, primarily equestrians

TRAIL SURFACE: Wide dirt

HIKING TIME: 1–1.5 hours

DRIVING DISTANCE: 44.5 miles from Millennium Park

ACCESS: Daily, 6:30 a.m.–sunset; no fees or permits

MAPS: On boards along the trails; interactive map at maps.lakecountyil.gov/trailmap; USGS *Grayslake, IL,* and *Lake Zurich, IL*

FACILITIES: Pit toilets and water at the trailhead. The preserve has picnic areas, shelters, playgrounds, and lakes for fishing; in winter, an ice-skating rink and a sledding hill open at the Millennium Trail Parking Area.

WHEELCHAIR ACCESS: None

CONTACT: 847-367-6640, lcfpd.org/lakewood

LOCATION: West Ivanhoe Road, Wauconda, IL 60084

COMMENTS: Dogs must be leashed. Most users of this trail are equestrians—always give them the right-of-way. On summer evenings as the sun goes down, check out the cluster of bat houses across Ivanhoe Road in the picnic area on the left. Across the park road from the bat houses, you can explore more than 3 miles of woodland trails.

From the parking lot, follow the wide trail on the right as it heads south alongside Heron Pond, named for the great blue herons often seen along its shore. At the first junction, take the trail to the left (east), and stay left as you pass a couple of junctions. While there are a handful of unmarked junctions throughout this hike, they're fairly easy to navigate. If you do get disoriented, trail boards showing your location are posted at most major junctions; keep in mind, though, that the boards don't show all of the short connector trails.

After dropping down a small hill and walking along the pond's wooded shore again, the trail rises steeply under a thick canopy of oak. The path curves right before arriving at a T-junction—hang a right (south) at the T, and then take an immediate left (south). This fairly flat stretch of trail runs through stands of quaking aspen and to the right of a spacious prairie dotted with black willows in the low spots. (To add 0.5 mile to your hike, take a left back at the T, and pass through oak woodland as you make your way near a couple of houses and a large horse facility.)

Continue straight ahead at the junction, passing a cattail marsh on the right; the landscape here becomes more rolling. Bur oaks multiply and provide more shade for the trail. Just before the trail turns right, you'll pass a marsh on the left thick with grasses and cattails. Stay left as the trail dips and rises to the next junction and then descends a big hill and passes a series of intermittent streambeds on both sides of the trail. After entering a savanna, the trail runs through clusters of buckthorn on its way to the next junction. Staying left (west) at the junction brings you through a short loop and close to the shore of a large marsh fringed with oak and cottonwood trees. While it's difficult to get much of a view of the marsh's open water through the thick cattails, you can do a little bushwhacking on the shoreline to seek out a better vantage point. This search may be rewarded by seeing a kingfisher, some waterfowl, or a

Lakewood Forest Preserve Loop

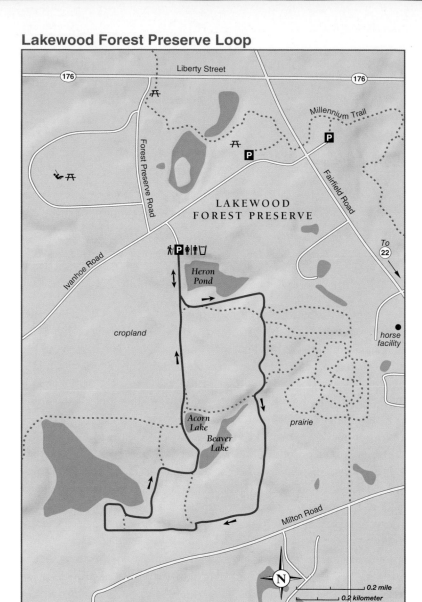

hawk perched in a tree above the edge of the marsh. Stay to the left as you complete the short loop and swing around to the other side of the marsh.

Continuing through a savanna, take the next right (east) on a short connector trail that leads to a couple of lovely little lakes. Beaver Lake offers grassy areas in which to sit down and enjoy the scene. The land around the lake is densely wooded, while the water's edge—stretching out of view to the left—is sprinkled with stumps and fallen trees. Heading left from the junction takes you through more savanna and past a junction on the left at Acorn Lake. This lake is smaller, largely covered with algae, and swampy in parts. Continuing straight ahead (north) past a couple of junctions on the right brings you back to the parking lot.

NEARBY ACTIVITIES

The **Millennium Trail** is a biking/hiking trail that's taking shape in the middle of Lake County. The Lakewood section runs through woodlands and savannas and next to a marsh and a few lovely lakes. While fairly popular with cyclists on warm weekends, the wide crushed-gravel trail offers plenty of room for hikers, too. Catch the trail from the parking lot at the corner of Ivanhoe and Fairfield Roads, just a half mile east of the trailhead for the previous hike. From this parking area, you can explore many miles within this gradually developing trail network.

• •

GPS TRAILHEAD COORDINATES N42° 15.296' W88° 06.404'

DIRECTIONS From the junction of I-90 and I-294, follow I-294 north for 12.4 miles; then merge onto I-94, and follow it 2.4 miles. Exit at IL 22/Half Day Road, and follow it west (left) for 6.8 miles. Turn right (northwest) on North Old McHenry Road, and follow it for 3.1 miles; then turn right (north) on North Fairfield Road, and follow it for 3.3 miles. Turn left on West Ivanhoe Road, and follow it for 0.5 mile. Park in the first parking area on the left, next to the service buildings.

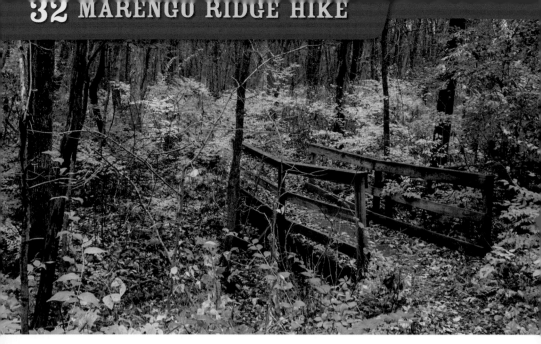

This rustic bridge crosses a dry streambed.   *Photo: Ron Ziolkowski/contemplativeimaging.zenfolio.com*

IF YOU ENJOY hiking through hilly terrain crisscrossed with intermittent streams and blanketed with dense groves of oak, hickory, and conifers, you'll be charmed by this hike in southwestern McHenry County. Situated up on a ridge left by the last glacier, this wonderfully wooded landscape provides visitors with an unusually isolated atmosphere.

DESCRIPTION

Rising a couple hundred feet above the surrounding agricultural land, 3-mile-wide Marengo Ridge runs north and south through western McHenry County to Kane County. A glacial moraine left by the last ice age, the ridge consists largely of sand, gravel, clay, and boulders. Situated nearly at the top of the ridge is 400 acres of hilly woods known as the Marengo Ridge Conservation Area. One of the many attractive features of this conservation area is the abundance of conifers. A former landowner, Emerson Kunde, planted the pine trees in 1955 with the hope that they would survive in the harsh soil, which had been damaged from overgrazing. Along with 15 species of conifers planted by Kunde—including Norway spruce, Douglas-fir, red pine, and Scotch pine—the woods are also thick with oak, hickory, poplar, sumac, and ash.

From the trailhead, located between the map board and the water pump, the gravel trail immediately climbs a hill through stands of oak, hickory, and conifer. At the top of the hill, continue straight (north) as you pass the trail heading to the right (with a few exceptions on the campground loop, stay to the left throughout this

DISTANCE & CONFIGURATION: 3.1 miles, 3 connected loops

DIFFICULTY: Moderate

SCENERY: Hilly woodland, pine plantations, numerous intermittent streams

EXPOSURE: Shaded

TRAIL TRAFFIC: Light

TRAIL SURFACE: Dirt, mowed grass

HIKING TIME: 2 hours

DRIVING DISTANCE: 57.5 miles from Millennium Park

ACCESS: Daily, sunrise–sunset; no fees or permits required except for camping, exclusive use of picnic areas/shelters, and groups of 16 people or more; see mccdistrict.org/rccms/permits for more information.

MAPS: On map board and at the website below; USGS *Marengo North, IL*

FACILITIES: Pit toilets, water, picnic tables, campground

WHEELCHAIR ACCESS: None

CONTACT: 815-338-6223, mccdistrict.org /rccms/marengo-ridge

LOCATION: 2411 N. IL 23, Marengo, IL 60152

COMMENTS: Dogs must be leashed. Marengo Ridge Campground (open May–October) offers 30 wooded sites, 6 of which are very nice walk-in sites.

hike). After you descend a small hill through stands of elm, cross a bridge over an intermittent, rocky-bottomed stream.

In the streambeds and scattered on the sides of the trail are boulders ranging in size from softballs to soccer balls. Known as glacial erratics, these rocks were carried here by the Wisconsin Glacier as many as 24,000 years ago and can be traced back to the bedrock around Lake Superior 350 miles to the north. Some of the boulders contain gneiss (pronounced "nice") or basalt, indicating that they came from central or eastern Canada. (Gneiss is coarsely textured with parallel streaks or bands, while basalt is dark and finely textured.)

At 0.6 mile into the hike, stay left (north) at the junction, and you'll soon pass stands of white and red pine as well as quaking aspen and sumac. The trail takes a short dip before rising to a large prairie blanketed with goldenrod and dotted with thistle plants for much of the summer. Quickly entering the woods again, you'll pass a cluster of erratic boulders before crossing another intermittent stream. The many intermittent streambeds throughout the conservation area carry meltwater or water from heavy rains to the nearby Kishwaukee River. When the streambeds are dry, there still may be puddles left in the them; the edges of these puddles are good places to look for animal tracks. Some of the deeper streambeds provide a glimpse of the layers of sand, rock, gravel, and dirt deposited by the last glacier.

Stay to the left (north) and start the next loop as the trail narrows and rises up a small hill. While the trail weaves through the trees on this less-used path, watch for boughs of thorny bushes hanging over the trail and occasional deadfall that must be stepped over. After you cross another bridge, a narrow side trail heads left to Collins Road. Growing near two bridges over intermittent streams are thick stands of elm and white oak. Nearby, you'll pass a pile of smaller boulders likely collected by an early farmer.

159

Marengo Ridge Hike

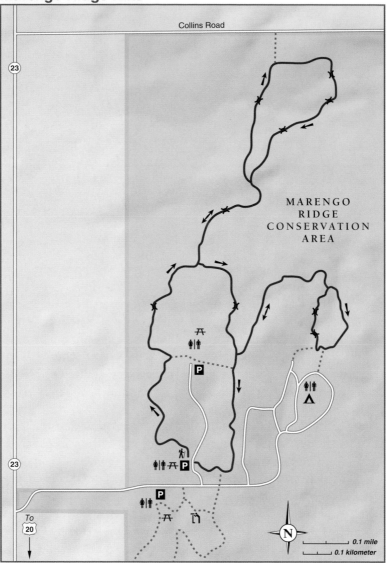

Keep to the left (east) as you finish the upper loop, backtrack along the connector trail, and then return to the lower loop. Turn left (southeast) on the lower loop, where the trail passes through a savanna and then enters a fragrant stretch where the sides of the trail are lined with wild raspberry, rose hips, gooseberry, and honeysuckle. After crossing a bridge, the trail rises to another pine plantation. Midway through the plantation, a marker indicates where you'll turn left (northeast) to start the campground loop.

The narrow connector trail takes you through rolling landscape on its way to the campground loop. Turning left on the loop, the trail makes a long, winding descent before passing two successive trails on the left, leading to the campground (the first trail provides access to restrooms and a water spigot). After the wide, grassy trail takes a couple of banked turns, you'll cross two bridges and then climb a hill before returning to the connector trail.

Once you've returned to the pine plantation via the connector trail, continue left (south) down the hill. Passing a few campsites through the trees on the left, the trail runs under a cluster of 60-foot Norway spruce trees with large, drooping branches. On the ground, you'll see the 6-inch-long cones that this tree produces (among spruces, Norways have the largest cones). The trail passes through groves of white pine and walnut trees before dropping you off in the picnic area by the parking lot.

After enjoying Marengo Ridge's main course, there are a couple of short walks that can serve as the dessert. To visit the small fishing lake, walk along the main park road toward the campground. Just before the RV dump station, take the trail to the right for a short trip down to the 1-acre lake. Directly across the main park road from the trailhead parking lot is the 1.25-mile South Hiking Loop, which leads mostly through open grassland and a bit of woods and takes you to a pleasant overlook.

NEARBY ACTIVITIES

The nearby town of **Union** hosts several fun historical attractions. A school built in 1870 now houses the **McHenry County Historical Museum** (6422 Main St.; 815-923-2267, mchenrycountyhistory.org). On the property, there's also a log home built in 1847 and a one-room schoolhouse from 1855. Check the website for seasonal hours and admission prices.

Donley's Wild West Town (8512 S. Union Road; 815-923-9000, wildwesttown .com) features a re-creation of a Gold Rush–era mining operation, along with a historic jail, saloon, and blacksmith shop. There are also pony rides, a train ride, a kiddie roller coaster, and a live stunt show, among other attractions. Check the website for schedules and ticket information.

• •

GPS TRAILHEAD COORDINATES N42° 17.102' W88° 36.058'

DIRECTIONS From the junction of I-90 and I-290, follow I-90 northwest for 25.6 miles. Exit on US 20 and head north (left) toward Marengo. Follow US 20 for 9.1 miles; then turn right (north) on IL 23. The entrance to Marengo Ridge is 2.5 miles ahead, on the right. After entering the park, park in the first lot on the left.

Expansive is the perfect word to describe Moraine Hills. *Photo: Elizabeth Vera*

IT'S A GOOD THING this hike is 8 miles long—the entire distance is needed for you to get a complete picture of Moraine Hills' mosaic of marshes, lakes, prairies, bogs, wooded hills, and streams.

DESCRIPTION

When glaciers receded from the landscape at Moraine Hills State Park some 15,500 years ago, they left behind the hills, the wetlands, and the centerpiece of the park: Lake Defiance, one of the few glacial lakes in Illinois that have remained undeveloped and in a near-natural state. Fed by a sprawling network of marshes, ponds, and old irrigation ditches, Lake Defiance was initially formed when a chunk of ice from a retreating glacier left a watery depression in the ground. Other highlights of the park, also the result of retreating glaciers, are the moraines, formed when an ice sheet stopped in its tracks and the idling glacier acted as a sort of conveyor belt, depositing gravel and rock at its edges and sides. The wooded hills and ridges at Moraine Hills serve as records of where glaciers paused during their retreat.

While you could begin this hike at any of several parking/picnic areas in the park, I recommend starting at Northern Woods, which has a playground, flush toilets, water, and plenty of picnic tables. It's also fairly close to the nature center, where you can stop to pick up a map and learn more about the park. At the Northern Woods

DISTANCE & CONFIGURATION: 8 miles, 2 loops, with several options for shorter hikes

DIFFICULTY: Moderate–strenuous

SCENERY: Woods, marshes, ponds, lakes, hills, prairies, and the Fox River

EXPOSURE: A mix of shaded and open

TRAIL TRAFFIC: Moderate

TRAIL SURFACE: Crushed gravel; 5 feet wide with mowed sides

HIKING TIME: 2–3 hours

DRIVING DISTANCE: 50.5 miles from Millennium Park

ACCESS: Park open daily, 6 a.m.–9 p.m.; nature center open Friday–Sunday, April–November, 9:30 a.m.–3:30 p.m.; no fees or permits

MAPS: Available at the park entrance, nature center, and website below; USGS *Wauconda, IL*

FACILITIES: Picnic areas, playgrounds, fishing, boat rentals, water, restrooms, and concessions; benches distributed throughout the trail system

WHEELCHAIR ACCESS: Yes

CONTACT: 815-385-1624, www.dnr.illinois.gov /parks/pages/morainehills.aspx

LOCATION: 1510 S. River Road, McHenry, IL 60051

COMMENTS: Dogs must be leashed. There are 800 acres of wetlands at Moraine Hills—be sure to bring mosquito repellent. Cross-country skiers and cyclists must follow the directional arrows; hikers may proceed in any direction. The non-profit group that supports the park has a website at friendsofmorainehillsstatepark.org.

picnic area, catch the access trail to the left of the restrooms. For now, follow the arrows by turning right on the main Leatherleaf Bog Trail, and then turn left when you reach the intersection for the Opossum Run picnic area. Right away, the trail starts to climb a hill through dense stands of oak and hickory.

At the bottom of the hill, a cattail marsh extends out to the left while Tomahawk Lake opens on the right. Without delay, the trail rises, granting a better view of the enormous marsh on the left. As the landscape flattens, you'll pass one of the sheltered benches that are widely spaced throughout the length of the trail. After skirting the edge of more open water on the right, the trail begins a half-mile stretch of twisting and turning in and out of prairies, savannas, and brief wooded sections while offering glimpses of Leatherleaf Bog and occasional patches of open water on the left. On this section, you may consider exploring the occasional narrow spur trails, which will allow you a closer view of the marshes and the bog.

Before reaching Junction B, the trail meanders through a wet prairie sprinkled with stands of cattails, then passes a drainage channel that cuts through the marsh on the left. At Junction B, stay to the right (south). Between Junctions B and C, the trail turns left sharply and then runs through dense woods and rolling terrain. At 2.9 miles into the hike, turn right (west) at Junction C, which takes you through a tunnel under River Road. After the tunnel, a large wetland appears on the left. Just ahead, at Junction D, continue straight (west) as the trail meanders alongside River Road and then runs by a viewing platform overlooking Black Tern Marsh.

At 4.1 miles into the hike, the trail meets up with the Fox River and the McHenry Dam picnic area. The dam, by far the busiest spot in the park, brings in a steady flow

Moraine Hills State Park Hike

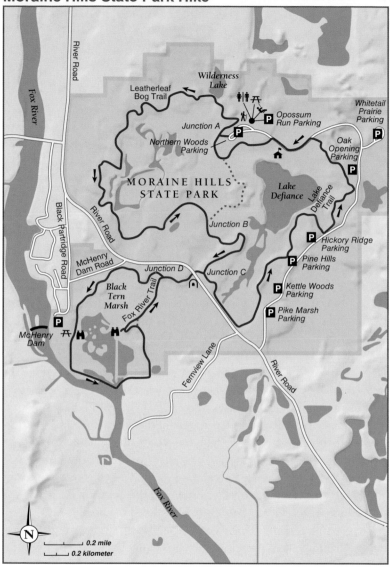

of anglers and picnickers on warm summer days. You can see the 4-foot-high dam by walking just 0.1 mile to the right along the edge of the parking lot. First built in 1907, the dam was reconstructed in 1934 by the Civilian Conservation Corps. Many different species of fish find the barrier of the dam hard to pass, so there's a tendency for catfish, drum, walleye, largemouth bass, and other species to congregate. In winter, the dam is one of the best spots in the area to catch a glimpse of bald eagles congregating. In 1939, the state acquired the dam and some surrounding property—the kernel of what would eventually become this 1,690-acre state park.

Following the dam, the trail runs between the Fox River and open marshes before passing a levee and a drainage channel on the left. Next, the trail mounts a couple of small hills that afford a good view of the large wetland you saw earlier (while on a summer walk on this trail, I counted several sandhill cranes and more than a dozen great egrets from these two hills). On the second hill, take the trail branching left, which leads to another viewing platform overlooking Black Tern Marsh.

Reaching Junction D again at 5.4 miles into the hike, turn right (east), pass through the tunnel, and then turn right again (east) at Junction C. For 0.35 mile after Junction C, the trail runs next to River Road and alongside a paved bicycle path that follows much of River Road through the park. For the remaining 2.1 miles of the hike, the trail passes eight separate parking and picnicking areas. Some are right at the edge of the trail, while others are a short walk off the trail; each is well marked and offers drinking water and pit toilets.

Beyond the left (north) turn for Pike Marsh, the trail skirts the edge of a marsh on the left and soon starts to roller-coaster up and down a series of small wooded hills (many of the steep sections are paved to prevent erosion). After passing the trail to the Pine Hills picnic area and a short spur on the left that provides access to Lake Defiance, the trail turns right and then accompanies the park road for a bit. Just beyond the spur leading to the Whitetail Prairie picnic area, the trail heads up a hill overlooking the 48-acre Lake Defiance. At the base of the hill, the trail again runs alongside the park road until you reach the nature center. Just to the west of the nature center are a series of boardwalks that will take you into the wetlands surrounding Lake Defiance. From the nature center, proceed west through the prairie for 0.3 mile to the Northern Woods parking lot.

· ·

GPS TRAILHEAD COORDINATES N42° 19.427' W88° 13.910'

DIRECTIONS From the junction of I-90 and I-294, follow I-294 north for 12.4 miles; then merge onto I-94, and follow it 2.4 miles. Exit at IL 22/Half Day Road, and follow it west (left) for 6.8 miles. Turn right (northwest) on North Old McHenry Road, and follow it for 5.8 miles. Turn right (north) on US 12 (South Rand Road), and follow it for 5.1 miles. Turn left on West Case Road, and continue for 4.6 miles. Turn right on Darrell Road, and then immediately turn left onto Neville Road. Follow Neville Road for 0.8 mile, and then turn left (south) on Dowell Road; in 1.2 miles, Dowell Road merges with South River Road—keep right where South River Road enters from the left. After 1.3 miles, enter the park on the right and proceed 2 miles north and west to the Northern Woods parking lot and picnic area.

Boardwalk along the Des Plaines River *Photo: Urbs in horto/Shutterstock*

THE TRAILS AT Edward L. Ryerson Conservation Area—known informally as Ryerson Woods—wind through some of the most stunning forestland in the Chicago region. Along the shore of the Des Plaines River and its backwater, expect to see waterfowl, wildflowers, and old rustic cabins left behind by the families that once owned the property.

DESCRIPTION

What was a once a weekend getaway for a local industrialist and his friends is now a hikers' heaven, with trails leading through one of the finest woodlands in northern Illinois. Much of what is now the southern section of Ryerson Woods was purchased in the 1920s by Edward L. Ryerson and his friends. Ryerson, who became president of Ryerson Steel Company upon the death of his father in 1928, built a rustic cabin on his riverside plot; in years to come, his friends built cabins of their own. In 1938, Ryerson bought 250 acres of farmland in what is now the northern section of the conservation area, and then a few years later he built a summer home that now serves as park offices. Motivated by a desire to maintain this forest sanctuary, Ryerson and his friends decided in the 1960s to donate and sell their land to the Lake County Forest Preserve District.

DISTANCE & CONFIGURATION: 4.5-mile loop within a loop

DIFFICULTY: Easy

SCENERY: Lush forest along Des Plaines River

EXPOSURE: Shady, with brief exposed stretches

TRAIL TRAFFIC: Moderate

TRAIL SURFACE: Dirt with numerous boardwalks and bridges

HIKING TIME: 3–4 hours for both loops

DRIVING DISTANCE: 31 miles from Millennium Park

ACCESS: Preserve open daily, 6:30 a.m.–sunset; visitor center open Tuesday–Saturday, 9 a.m.–

5 p.m., 11 a.m.–4 p.m. Sunday (closed major holidays); no fees or permits

MAPS: Available at the visitor center and on map boards at trailheads/trail intersections; online trail map at maps.lakecountyil.gov/trailmap; USGS *Wheeling, IL*

FACILITIES: Water, restrooms, visitor center

WHEELCHAIR ACCESS: None

CONTACT: 847-367-6640, lcfpd.org/ryerson

LOCATION: 21950 N. Riverwoods Road, Riverwoods, IL 60015

COMMENTS: No pets, bicycling, or picnicking allowed. Visit brushwoodcenter.org to learn about the nature hikes, art classes, and other events offered at Ryerson Woods.

Given Ryerson Woods' startling beauty and its proximity to Chicago, one would expect it to be swarming with hikers and nature watchers. Fortunately, this is not the case—perhaps it's the restrictions on pets, bicycles, and picnicking that keep the crowds away. Despite its lack of traditional park amenities, Ryerson Woods is still a great place to bring the family. At the farm exhibit in the north section of the conservation area, kids will enjoy the sheep, goats, and chickens. Also, the layout of trails allows for easy shortening or lengthening of a hike.

Map boards are posted at trailheads and at a handful of trail intersections, but picking up a map at the visitor center will ensure that you always know where you are.

The first part of this hike, which starts at the parking area near the Brushwood Center, takes you on a 1.5-mile loop through the northern section of the conservation area. The second part of the hike, which starts near the farm and welcome center, takes you on a 3-mile loop more or less along the perimeter of the preserve. Catch the beginning of the hike's first part just left of the driveway that leads into the parking lot near the Brushwood Center. Right away on the trail, on the right, you'll notice a high fence, which allows Ryerson Woods staff to monitor the amount of browsing done by deer.

At about 0.2 mile, near a couple of boardwalks spanning intermittent streams, you'll get a taste of what makes the Ryerson Woods landscape so beautiful: tall oaks, hickories, elms, dense canopies, minimal understory, and a lush, leafy ground cover. Coming out of the woods, the trail takes a sharp right turn as it begins to run alongside a park road that borders the farm property. Keep going on this mowed path, passing the intersection with the perimeter loop trail and then crossing the park entrance road. In the clearing across the road, keep an eye out for bluebirds and indigo buntings, and—if it's dusk—for the bats leaving the bat house. The trail continues to the

Ryerson Woods Hike

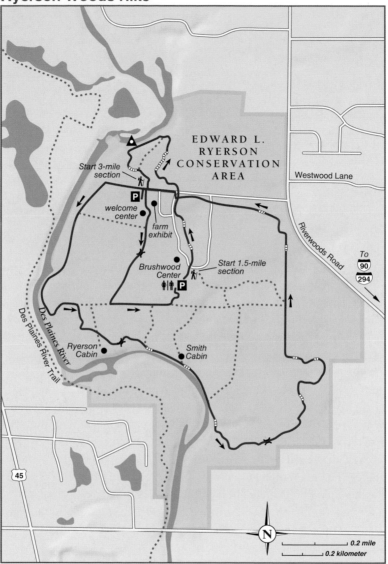

left, running between the two cabins, which are used for programs and exhibits when school groups visit.

At the next junction, turn right (north) and cross a boardwalk. After you walk through a grove of large shagbark hickories and cross a bridge next to a couple of sizable oaks, the Des Plaines River will appear on the right. In a short distance, you'll find a bench at a modest overlook of the river. After the overlook, take the next trail to the right, which takes you back to the park entrance road. The hike continues on the other side of a parking lot and the farm building in front of you. Before getting back to the trail, you may want to stroll around the farm to see the livestock. Although Edward Ryerson kept dairy cattle and Yorkshire pigs, his main interest was Arabian horses, which were kept in these structures designed by Edwin Hill Clark, the architect who designed the famous Brookfield Zoo in suburban Brookfield.

Back on the trail, you'll cross a bridge and enter the forest. In this area and in others, don't be alarmed when you see garbage bags on the trail waiting to be picked up. Most likely the bags contain an invasive, quickly spreading plant called mustard garlic, which has been pulled up by volunteers. Turn left at the T-intersection and continue along this wide gravelly path until coming to a trail branching left. Follow this short trail through an open area and back to the parking lot.

Pick up the 3-mile perimeter hike at the parking lot by the farm and the welcome center. Starting in the corner of the parking lot closest to the woods, this trail traverses the edges of the open space for a quarter mile, then rambles alongside the backwater of the Des Plaines River. During spring and summer, watch for trilliums as well as irises, which are called blue flags and yellow flags. At about 0.4 mile into the hike, as the trail approaches the main thread of the river, consider slowing your pace: it's a favorite place for great blue herons. In the low spots, receding water has left logs strewn about.

Stay to the right (southeast) at the intersection, and at 0.9 mile you'll reach Ryerson Cabin and a small dam in the river. From the back-right corner of the cabin, continue on the trail as it runs along the bank of the river and over a boardwalk that protects the softer, erosion-prone areas of the riverbank. Ahead is the intersection with another trail and the Smith Cabin, as well as a bench and map board. Beyond the Smith Cabin, cross a bridge over a twisting stream, and head back into the forest. If rain has recently fallen, hikers in Ryerson Woods should expect to get mud on their shoes, particularly on this section of the trail, as it weaves among small marshes and intermittent ponds. After crossing the stream again, you'll pass through groves of elms, patches of mayapples, and towering oaks.

At 2.3 miles, you'll see another map board and bench at a trail intersection—continue straight ahead through more dense woodland and marshy areas with boardwalks. The path turns left just before reaching a metal gate and soon runs alongside the park entrance road. A short way up, pass a trail intersection on the left, and come out on the road that borders the farm area. Return to the parking lot by following the road on the right to the other side of the farm.

NEARBY ACTIVITIES

The **Brushwood Center,** which occupies Edward Ryerson's former summer home on the property, invites visitors to come inside, visit its galleries, and participate in programs. It hosts speakers and programs throughout the year on a variety of subjects, ranging from botany courses, art classes, and book groups run by local college professors to guided owl hikes and an annual environmental-film festival. Learn more about this local treasure at brushwoodcenter.org.

Just across the river from Ryerson Woods is the **Des Plaines River Trail,** a crushed-limestone trail that runs along the river and through a number of forest preserves. For a taste of this long trail, see Hike 27, page 136.

• •

GPS TRAILHEAD COORDINATES N42° 10.725' W87° 54.757'

DIRECTIONS Just north of the junction of I-90 and I-294, bear right onto Exit 24; at the end of the exit ramp, turn left (west) on Deerfield Road, and proceed 0.5 mile. At Riverwoods Road, turn right (north). Two miles ahead, turn left at the sign for Edward L. Ryerson Conservation Area. Park in the main parking area near the visitor center.

PUBLIC TRANSPORTATION Ryerson Woods is a 3.5-mile bike ride from **Metra**'s Deerfield Station on the Milwaukee District/North Line and the Buffalo Grove Station on the North Central Service Line. See the **Active Transportation Alliance**'s *Chicagoland Bicycle Map* ($8; activetransreg.org/shop) for good routes between Ryerson Woods and these stations.

35 VETERAN ACRES–STERNE'S WOODS HIKE

Hikers enjoy a variety of scenery at Veteran Acres and Sterne's Woods.   *Photo: John Baker*

THIS HIKE OFFERS a surprisingly varied patchwork of scenery featuring beautiful rolling prairie, hilly oak woodlands, pine plantations, a cattail-fringed pond, and a rare type of wetland called a fen.

DESCRIPTION

Both of these parks—Veteran Acres and Sterne's Woods—are individually charming, and each is well worth a visit. But taken together, they offer an array of scenic landscapes and many miles of enjoyable rambling through quiet woodlands, rolling prairie, and expansive wetlands. The western side of Veteran Acres along Walkup Road hosts typical city-park offerings such as playgrounds, ball fields, and basketball and tennis courts. Oak woodlands occupy the middle section of the park, while the west side is home to the Wingate Prairie. Northeast of Veteran Acres at Sterne's Woods and Fen, you'll find more woodland, steep hills, and an unusual wetland environment.

Before starting the hike, duck into the Crystal Lake Park District Nature Center at Veteran Acres to see a collection of live animals. Mixed in with the fauna are a small gift shop, an array of children's exhibits, and a collection of birds' nests. From the front door of the nature center, look for the wood-chip trail on the left heading north into the woodland. Taking the second junction on the right (east) brings you into the rolling grassy hills of Wingate Prairie.

DISTANCE & CONFIGURATION: 3.5-mile loop

DIFFICULTY: Easy–moderate

SCENERY: Oak-and-conifer woodland, open parkland, prairie, pond, marshland, stream, fen

EXPOSURE: Prairie section is exposed, while woodland is shaded

TRAIL TRAFFIC: Light

TRAIL SURFACE: Wood chips, grass, and dirt

HIKING TIME: 2 hours

DRIVING DISTANCE: 52.5 miles from Millennium Park

ACCESS: Both Veteran Acres Park and Sterne's Woods and Fen are open daily, sunrise–sunset; the Crystal Lake Park District Nature Center at Veteran Acres is open Monday–Saturday, 9 a.m.–5 p.m., Sunday 11 a.m.–5 p.m.; no fees or permits for either park

MAPS: Available at the nature center at Veteran Acres, the Sterne's Woods parking area, and the website below (under "Places to Go," choose "Interactive Map"); USGS *McHenry, IL*

FACILITIES: Veteran Acres has a nature center, ball fields, tennis courts, picnic shelters, restrooms, playgrounds, and ice skating during winter; Sterne's Woods has pit toilets and picnic tables

WHEELCHAIR ACCESS: None

CONTACT: 815-459-0680, crystallakeparks.org

LOCATION: Crystal Lake Park District Nature Center (Veteran Acres Park), 330 N. Main St., Crystal Lake, IL 60014; Sterne's Woods and Fen, 5617 E. Hillside Road, Crystal Lake, IL 60014

COMMENTS: Dogs must be leashed. Watch for cyclists on the Prairie Trail.

Among the many prairie remnants in the Chicago region, this 33.5-acre prairie is unique for its beautiful hilly topography and stands of pine. The prairie was named after Bill Wingate, who worked for nearly 30 years with volunteers restoring this prairie and establishing it—as well as Sterne's Woods and Fen—as Illinois Nature Preserves. Once in the prairie, turn right toward the prairie's southern boundary. Along the way, look for summertime plants such as big bluestem grass, goldenrod, and rattlesnake master (stalks topped with prickly balls containing dense clusters of tiny flowers). At the southern boundary of the prairie, turn left (east) and pass through groves of red pine on your way to the parking lot for the Prairie Trail at the corner of Lorraine Drive and View Street.

The Prairie Trail runs for 25.9 miles from Algonquin to the Illinois–Wisconsin border through areas that are both urban and rural. This hilly, nearly mile-long segment of the Prairie Trail—one of its best parts—starts off heading left (north) in a grove of red pine before descending a steep hill. As the path swings right to accompany a power line right-of-way, yellow-flowered compass plants line the trail. After passing an industrial building beyond the trees on the right, the ribbon of pavement angles into Sterne's Woods and Fen through stands of pine (planted by the previous landowner, Ted Sterne), hickory, and giant black and white oak trees with gnarled limbs reaching out over the trail. While the landscape rises and dips, look for short side trails on the right that drop down next to a pleasant little stream running beside a set of railroad tracks.

After following the Prairie Trail 0.9 mile, look for a wide gravel trail that runs parallel to you on the left. Taking this gravel trail to the right (west), you'll see numerous marked side trails heading up the hill to the left. Stay on the gravel trail until you

Veteran Acres–Sterne's Woods Hike

come to a junction with another wide gravel trail. Turning right (north) on this gravel trail takes you into a 40-acre wetland, a portion of which is known as a fen. As a result of their unusual soil and water conditions, fens often host an uncommon assortment of plants. This fen is home to two types of orchids: the lady's slipper and the state-endangered grass-pink orchid. Other flowers include fringed gentians, cup plants, liatris, and shrubby cinquefoil.

173

At the other side of the fen, before the house, turn left (west) into a parking area with picnic tables, pit toilets, and a map board. From the back of the map board, follow the two-track road (southwest) as it runs between stands of walnut trees on the right and marshland on the left. Keep straight ahead as you pass a major junction on the left, and then climb a big hill.

If you have the inclination to do some wandering, some of the best hiking in Sterne's Woods is found among the maze of side trails on the left. Within this area, dozens of short trails run through pine plantations and rolling savannas and to the top of a 70-foot bluff that is the former location of a gravel-mining operation. While a GPS device may be useful here, it's not a necessity due to the size of the area and the wide, easy-to-find gravel trail that surrounds it.

After climbing the big hill, continue straight as you pass another wide gravel trail heading left. This brings you back to the power-line right-of-way, where you can see the Prairie Trail heading up the hill on the left. As you pass through the right-of-way and enter Wingate Prairie straight ahead, skip the first trail on the right heading into the woods, and follow the next right, which cuts through open prairie toward the oak woods. Along the way, you'll notice there are a number of short connector trails that would allow you to zigzag for a mile or two through this attractive swath of grassland. Once you've arrived at the stand of oak trees on the western side of the prairie, keep straight ahead and drop down the hill to the ball fields. At the ball fields, head left toward the right shoreline of the pleasant little pond. Take the bridge that runs next to the willows growing on a couple of islands. As you get closer to the fishing pier, the nature center and the parking lot are straight up the hill.

• •

GPS TRAILHEAD COORDINATES N42° 15.011' W88° 18.980'

DIRECTIONS From the junction of I-90 and I-290, head west on I-90 for 2.1 miles. Exit right (north) onto North Roselle Road and, in 1 mile, turn left (northwest) on IL 62/West Algonquin Road). Drive 13.8 miles, and then turn right (north) on Pyott Road. After 3 miles, Pyott Road becomes Main Street, which you'll follow for 2.3 miles. Look for the Crystal Lake Park District Nature Center on the left, after Main Street crosses East Terra Cotta Avenue.

PUBLIC TRANSPORTATION The Crystal Lake Station on **Metra**'s Union Pacific/Northwest Line is just 0.5 mile from the trailhead. From the station, walk southeast on Railroad Street, and turn left (north) on North Main Street. Cross East Terra Cotta Avenue, and the nature center is on the left.

36 VOLO BOG STATE NATURAL AREA HIKE

The Interpretive Trail winds through a veritable hallway of shrubs.   *Photo: Elizabeth Vera*

AS ONE OF THE most noteworthy wetlands in all of Illinois, Volo Bog hosts an unusual assortment of plants and animals. Its outlying areas feature rolling hills, thick woods, and open prairies.

DESCRIPTION

Owned by a dairy farmer until 1958, when it was purchased by the Illinois Nature Conservancy, Volo Bog was transferred to the state in 1970, and in 1973 it was registered as a National Natural Landmark. One reminder of the park's earlier life is a renovated dairy barn that now serves as a park office and visitor center. Sometime during your visit to Volo Bog, take a moment to drop by the visitor center, where you'll see preserved specimens of various birds and mammals found within the park's 1,200 acres, including a sandhill crane (which is often confused with the blue heron), a beaver, a coyote, and several owls.

To begin, pick up the beginning of the Interpretive Trail at the bottom of the hill next to the visitor center. This half-mile loop—entirely on a boardwalk—gives you a close-up view of the plants and trees typical of a bog (*note:* pets aren't allowed here).

DISTANCE & CONFIGURATION: 5.75 miles, 2 sets of loops joined by a connector trail

DIFFICULTY: Easy–moderate

SCENERY: Hilly with marshes, prairies, forests, and a boardwalk to the center of a bog

EXPOSURE: Roughly an equal amount of exposed and shady areas

TRAIL TRAFFIC: Moderate

TRAIL SURFACE: Mowed grass, dirt, boardwalk

HIKING TIME: 2–3 hours

DRIVING DISTANCE: 52 miles from Millennium Park

ACCESS: Daily, 8 a.m.–8 p.m. Memorial Day–Labor Day, until 6 p.m. the rest of the year; no fees or permits

MAPS: Available outside the front door of the visitor center and at the first website below; USGS *Wauconda, IL*

FACILITIES: Water, restrooms, picnic tables, parking, and visitor center

WHEELCHAIR ACCESS: None

CONTACT: 815-344-1294, www.dnr.illinois.gov /parks/pages/volobog.aspx, friendsofvolobog.org

LOCATION: 28478 W. Brandenburg Road, Ingleside, IL 60041

COMMENTS: Dogs are prohibited on Interpretive Trail boardwalk; they must be leashed on other trails. Volunteer naturalists lead 1-hour public bog tours on Saturdays and Sundays at 11 a.m. and 1 p.m.; call the number above for visitor-center hours.

Heading out on the boardwalk, you can see plenty of bright green duckweed floating on the surface of the water. Keep an eye peeled for muskrat lodges as you enter an area dense with 10- to 12-foot shrubs. The winterberry holly, European buckthorn, and poison sumac seem to create a hallway of shrubs. Be sure to keep your distance from the poison sumac, a tall shrub or small tree with paired leaflets and a single leaflet at the end of the midrib. Whitish-green fruits that hang in loose clusters distinguish poison sumac from the nonpoisonous variety that produces red fruits. Just touching the bark or leaves can give some people a rash.

This area also contains red dogwood and, during the summer, five different types of ferns, some of which reach heights of 6 feet. Moving farther into the shrubs, you'll see the moss-covered hummocks, which are floating mounds of decomposing plant material. If you step on a mound, the hummocks will sway and shake—this is why Volo Bog is called a "quaking bog."

Next you'll see tamarack trees, conifers that lose their needles each year. Near the tamaracks, watch for the insect-eating pitcher plant, which looks like a cluster of 4- to 6-inch green-and-red bulbous tubes that are open at one end. At 0.3 mile, you'll reach the open water that marks the center of the bog. During spring and summer, you might catch a glimpse of a green heron here. Complete the loop by hiking 0.2 mile to the end of the Interpretive Trail, emerging on solid ground close to where the Tamarack View Trail begins, at the bottom of the hill next to the visitor center.

Turn left (south) on the 2.75-mile Tamarack View Trail, which offers a pleasant stroll around the larger basin that includes the bog. The first leg of the hike takes you between the marsh and Sullivan Lake Road. As you enter the wooded area thick with white oaks and box elders, keep an eye out for downy woodpeckers flitting

Volo Bog State Natural Area Hike

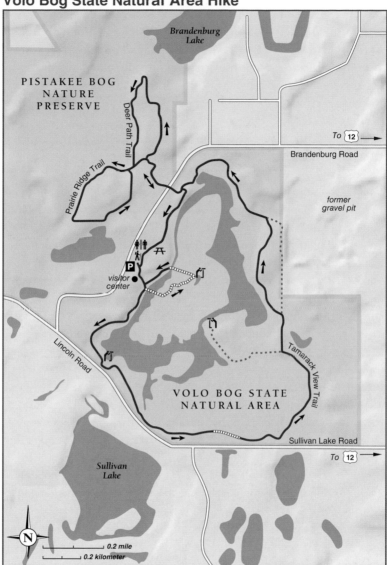

among the trees. In spring, expect to see plenty of sparrows, warblers, and other songbirds along this stretch. In spring, summer, and fall, expect to see a variety of waterbirds in the marsh: kingfishers, mute swans, white egrets, Canada geese, mallard ducks, and great blue herons.

After 0.4 mile, you might see a beaver lodge in the water before crossing the bridge over the stream that runs from the marsh toward Sullivan Road.

While following a section of the trail with woods on one side and savanna on the other, you'll come upon stands of walnut trees and willows, then take a short trip over a boardwalk through a marsh. Beyond the boardwalk, follow a trail to the left to an observation tower for a bird's eye view of the bog. While on the tower, keep an eye out for sandhill cranes. Some bird-watchers maintain that Volo Bog is one of the most dependable locations in northeastern Illinois for seeing these large, beautiful birds. Also keep watch for the inhabitants of the bluebird houses that are mounted on posts along the trail.

Two miles from the trailhead, you'll leave the prairie-savanna and enter a wooded area. Descend a gentle ravine that leads to an attractive spot with a small pond on one side of the trail and the marsh on the other. Farther ahead, take a left turn, and follow the trail along the edge of the water. At the top of a small hill, you'll have the opportunity to hike two more trails and a connector trail, adding another 2.5 miles to your hike. (If you're bound for the parking lot, it's only 0.3 mile from this intersection. After passing a collection of wood benches located within a grove of Scotch pines, the trail drops you off across the parking lot from the visitor center.)

To hike the Deer Path and Prairie Ridge Trails, located in the Pistakee Bog Nature Preserve, follow the mowed connector path a quarter mile across Brandenburg Road, then into a savanna and part way up an incline until you see a trail marker. Turning right (north) for the 1.2-mile Deer Path Trail and continuing up the hill, you'll pass through an area thick with young trees and soon reach a section of the trail that runs alongside stands of older-growth trees. After the hairpin turn going left, you might be able to see Lake of the Hollow through the trees to the right. The trail then descends into a low wooded area thick with box elder, oak, and hickory. If rain has fallen recently, this area likely will be muddy. On your right is an extensive marsh containing two more bogs. Soon, a trail sign indicates that the 0.8-mile Prairie Ridge Trail is to the right.

On the Prairie Ridge Trail, a picturesque hilly prairie immediately opens in front of you. Taking the trail counterclockwise (west) leads you alongside the marsh again. In the open space, look for swallows performing their aerial acrobatics. Following the edge of the woods, you'll eventually turn to walk along a small ridge. Reaching the highest section of the ridge gives you an expansive view overlooking a cattail marsh that is active with water birds. Beyond the marsh is the entrance to Volo Bog. Coming down from the ridge, the trail turns left and then drops you off where you left the Deerpath Trail. Follow the signs back to the connector trail that will take you across the road to the Tamarack View Trail and back to the parking lot.

NEARBY ACTIVITIES

In the mood for more hiking? If so, you're lucky, because Volo Bog is situated within a cluster of other hiking destinations. Just a few miles to the southwest is **Moraine Hills**

The trail wends its way through a wooded area.   *Photo: Elizabeth Vera*

State Park (Hike 33, page 162). Four other hikes in this chapter are located about 10 miles away: to the southeast is **Lakewood Forest Preserve** (Hike 31, page 154), to the northwest is **Glacial Park** (Hike 30, page 150), and directly north is **Chain O' Lakes State Park** (Hike 26, page 132).

• •

GPS TRAILHEAD COORDINATES N42° 21.130' W88° 11.301'

DIRECTIONS Where I-294 and I-94 merge, head north on I-94 for 13.7 miles. Exit left (west) onto IL 120/Belvidere Road, and drive 13.1 miles; then turn right (north) on IL 59/US 12, and travel 2.5 miles until you reach West Brandenburg Road. Turn left (west), and 1 mile ahead on the left is the entrance to Volo Bog State Natural Area.

NORTHWEST INDIANA AND ENVIRONS

Contrary to its name, Deep River actually isn't very deep.   *Photo: Lynne Dohner*

THIS HIKE TAKES you along the edge of the Deep River as it meanders through a large, diverse hardwood forest. At some point during your visit, stop in at the gristmill that was first built next to the river in 1837.

DESCRIPTION

At the entrance to Deep River County Park sits an old church that now serves as the park's visitor center and gift shop. Built in 1904, the inside of this former church now looks like an old-fashioned general store, with jars of candies and preserves, wooden toys, maple syrup, handcrafted items, and various souvenirs stacked high up on shelves. After picking up a map and perhaps a few pieces of hard candy for the hike, take a walk next door to the brick gristmill.

In 1837, John Wood built his gristmill on the banks of the Deep River using native white oak; he also built a sawmill that still stands on the other side of the river. After grinding grain into flour for nearly 20 years, 56-year-old Wood decided to sell the operation to his sons Nathan and George. Several years later, Nathan bought out George, and 16 years later, Nathan decided to tear down the wooden mill and erect one of the finest mills in the county. This new brick mill could grind 12 bushels of corn, wheat, rye, or buckwheat per hour. Nathan sold the mill in 1908, and it passed

DISTANCE & CONFIGURATION: 2.9-mile out-and-back with 2 loops

DIFFICULTY: Easy

SCENERY: River, woodland, grassland, restored gristmill

EXPOSURE: Mostly shaded

TRAIL TRAFFIC: Light

TRAIL SURFACE: Dirt

HIKING TIME: 1.5 hours

DRIVING DISTANCE: 46.5 miles from Millennium Park

ACCESS: Daily, 7 a.m.–sunset; mill and gift shop/visitor center open May 1–October 31; no fees or permits

MAPS: Available at the gift shop/visitor center and the website below; USGS *Plamer, IN*

FACILITIES: Restrooms, picnic area, gift shop/visitor center, historic gristmill, and sawmill

WHEELCHAIR ACCESS: Yes

CONTACT: 219-947-1958, lakecountyparks.com/151/deep-river-county-park

LOCATION: 9410 Old Lincoln Highway, Hobart, IN 46342

COMMENTS: Dogs must be on leash no longer than 6 feet. For information about the Deep River Grinders Vintage Base Ball Team, see lakecountyparks.com/172/deep-river-grinders-vintage-baseball.

through the hands of many owners. By 1930, the mill lay abandoned and forgotten until it was renovated by the county and opened to the public in 1977.

On the first floor of the mill, you can watch the 4,000-pound millstone (now powered by electricity rather than the river) pulverizing various grains that are loaded into cotton bags and offered for sale. A volunteer is on hand to demonstrate the grinding process and describe how it worked. In front of the grinding platform, a drawing shows which millstones—each with a different pattern etched in the stone—were used for grinding different grains. Upstairs, quilts and 19th-century furniture and fashions are on display, and the third floor contains a gallery for local artists.

A picturesque gazebo surrounded by plantings of flowers and prairie grasses sits next to the gristmill. From the gazebo, head left (north) across the footbridge to the open area, which is the home field for the Deep River Grinders, a "vintage base ball" team that plays according to rules from 1858 (back when *baseball* was still *base ball*) and wears period uniforms as they take on other teams from across the Midwest. Before the Grinders' season starts, during the second and third weekends in March, the building on the right hums with activity as park staff and volunteers use the wood-fired evaporator to create maple syrup from sap collected in the park. To the left of the sugar shack is the sawmill built by John Wood in 1837.

Continuing left, across another footbridge, follow the dirt trail to the right as it weaves alongside the sandy-bottomed river. From the footbridges and the trailside observation platform overlooking the river, it may be apparent that this is not a particularly deep river. Its name, Deep River, was inspired by deeper stretches of water downstream. Stay to the right (north) at the junction at 0.3 mile. After the junction, an Indian mound marked with a sign rises on the bank of the river. The mound—70 feet long and 30 feet high—is likely the handiwork of Potawatomi Indians who set

Deep River Hike

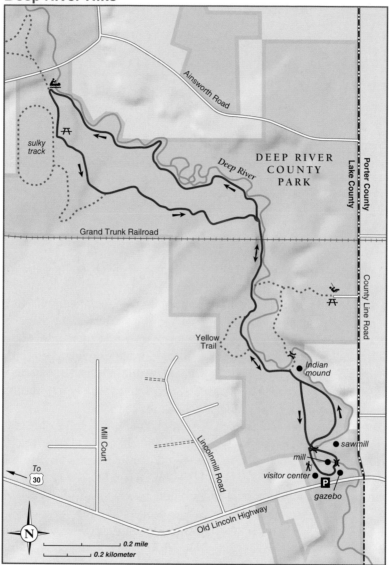

up summer encampments along Deep River before white settlers came to the area. After the Indian mound, a trail breaks off to the right, heading over a footbridge toward a playground and picnic area on the other side of the river. Continuing ahead on the main trail, you'll pass an open field and a grassy marsh on the left, and signs for the two ends of the short loop called the Yellow Trail.

After the railroad underpass at 0.6 mile, take the narrow trail on the right (northwest) as it continues near the river. In this more-remote section of the park, the river winds through a deeper channel. For anyone who likes to admire and identify trees, hiking along the Deep River is a treat: substantial cottonwood, sycamore, basswood, swamp white oak, sweet gum, shagbark and bitternut hickory, and Kentucky coffee trees all grow in the moist riparian soil. While it's not the largest of Lake County's parks, Deep River's 1,400 acres easily take the prize for the greatest variety of trees.

At the hike's halfway point, the trail ends at the canoe launch alongside the park driveway that leads to the sulky horse track. (In case you're wondering, a sulky is a lightweight single-seat cart used for harness racing.) If you're in the mood to explore a less-used section of the park, check out the trails north of Ainsworth Road near the entrance to the sulky track. While these trails can be overgrown in places, the hiking is pleasant, and, with a little exploration, you'll find a scenic overlook. But to continue on the next part of this hike, take a left (west) at the canoe launch, following the park road toward the sulky track. When you reach the small picnic area on the left, look for the trail leading into the woods.

Now heading back toward the mill, the trail runs next to a marsh before reaching an agricultural field flanked by train tracks on the far side. After you walk 0.2 mile between the agricultural field on the right and stands of cottonwood and apple trees on the left, the trail reenters woodland. This hilly swath of woodland is dense with large oak, walnut, and hickory trees—many with vines hanging from their branches or snaking around their trunks. During the summer, look for wildflowers such as white and purple asters. After finishing the loop, passing underneath the train tracks, and going by the Indian mound, take the fork to the right marked LOOP. This short trail takes you next to a large, grassy field and through a picnic area on the way back to the parking lot.

• •

GPS TRAILHEAD COORDINATES N41° 28.600' W87° 13.334'

DIRECTIONS From the junction of I-90 and I-65 in Gary, Indiana, go south on I-65 for 8.5 miles. At Exit 253, follow US 30/East Lincoln Highway to the left (east) for 4.5 miles, and then turn left (north) on Randolph Street. Proceed along Randolph Street for 0.3 mile before taking another right (east) on Old Lincoln Highway/East 73rd Avenue. The park is 0.9 mile ahead on the left.

A peaceful scene on the banks of a pond at Grand Kankakee Marsh County Park   *Photo: Kristina Januski*

LITTLE KNOWN OUTSIDE of its immediate area, Grand Kankakee Marsh County Park is huge, quiet, and persistently charming. The first part of this hike runs alongside the Kankakee River and through a vast marshland. The return trip takes you through a prairie and along the extensive network of drainage ditches dug when the park was all farmed.

DESCRIPTION

At one time, the Kankakee River made 2,000 bends as it traveled from its source near South Bend, Indiana, to the Illinois state line. The river slowly meandered through an area roughly 75 miles long and 30 miles wide known as the Grand Kankakee Marsh. After farming interests straightened and channelized the Kankakee, the river's length dropped from 240 miles to 85 miles. The next step in making the land suitable for farming involved draining the enormous marshland through an elaborate system of ditches. After all the work of draining the marshes, farmers discovered that swaths of the former marsh were still terrible for farming. Crops drowned in wet years and burned out in dry years. Some of these tracts of marginal farmland were then set aside as nature refuges.

On this hike, you'll get a chance to tour some of the wetlands that have been restored along the Kankakee River, as well as an extensive system of ditches and

DISTANCE & CONFIGURATION: 7.3-mile double loop

DIFFICULTY: Moderate–strenuous due to length

SCENERY: Kankakee River, an enormous marsh, a maze of drainage ditches, bottomland forest, and an abundance of birds

EXPOSURE: Primarily shaded

TRAIL TRAFFIC: Very light

TRAIL SURFACE: Sandy doubletrack road, mowed grass

HIKING TIME: 3 hours

DRIVING DISTANCE: 61.5 miles from Millennium Park

ACCESS: January–September, daily, 7 a.m.–sunset; no fees or permits

MAPS: On board near restrooms and at the website below; USGS *Shelby, IN,* and *Demott, IN*

FACILITIES: Pit toilet, map board, drinking water, boat launch

WHEELCHAIR ACCESS: None

CONTACT: 219-552-0033, lakecountyparks .com/153/grand-kankakee-marsh

LOCATION: 21690 Range Line Road, Hebron, IN 46341

COMMENTS: Dogs must be on leash no longer than 6 feet. The park is closed to the public during hunting season (October–December). The two-track roads that this hike follows are for authorized vehicles only. Once you get away from the fishing spots and boat launch, expect to have this park all to yourself. For another great hike through the Kankakee Marshes, see the LaSalle Fish and Wildlife Area Loop (page 216).

levees. Because two-track roads accompany many of these ditches, the 1,900-acre park offers plenty of opportunities for exploration along established routes—just bring your map and compass or GPS device.

Start the hike by heading to the right (south) from the parking lot along Range Line Road toward the one-lane iron bridge over the Kankakee River. Just before the bridge, turn left (west) on the dirt road that runs alongside the river toward the boat launch. The boat launch's gravel parking lot can be a busy place on summer afternoons, with fishermen showing off stringers of smallmouth and largemouth bass, walleye, bluegill, and pickerel. On the other side of the parking lot, pass through the gate and follow the sandy two-track road running along the levee. On the left, the bottomland forest contains patches of dense shrubs, occasional marshy spots, and thick stands of maple, cottonwood, and quaking aspen.

At 0.4 mile into the hike, a small pipeline is suspended with cables across the river between the wooded banks. Plenty of openings along the bank provide good views of the river and the opposite shore. You may notice that the two sides of the river look similar, each with a trail running on top of a levee. In spots on the other side of the river, small rocks reinforce the riverbank to prevent erosion. At the river's edge—about 15 feet below the level of the trail—look for painted and softshell turtles basking on logs (painted turtles have dark, smooth, rounded shells; softshells are flatter and larger with lighter coloring).

Keep straight when you encounter a two-track road on the left at 0.6 mile into the hike. Farther ahead, also on the left, you'll see occasional patches of agricultural land

Grand Kankakee Marsh County Park Hike

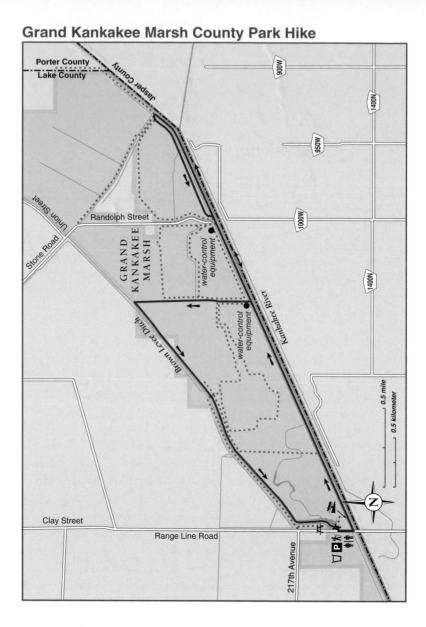

alternating with more bottomland forest and marshy areas. At 1.7 miles, the trail passes some water-control devices that pump water back and forth between two drainage ditches and the river. Remember this spot: after taking a loop through a marsh ahead, you'll return here and head away from the river.

At 2.3 miles into the hike, you'll see more pumps and pipes, as well as the beginning of a restored portion of the Grand Kankakee Marsh. Keeping straight ahead on the levee for now, you'll begin to see small houses, some with homemade river docks, sprouting up on the opposite bank of the river. At 3.1 miles into the hike, take a sharp turn left (north) at the two-track road on the left for a hike through an expansive marsh. Bring your field glasses to see herons, ducks, and geese among fields of lush marsh grass and the scattered stands of cattails. Also, look for hawks perched in the cottonwoods and sand willows to the left. Far in the distance across the marsh, a farm serves as a reminder of this land's agricultural history.

Once you return to the river levee, follow the trail 0.6 mile to the right (west) back to the first set of water-control devices you passed earlier. Here, take the middle trail to the right (north) away from the river. On this section of the hike, there's a ditch on each side of the two-track for the first half mile. After the ditch on the left cuts away, a picturesque tallgrass prairie develops on the left, and an agricultural field is visible on the right through the trees, again with the farm in the distance. Sections of this trail are bordered by thick stands of shrubs; watch out for stinging nettles hanging in your path—the 2- to 4-foot-tall plants have heart-shaped, coarsely toothed leaves.

Reaching the Brown Levee Ditch at 5.2 miles into the hike, turn left (southwest) and continue along another levee. Look for waterbirds hanging out in the lily pads and perched on occasional logs on the edge of the bank. While the prairie continues on the left, another levee appears on the other side of the ditch, as well as thick stands of cottonwood trees. Nearly a mile after the last turn, there's a hedgerow and the end of a ditch on the left, followed by a bridge over the ditch on the right. Across the bridge are short grain silos and a windmill with the blades removed. As you pass several side trails on the left, you'll also pass more ditches and hedgerows.

At 7 miles into the hike, you'll know you're getting close to the end when the trail becomes mowed turf. With open water on both sides of you, the trail curves back toward the Kankakee River. Pass a few picnic tables and possibly a few anglers on your way to the bridge that leads toward the parking lot.

• •

GPS TRAILHEAD COORDINATES N41° 13.235' W87° 16.566'

DIRECTIONS From the junction of I-90 and I-65 in Gary, Indiana, go south on I-65 for 21 miles. At Exit 240, follow IN 2 for 1.2 miles to the left (east), and then follow Clay Street/Range Line Road to the right (south) for 6 miles. The parking area is on the right, just before the old iron bridge over the Kankakee River.

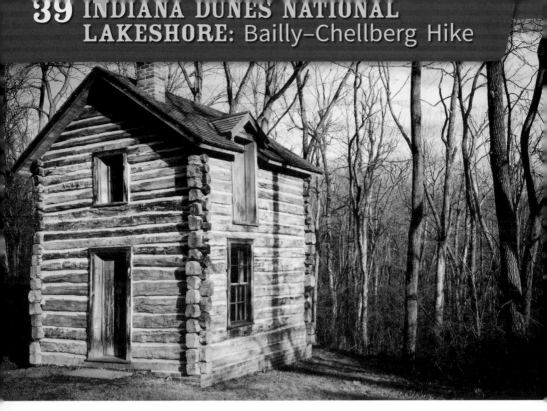

The Bailly Homestead was built in 1835. *Photo: Mikhail Siskoff*

GET A GLIMPSE of early settlement life in northwestern Indiana by touring the homesteads of two frontier families. You'll also see wooded ravines, rich bottomland forest that grows beside the Little Calumet River, and a curious old cemetery.

DESCRIPTION

In 1874, 10 years after emigrating from Sweden, Anders and Johanna Kjellberg, who Americanized their surname to Chellberg, were farming 80 acres within a growing Swedish community in northwest Indiana. Over the years, three generations of Chellbergs made their living on the farm growing wheat, oats, corn, and rye and keeping farm animals. The Chellbergs farmed the land until 1972, when the National Park Service bought their property. To preserve the past, the park service continues operating this typical northwest Indiana farm from the late 1800s.

The hike starts 100 yards south of the farm, at the back of the former visitor center, where you'll follow the trail to the right (north) as it runs along the top of a 40-foot wooded ravine. The first farm building you'll pass is the maple-sugar house, followed by a windmill with a pump house, a harness shop, a corncrib, a chicken house, the

DISTANCE & CONFIGURATION: 3.3-mile balloon loop

DIFFICULTY: Easy

SCENERY: Bottomland forest, marshland, oak woodland, Little Calumet River, a 19th-century working farm, and an early trader's homestead

EXPOSURE: Shaded except through the prairie

TRAIL TRAFFIC: Moderate

TRAIL SURFACE: Dirt, grass

HIKING TIME: 2 hours

DRIVING DISTANCE: 46 miles from Millennium Park

ACCESS: Daily, 7 a.m.–30 minutes past sunset; no fees or permits

MAPS: Posted on trail board and available at the visitor center and the website below; USGS *Chesterton, IN*

FACILITIES: Picnic tables and shelters, visitor center, restrooms

WHEELCHAIR ACCESS: None

CONTACT: 219-395-1882, nps.gov/indu

LOCATION: Mineral Springs Road just north of US 20, Porter, IN 46304

COMMENTS: Dogs must be on leash no longer than 6 feet. The Chellberg Farmhouse and the Bailly Homestead are occasionally open to the public for special events.

restored brick farmhouse built in 1885, and the large 100-year-old barn. Kids will enjoy the farm animals in the pens the barn. Inside the farmhouse, visitors can tour the parlor, the kitchen, and a bedroom as they looked in the early days of the farm.

Continuing on the trail, cross a bridge and then follow a set of steps down into a pleasant wooded ravine carved by a running stream. Crossing several more bridges, the trail runs along the bottom of the ravine for a short stretch until a flight of stairs brings you back up to flat ground. Cross another bridge and then turn right (north) at the junction for the out-and-back trail to the Bailly Cemetery. On the way to the cemetery, cross Oak Hill Road and a crushed-gravel trail, and then hike 0.3 mile through bottomland forest. The cemetery—a walled-in earthen area built on a small hilltop—has a tomblike quality to it. The wall was built in 1885 on what archeologists have surmised to be an existing cemetery: bones thought to predate European settlement have been uncovered at this site. After circling the cemetery, retrace your steps back to the main trail.

Back on the main trail, cross a bridge and then stay to the right (west) at the next junction. Soon the trail crosses Howe Road and a crushed-gravel trail that leads to the Indiana Dunes Environmental Learning Center, a frequent stop for school groups visiting the dunes. After passing a spur trail on the left leading to the learning center, you'll see the building on the left through stands of hickory, maple, and locust trees. After passing between a few big white oaks on both sides of the trail, the trail turns left toward the Little Calumet River. From here, the woodland becomes shrubby savanna as the trail runs through a few small ravines.

At 1.9 miles into the hike, a 0.2-mile boardwalk carries you through a wet bottomland forest and a marshland and ends at a scenic spot where a metal footbridge spans the Little Calumet. Stay to the left (east) at a junction 0.2 mile beyond the bridge. After the trail curves left, you'll have sporadic views of the river, marshy

Indiana Dunes National Lakeshore: Bailly–Chellberg Hike

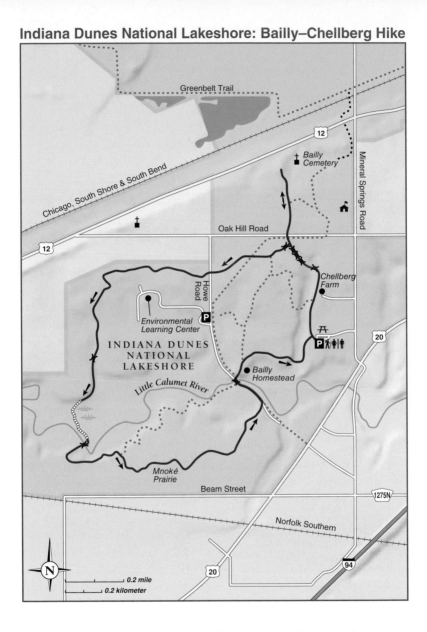

areas, and the cattails at the bottom of the ravine. In the riverside areas, ground-cover plants are scarce due to the dense, leafy canopy above. Soon, the trail leaves the riparian landscape behind and enters the 120-acre Mnoké Prairie. After passing through this picturesque prairie and a short stretch of woodland, the trail arrives at a parking area. From the parking area, descend the hill and then stay to the left, heading toward the bridge on Howe Road.

On the other side of the bridge, immediately turn right (northwest) on the brick road that heads up the hill to the Bailly Homestead. Montreal-born Honoré Gratien Joseph Bailly de Messein was one of the first settlers in northwest Indiana when he arrived in 1822 to start a trading post; here, he exchanged blankets, guns, and cooking pots for skins of beaver, muskrat, and mink. As animals became scarce and the trading slowed, Bailly turned his attention to operating a local tavern and establishing a small community named after him, which was on land now occupied by Bethlehem Steel.

On the right is the restored wooden frame house built by the Bailly family in 1835. Though Bailly died before construction of the house was finished, his family occupied the house until 1917. Over the years, the six-bedroom house has been a restaurant, an antique shop, and a Catholic retreat. The ground floor, unfurnished except for a beautiful fireplace mantel built by a local craftsperson, is occasionally open to the public.

Beyond the house and the cabins, the path on the left, which leads to the Bailly Cemetery, is said to be part of an old Indian trail. The hike continues on the right (east), just beyond the wigwam frame and the National Historic Marker plaque. From the Bailly Homestead, it's a short woodland hike back to the parking lot.

NEARBY ACTIVITIES

Just a few miles away in Chesterton, **Lucrezia Café** (428 S. Calumet Road; 219-926-5829, lucreziacafe.com) serves authentic Italian cuisine, and **The Port Drive-In** (419 N. Calumet Road; 219-926-3500 theportdrivein.net) brews its own root beer and is known for its chili dogs. To reach them from the trailhead parking lot, turn right (south) on North Mineral Springs Road, then left (east) on West Beam Street, and then right (south) on Wagner Road), which quickly turns into North Jackson Boulevard. Turn left (east) on Broadway Avenue and then either right (south) on South Calumet Road to reach Lucrezia Café or left (north) on Calumet to reach The Port Drive-In.

• •

GPS TRAILHEAD COORDINATES N41° 37.472' W87° 05.362'

DIRECTIONS From the junction of I-90 and I-94 in Gary, Indiana, follow I-94 east for 6.2 miles. At Exit 22B, follow US 20/Melton Road east for 1.9 miles; then turn left (north) on North Mineral Springs Road, and immediately look for the entrance to the parking lot on the left.

PUBLIC TRANSPORTATION Take the **South Shore Line** to the Dune Park Station at IN 49 and US 12. Follow the Calumet Bike Trail west for 1 mile as it runs alongside the railroad tracks. Turn left (south) on Mineral Springs Road and, in 0.7 mile, turn right to reach the trailhead parking lot. Plan your trip at mysouthshoreline.com.

The plant life at Cowles Bog ranges from ferns to hardwoods to beach grasses.   *Photo: Peter Musolino*

COWLES BOG TRAIL runs past wetlands, through oak forests, and over wooded dunes that increase in height as you approach the sandy beach.

DESCRIPTION

As one of the more famous spots at Indiana Dunes National Lakeshore, Cowles Bog is well known for its beauty and historical significance in the field of environmental science. Shortly after starting the hike from the Cowles Bog Trail parking lot, you'll pass a plaque on the right honoring Henry Cowles, the trail's namesake. His work in the early 20th century helped establish the science of ecology. Cowles, a professor at the University of Chicago, was drawn to Cowles Bog—and Indiana Dunes in general—partly because of its impressive variety of plants. According to botanical surveys, there are more types of plants within the 12,000 acres of Indiana Dunes National Lakeshore than there are in the 500,000 acres within Great Smoky Mountains National Park.

At 0.3 mile, a 200-foot-long boardwalk leads hikers through a lush marshy area. After the boardwalk, the trail runs close to the shore of more marshland. Although the

DISTANCE & CONFIGURATION: 4-mile balloon

DIFFICULTY: Moderate

SCENERY: Dunes, beach, marshes, woods, and savannas

EXPOSURE: Shady except for 0.2 mile along the beach

TRAIL TRAFFIC: Moderate

TRAIL SURFACE: Dirt, sand

HIKING TIME: 1.5–2 hours

DRIVING DISTANCE: 47 miles from Millennium Park

ACCESS: Daily, sunrise–30 minutes past sunset; no fees or permits

MAPS: On trail board and at the website below; USGS *Dune Acres, IN*

FACILITIES: Parking, restrooms

WHEELCHAIR ACCESS: None

CONTACT: 219-395-1882, nps.gov/indu

LOCATION: Mineral Springs Road, Dune Acres, IN 46304

COMMENTS: Dogs must be on leash no longer than 6 feet. Consider a picnic at the beach.

interior of this wetland is called Cowles Bog, it's actually a fen. Fens have soil and water that are alkaline, whereas bogs are acidic; different plant communities inhabit each.

Turn left (southwest) at the first trail junction, which appears at 0.8 mile. After skirting the west side of the large marsh for 0.3 mile, turn right (north) at the next junction. Intermittent marshes with cattails and sedges appear on each side of this trail. Also on this stretch of the trail, you'll see some of the heavy industry that makes the existence of the National Lakeshore such an unlikely prospect. The behemoth on the left is Northern Indiana Public Service Company, a coal-fueled power plant that provides electricity to the local steel industry.

Keep straight ahead when you reach a connector trail on the right at 1.7 miles. As the oak forest becomes thicker, the dunes start to bulge upward. The dunes come and go quickly, creating sudden dramatic shifts in the terrain, steeply sloping in one direction and then another. As you get closer to the lakeshore, the dunes begin to soar—and so does your heart rate as you climb these steep, sandy slopes. If it's a hot summer day, keep in mind there's a cool, wet reward at the bottom of the last dune.

At 2.2 miles, the trail descends to Bailly Beach, where, on a clear day, the sky-scrapers of downtown Chicago are visible to the northwest. This beach is a popular spot for boaters on summer weekends; during the rest of the year and on weekdays, however, this beach is seldom used because it can't be reached by car. If a picnic or sunbathing is on the agenda and boats are anchored offshore shoulder-to-shoulder, look for a quieter stretch of beach a half mile or so to the right. Try walking just beyond the fenced-in area that serves as a nesting site for the federally endangered piping plover, a pale-whitish sparrow-sized bird sporting a black breast band.

The trail continues up a dune 0.2 mile to the right (east) of where you arrived on the beach. Back on the trail, take note of how quickly the vegetation changes from hearty dune grass toward the beach to oak woods at the top of the first dune. This swift transition fascinated Henry Cowles and prompted him to investigate why oak trees didn't grow closer to the lake. In the course of his research here, he observed

Indiana Dunes National Lakeshore: Cowles Bog Hike

that oak trees and other plants need decomposed plant material in which to grow. As dune grasses die and add organic material to the sand, groundwork is laid for oak trees to sprout. In time, oak trees and other plants replace the dune grass. Through such observations, Cowles pieced together one of the major concepts in the field of ecology: as plants grow on a site, they change it.

As you drop down on the back side of the first dune, the sound of wind and water is hushed by the mounds of sand. Amid the stands of black oak and jack pine, look for flora rarely seen in the Chicago region, including the prickly pear cactus (it blooms yellow flowers in midsummer), blueberries, and, closer to the marshes, birch trees and large ferns. Continue straight ahead as you pass the first connector trail on the right, at 0.4 mile beyond the beach. Except for a few open spaces littered with large fallen branches, the trail in the summer is shaded under a canopy of oak leaves. Passing the second connector trail at 0.9 mile beyond the beach, the terrain flattens and leads you along the marsh and back to the parking lot.

• •

GPS TRAILHEAD COORDINATES N41° 38.705' W87° 05.186'

DIRECTIONS From the junction of I-90 and I-94 in Gary, Indiana, follow I-94 east for 6.2 miles. At Exit 22B, follow US 20/Melton Road east for 1.9 miles; then turn left (north) on North Mineral Springs Road. The Cowles Bog parking lot is 1.5 miles ahead on the right, just before the Dune Acres guardhouse.

PUBLIC TRANSPORTATION Take the **South Shore Line** to the Dune Park Station at IN 49 and US 12. Follow the Calumet Bike Trail west for 1 mile as it runs alongside the railroad tracks. Turn right at Mineral Springs Road, and follow it 0.5 mile north to the trailhead. Plan your trip at mysouthshoreline.com.

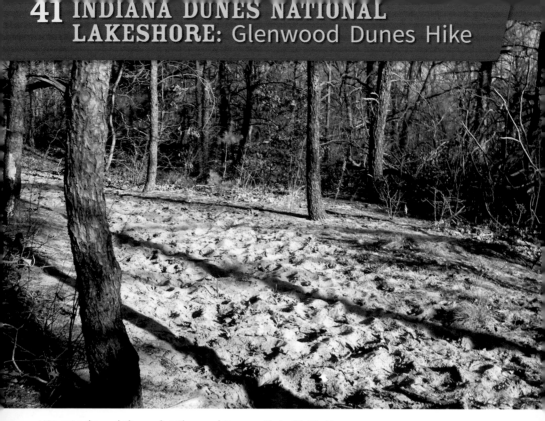

Horse tracks mark the sand at Glenwood Dunes.   *Photo: Clint Hadden*

THIS SANDY TRAIL allows you to explore miles of deep woods, gentle dune ridges, and marshy thickets. Given the ample mileage and the sand-covered surface, you'll likely find yourself at the end of this hike with a type of blissful exhaustion that comes from scaling a mountain, or perhaps running laps in a sandbox. If you'd prefer a shorter walk, trim some mileage by heading back at one of the many trail junctions.

DESCRIPTION

While you won't be climbing over monstrous sand dunes at Glenwood Dunes, you will follow a couple of gentle dune ridges as they gradually rise and fall. Like other sandy ridges in the area, these mild slopes mark the shores of a once larger version of Lake Michigan. In between the pleasant, tree-covered ridges are dense woods, shrubby wetlands, and open areas sprinkled with oaks and patches of exposed sand.

A quick look at a map of the Glenwood Dunes Trail reveals multiple trail junctions throughout the hike—often less than a half mile apart. With so many junctions, I suggest keeping the navigation simple by staying to the right. This will also keep

DISTANCE & CONFIGURATION:
12.2-mile series of connected loops with
2 out-and-back segments

DIFFICULTY: Strenuous due to length and
sandy trail surface

SCENERY: Savannas, hardwood forests,
wooded dunes, creeks, and marshes

EXPOSURE: Mostly shaded

TRAIL TRAFFIC: Light–moderate

TRAIL SURFACE: Sand, both loosely and
firmly packed, plus a short paved section

HIKING TIME: 4–5 hours

DRIVING DISTANCE: 53 miles from
Millennium Park

ACCESS: Daily, 7 a.m.–30 minutes past sunset;
no fees or permits

MAPS: Available at trailhead, visitor center,
and the website below; USGS *Dune Acres, IN,*
and *Michigan City West, IN*

WHEELCHAIR ACCESS: None

FACILITIES: Restrooms, water, shelter,
map board, and visitor center

CONTACT: 219-395-1882, nps.gov/indu

LOCATION: County Road 275 East at US 20,
Chesterton, IN 46304

COMMENTS: Dogs are prohibited. Sections of this
trail regularly flood. You can usually take
a short detour to avoid the water. Most of this
hike is open to horses mid-March–mid-December—
give them the right-of-way. The gentle terrain
and many straightaways allow for good cross-
country skiing. In recent years, the park
service changed the name of this trail from
Ly-co-ki-we to Glenwood Dunes.

you with the flow of equestrians and cross-country skiers, who are required to stay right throughout these multiple loops.

From the parking area just off US 20, this hike starts in a hardwood forest with scattered deadfall and stands of shrubs. After passing the first trail junction just beyond the trailhead and another junction at 0.5 mile, the flat terrain gives way to a lightly rolling landscape of low, wooded dunes. Before and after crossing Furnessville Road at 0.7 mile, you'll follow a couple of short boardwalks over marshy areas.

In this next section of the trail, look for small American holly trees, a conifer that rarely grows in this part of the Midwest. The green leaves of the American holly, often used for Christmas decorations, are broad, stiff, and leathery, with sharp spines on the edges; birds love the bright red berries that develop into flowers. Hollies are easiest to spot in fall, winter, and early spring, when it appears they are the only trees still bearing green leaves.

At 1 mile, stay right (north) at a junction that appears in an open sandy area with small bare dunes on the left. After the next junction, the trail closely follows US 12 before crossing Teale Road and meeting another junction. Here, the path mounts a hill topped with a cluster of pine trees and then passes several knolls and small ravines before dropping into a hardwood forest bordered on the right by a large marsh. This shrubby wetland will accompany the trail intermittently for the next few miles of hiking. At 2.3 miles into the hike, the trail meets with the 0.4-mile-long paved trail that loops in back of a former visitor center (see Nearby Activities for directions to the new park visitor center). A short walk to the right along the paved trail brings you to the

Indiana Dunes National Lakeshore: Glenwood Dunes Hike

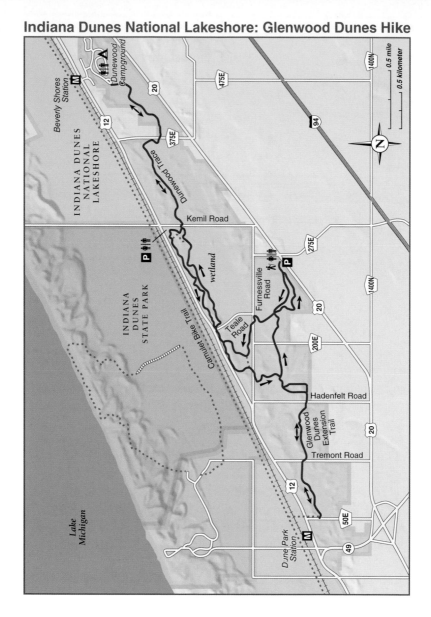

beginning of the 1.8-mile-long Dunewood Trace, an out-and-back trail that leads to the Indiana Dunes National Lakeshore's Dunewood Campground.

After crossing Kemil Road, the first half mile of the Dunewood Trace passes through a few open sandy areas bordered by hardwoods. In the open sand, look for a small brownish-tan fungi called earthstar. When there's enough moisture in the air, the rays of this star-shaped fungus open several inches across; when the air is dry, it curls up into a ball. Much of Dunewood Trace runs next to wetland on the right; now and then you'll also pass sections of a stream bed. After hiking 0.9 mile on the Trace, the path reaches County Road 375 East. To catch the rest of the trail, turn right (south) on the road, follow it 0.1 mile, and look for the continuation of the trail on the left side of the road at the small brown sign for the Dunewood Campground. You'll soon cross a two-track, and then arrive in an open savanna. As the trail enters the savanna, look to the left for a bevy of prickly pear cacti. After passing through a dense bottomland forest, the trail snakes by a series of irrigation ditches and a small pond. Just beyond the ditches, the trail ends at a campground road, where you'll turn around and retrace your steps back to the paved path near the visitor center.

At 6.1 miles into the hike, you'll return to the paved path. Follow it on the north side of the building near the restrooms, and then take the first right (west). Soon you'll cross a two-track and enter the familiar rolling terrain. Although much of this section of the hike runs closely to US 12, the road is not overly busy and takes little away from the tranquility of these woods. The trail continues along the wooded dune ridges and through gently sloping savannas with the occasional open sandy spots. Throughout this hike, keep your eyes peeled for deer: if you're ambling close to dusk or dawn, you're virtually guaranteed to spot their bushy white tails as they scamper off into the woods. Stay to the right at a couple of trail junctions.

At 8.2 miles into the hike, you'll arrive at the Glenwood Dunes Extension Trail, an out-and-back trail that is 1.2 miles each way. In the first half mile of the extension, you'll stay right at a couple more junctions and then cross Hadenfelt Road and a stream called Munson Ditch, which winds through a beautiful wooded ravine. Beyond the stream, the trail straightens out on its way to Tremont Road. At Tremont Road, the trail continues 20 yards to the right (north) with a short boardwalk. The final segment of the extension trail passes through flat terrain, with sections both open and wooded, before reaching County Road 50 East/Main Street, which is where you'll turn around and retrace your steps.

After crossing Hadenfelt Road, you'll be back at the beginning of the extension trail. Stay to the right at the next three junctions before crossing CR 200 East. While staying right at two more junctions, the trail passes over lightly rolling terrain on your way back to the parking lot. During this deeply wooded section of the hike, look for black oak, white oak, tulip, sugar-maple trees, and the flowering dogwood tree, which is especially captivating in the spring.

NEARBY ACTIVITIES

Dunewood Campground has 12 walk-in sites and 54 drive-in sites. While the sites here aren't set against the dunes or along the lakeshore, they're bigger and more private than those at nearby **Indiana Dunes State Park Campground.** During the summer, both campgrounds fill up fast; sites at Dunewood are strictly first-come, first-served, but those at the state park can be reserved (call 877-444-6777 or visit reserveamerica.com).

The **Indiana Dunes National Lakeshore Visitor Center,** 2.5 miles from the Glenwood Dunes Trailhead (1215 N. IN 49; 219-926-2255, indianadunes.com), features displays about the park, a bookstore, and art exhibits. From the trailhead, turn right (southwest) on US 20. A couple of miles ahead, turn left (south) on North Tremont Road. In 0.5 mile, turn right (northwest) on IN 49 and, in another 0.3 mile, turn right again into the visitor-center parking lot.

• •

GPS TRAILHEAD COORDINATES N41° 38.887' W87° 00.935'

DIRECTIONS From the junction of I-90 and I-94 in Gary, Indiana, follow I-94 east for 6.2 miles. At Exit 22B, follow US 20/Melton Road east for 5.8 miles, and then turn left to reach the Glenwood Dunes Trail parking lot, immediately on your left.

PUBLIC TRANSPORTATION Take the **South Shore Line** to the Dune Park Station at IN 49 and US 12. The west end of the Glenwood Dunes Extension Trail is less than 0.5 mile away—from the station, head northeast on US 12, and then turn right (south) on CR 50 East/Main Street. The extension trail starts about 0.1 mile ahead on the left (see last two paragraphs of the Description for how to reach the beginning of the main trail). Plan your trip at mysouthshoreline.com.

Colorful wildflowers and grasses adorn the trail.   *Photo: Ted Villaire*

THIS HIKE AT the Indiana Dunes National Lakeshore reveals another reason that the dunes are a local treasure. End to end, the hike persistently captivates, with its rolling dunes landscape dotted with ponds and marshes, pristine oak savannas, prairie grasses, abundance of wildflowers, sprawling lagoon, and windswept Lake Michigan shoreline.

DESCRIPTION

Occupying an unlikely spot in northeast Gary, Indiana, Miller Woods sits between the sprawling U.S. Steel mill and the residential neighborhood of Miller Beach. But that's the story with so much of the Indiana Dunes: breathtakingly beautiful spots sandwiched between heavy industry, residential areas, and the big lake. As with other hikes at the dunes, the variety along this trail is riveting. The question of what's around the next corner pushes you forward constantly.

In the spring, Miller Woods rewards visitors with impressive displays of wildflowers such as columbine and Indian paintbrush. In the fall, hikers will see bracken ferns turning gold, along with asters, goldenrods, sunflowers, grapevines, fringed

DISTANCE & CONFIGURATION: 3.2-mile loop with long out-and-back spur

DIFFICULTY: Easy–moderate

SCENERY: Dunes, marshland, ponds, oak savanna, lagoon, sandy beach, Lake Michigan

EXPOSURE: Mostly open

TRAIL TRAFFIC: Moderate

TRAIL SURFACE: Sand and dirt

HIKING TIME: 3 hours

DRIVING DISTANCE: 21 miles from Millennium Park

ACCESS: Daily, 7 a.m.–30 minutes past sunset; no fees or permits

MAPS: Available at the website at right; USGS *Gary, IN*

FACILITIES: Restrooms, nature center, picnic tables, benches, beach

WHEELCHAIR ACCESS: Most of the main hike is not accessible. A short accessible trail starts from the back of the nature center; just off of this trail, a ramp leads to an accessible boardwalk that bisects the marsh.

CONTACT: 219-395-1882, nps.gov/indu

LOCATION: 100 N. Lake St., Gary, IN 46403

COMMENTS: Dogs must be on leash no longer than 6 feet. Please stay on the official trail—hikers damage the fragile dunes ecosystem when they stray from it. Another reason to stay on the trail: poison ivy grows in abundance here. Leave the car at home and take the South Shore Line, which is a pleasant 15-minute walk from the trailhead.

gentians. Miller Woods hosts a number of rare flowers, including the fame flower, which exists nowhere else in the Indiana Dunes. If you keep your eyes peeled, you'll see prickly pear cactus growing along the trail, and you may see the local lizard species called the six-lined race runner. Miller Woods is also home to the fragile and federally endangered Karner blue butterfly, which has a lifespan of only three to five days.

Starting out from the nature center, take the trail on the right, which follows a counterclockwise route around the large cattail pond. Immediately, you're walking in the shadow of massive oaks hanging over the trail. Not quite a quarter mile ahead, a boardwalk stretches across the marsh to the left, providing a view of a possible beaver lodge in the pond.

Beyond the boardwalk, a gently rolling savanna sprinkled with oaks flattens out as you reach a marshy area—one of what seems like dozens of ponds and marshes on this hike. At about a quarter mile into the hike, turn right at the junction and follow the sign pointing to the beach. After taking this out-and-back spur trail to the beach, you'll finish the loop around the large pond.

On the trail to the beach, the landscape opens up more as you brush against a swath of cattails, and for the next mile or so, the trail snakes among a series of ponds and marshes, many with stands of fluffy-topped sedge grasses swaying in the breeze. These ponds—dominated by thick rushes, sedges, and shrubs—have a particular name: interdunal wetlands. The insects, amphibians, and other small animals teeming within these shallow wetlands provide an all-you-can-eat buffet for local birds.

Soon, you'll cross a former railroad embankment that will eventually become part of the Marquette Greenway, a multiuse path along the south shore of Lake

Indiana Dunes National Lakeshore: Miller Woods Hike

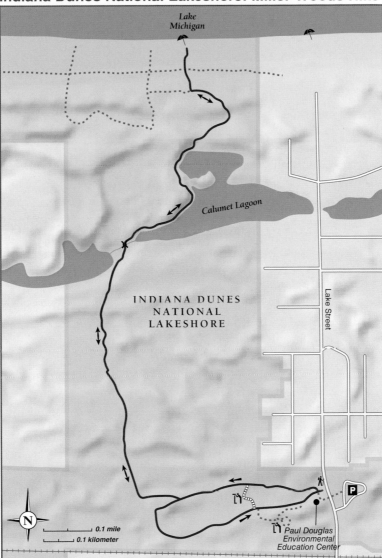

Michigan that will connect Chicago with New Buffalo, Michigan. While some sections of this trail have already been built, much of the trail, including this section, will be built in the future (go to nirpc.org for more information).

As the oaks get sparser and grasses get thicker, the landscape rolls and undulates like a snake wriggling in the grass. At about 1 mile into the hike, you'll reach the Calumet Lagoon, a peaceful body of water surrounded by dunes topped with black oak trees. The lagoon stretches nearly a couple of miles from between a steel mill on the west to the lovely grounds of Marquette Park to the east. The acclaimed Chicago writer Nelson Algren owned a cottage close to the north shore of the lagoon just to the east.

The next section of the hike follows a narrow path that curls around the edges of the sprawling lagoon. The lagoon, edged with cattails and sedge grasses, is literally one step to the right of the trail while 50-foot-high dunes immediately shoot up on the left. The sand dunes rising above the placid water of the lagoon give this spot a serene beauty (Please observe the signs asking hikers to stay on the trail to avoid damaging the fragile dune grasses.)

Leaving the lagoon behind and now getting closer to the beach, the trees grow sparse. It's all marram grass with the occasional cottonwood tree, known for preferring wet, sandy soil and leaves that rattle in the wind. Passing over a series of low dune ridges, you'll catch your first glimpse of the U.S. Steel plant to the west. Keep straight ahead when you come to a junction with a trail that parallels the shoreline.

Arriving at the beach, it's time to unpack your picnic and—if it's summer—take a dip in the water. Of course, you can always add mileage to your hike by taking a stroll on the beach. Once you've reached a proper state of relaxation while taking in the sound of the waves and enjoying the view of the Chicago skyline 25 miles to the northwest, you can head back on the same trail that brought you here.

Arriving back at the initial loop near the nature center, turn right at the junction, and you're immediately on top of the 40-foot dune, overlooking an oak savanna, ponds, wetlands within a rolling landscape. To the south, you'll see a very active railroad that connects some of the heavy industry in northwest Indiana.

Just ahead, you'll encounter the other end of the boardwalk crossing the pond and an accessible trail that runs from the back of the nature center. The accessible trail also leads to a pleasant picnic area behind the nature center. If you have kids along, be sure to step inside the nature center to enjoy the interactive exhibits.

NEARBY ACTIVITIES

Faced with some of the worst effects of Rust Belt deindustrialization, Gary has lost more than half of its population since the 1960s. The Miller Beach neighborhood, where this hike takes place, was never hit as hard as the rest of Gary because of its desirable location on the shore of Lake Michigan. Its business district, revitalized in recent years, features an arts center and several restaurants. The **18th Street Brewery** (5725 Miller Ave.; 219-939-8802, 18thstreetbrewery.com) serves burgers and sandwiches along with its signature beers. The **Miller Bakery Cafe** (555 S. Lake St.; 219-427-1446, millerbakerycafe.com), housed in a historic former bakery, serves upscale American dishes.

The main attraction along the Miller Beach lakefront is **Marquette Park,** a national landmark containing some beautiful historical structures and bronze sculptures; it was also the location of early experiments in aviation predating the Wright Brothers' flights. **Carmella's Cafe** (7010 Oak Ave.; 312-401-7401, carmellas.info), a seasonal beachside restaurant inside the park, frequently presents live music.

• •

GPS TRAILHEAD COORDINATES N41° 36.405' W87° 16.112'

DIRECTIONS From I-90/I-94, take the Chicago Skyway (I-90) toll road 7.8 miles southeast into Indiana; at the state line, I-90 becomes the Indiana Toll Road. In 16.5 miles, take Exit 17 east onto US 12/US 20/East Dunes Highway. In 2.1 miles, stay left on US 12 as US 20 branches right. A half mile ahead, turn left (north) on South Lake Street. Three-quarters of a mile ahead, look for the Paul A. Douglas Environmental Education Center on the left, at 100 N. Lake St. A small parking area is just past the building on the left; a larger lot is located just before the education center on the right.

PUBLIC TRANSPORTATION Take the **South Shore Line** to the Miller Station. From here, the trail is a pleasant 15-minute walk along the Miller Beach commercial strip—note, however, that the Miller Station does not allow passengers to board or disembark with bicycles. From the station, walk east on US 12/East Dunes Highway to the traffic light at South Lake Street. Turn left (north) at South Lake Street, and continue for 0.6 mile to reach the trailhead. Plan your trip at mysouthshoreline.com.

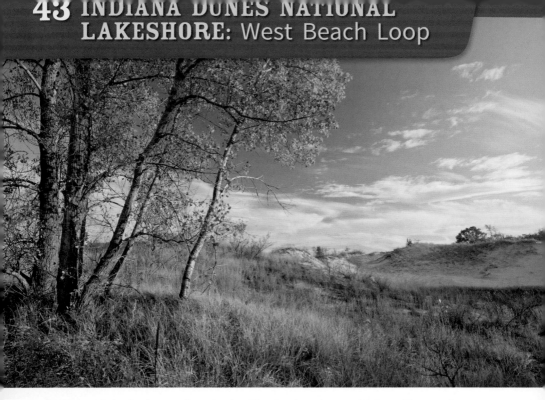

Cottonwoods dot the dunes and grasslands at West Beach.   *Photo: Hank Erdmann/Shutterstock*

TAKE IN GREAT views on high dunes topped with marram grass, jack pine, and cottonwood trees. Coming off the dunes, the trail runs along a scenic lake, through a sandy savanna, and into dense woodland.

DESCRIPTION

It's not just the high dunes and a long, sandy beach that make hiking at West Beach such a satisfying experience. What makes this hike so engaging is how the landscape and plants magically transform every half mile or so. As you move from the beach to the dunes to the wooded ridges to the savanna to a large lily-pad pond, it seems the landscape is always changing.

Note: If you've brought along a canine hiking companion, the first segment of the hike, which accesses West Beach, is off-limits. In this case, start by heading right (east) from the trailhead on the connector trail and, in about 0.1 mile, turn right (south) at the next intersection to pick up the segment that accesses Long Lake (see fourth paragraph following).

Otherwise, start by heading left (north) from the trailhead on the wide, paved path heading toward Lake Michigan. You'll pass a wind-scoured, bowl-shaped depression on the right. Known as a blowout, this depression contains a pond, because the

DISTANCE & CONFIGURATION: 3.15-mile loop

DIFFICULTY: Moderate

SCENERY: High dunes, small lake, sand savanna, wooded ridges and ravines, and an unusual array of plants

EXPOSURE: Mostly exposed

TRAIL TRAFFIC: Moderate

TRAIL SURFACE: Sand, wooden boardwalk, and dirt, plus short paved section at the beginning

HIKING TIME: 1.5 hours

DRIVING DISTANCE: 40.5 miles from Millennium Park

ACCESS: Daily, 8 a.m.–10 p.m. Memorial Day–Labor Day (7 a.m.–30 minutes past sunset the rest of the year); admission: $6/car Memorial Day–Labor Day (free the rest of the year)

MAPS: Available at the guardhouse and the website below; USGS *Portage, IN*

FACILITIES: Bathhouse, picnic areas, restrooms, snack bar

WHEELCHAIR ACCESS: Only the initial paved section

CONTACT: 219-395-1882, nps.gov/indu

LOCATION: West Beach Access Road, Gary, IN 46403

COMMENTS: Dogs are prohibited on the section of the trail that runs along the beach but permitted elsewhere on the trail (on leash no longer than 6 feet). Watch for cars while making 3 crossings of the main park road. Please stay on the trail to prevent erosion of the dunes.

wind has swept the sand away down to the water table. After passing through the center of the bathhouse and reaching the white, sandy beach, look for the boardwalk on the right (east), which leads over the small foredune. This part of the hike, called the Dune Succession Trail, gives you a sense of how prevailing winds and plants change the bare beach into dense groves of oak, hickory, and basswood in the span of only a few hundred yards. Where the trail drops between a couple of gentle dunes, you'll see clusters of jack pines, which typically grow farther north but also thrive in the harsh conditions at the dunes.

At 0.3 mile into the hike, another boardwalk takes you through the bottom of an old blowout. Stairs lead from the blowout to the dune, wrapped in marram grass and topped with cottonwood trees. Cottonwood trees deal with the constantly shifting sand remarkably well: when their limbs are covered with blowing sand, the limbs sprout roots; likewise, when blowing sand exposes the roots, the roots grow stems and leaves. Some of the small cottonwoods at the tops of dunes may actually have 60 feet of trunk below the surface.

From the top of the dune, the trail drops and then quickly enters a woodland dense with oak, wild grape, basswood, and more cottonwood. Rising again to the top of a dune, you'll have a fine view of the relatively flat area containing the parking lot and the lower dunes and wooded areas to the south. Before becoming parkland, the sand in this area as well as other spots along the Dunes Lakeshore was hauled away for making bricks and glass and for filling in wetlands, as was done at Jackson Park in Chicago in preparation for the 1893 World's Columbian Exposition.

At the bottom of a long flight of stairs, immediately turn left (south) on a faint trail (you'd probably miss it unless you were looking for it). This wide, grassy trail

Indiana Dunes National Lakeshore: West Beach Loop

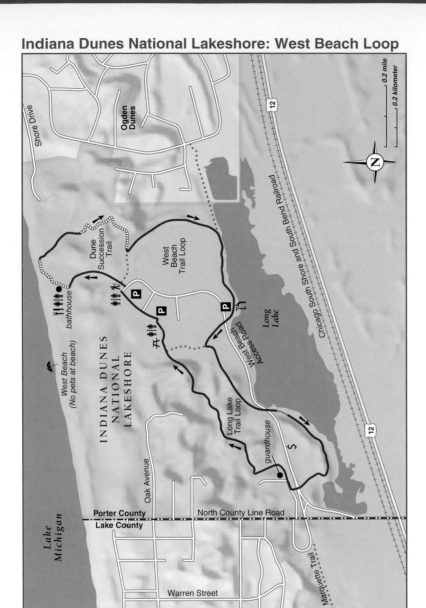

runs through a savanna between a large dune rising on the left and a small ridge on the right. During the summer, goldfinches and king birds (dark gray on top, white below) dart among the poplar, white oak, and sumac trees. Closer to the ground, look for ferns, prickly pear cacti, and a variety of wildflowers. At the junction, turn right (west) so that you're walking alongside 60-acre Long Lake, blanketed by lily pads, fringed with cattails, and frequently visited by waterbirds. The trail to the left runs 0.25 mile to the community of Ogden Dunes. Before crossing the park road, don't miss the observation deck overlooking the pond.

In the sand prairie across the park road, prickly pear cacti line the sides of the trail; closer to the woods, plenty of milkweed plants and small sassafras trees push up through the sandy soil. Turn left (southwest) at the junction and continue between the steep, wooded dune on the right and a small sand ridge on the left. Crossing the park road again, the trail follows the spine of an oak-covered dune ridge that drops steeply 50 feet or so on each side. From the winding trail, you'll have a fine view of a section of Long Lake sprinkled with small, grassy islands. Coming down from the ridge through dense, shrubby woodland, cross the park road again. The trail turns right along the chain-link fence and passes a few park-service buildings and a parking area before crossing a paved service road.

From the service road, the trail climbs a dune ridge under a thick oak canopy. In many places, you can see marshland—probably former blowouts—at the bottom of the wooded ravine. At the junction, stay to the right (east). (The trail to the left continues 0.2 mile through wooded dunes to Wabash Avenue.) From the junction, the trail drops alongside a marsh before making a steep, sandy climb to the top of a dune overlooking a group of picnic pavilions and the parking lot. From the top of the dune, you can descend straight down through the open sand or, for a more gradual descent, follow the trail down to the left.

• •

GPS TRAILHEAD COORDINATES N41° 37.352' W87° 12.488'

DIRECTIONS From I-90/I-94, take the Chicago Skyway (I-90) toll road 7.8 miles southeast into Indiana; at the state line, I-90 becomes the Indiana Toll Road. In 16.5 miles, take Exit 17 east onto US 12/US 20/East Dunes Highway. In 2.1 miles, veer right to stay on US 20 as US 12 branches left; then, 3.1 miles past the fork, turn left (north) on North County Line Road. The entrance to West Beach is 0.2 mile ahead on the right. After stopping at the guardhouse to pick up a trail map and pay the entrance fee, follow the park road 1 mile to the main parking lot, on your left. The trailhead is just north of the parking lot.

The state park's namesake dunes create an otherworldly scene.   *Photo: Dorothy Weatherly*

INDIANA DUNES BOASTS one of the most beautiful and dramatic settings in the Chicago region. This hike is especially notable for its variety: after you trek through forest, wetland, and wooded dunes, you'll pass over spectacular sand dunes bordering the shoreline.

DESCRIPTION

For more than a century, Indiana Dunes State Park has captured the interest of local people looking for a spot close to home where they can experience breathtaking beauty. One person drawn to the dunes was the poet Carl Sandburg, who once wrote, "The dunes are to the Midwest what the Grand Canyon is to Arizona. . . . They constitute a signature of time and eternity." Overstatements aside, this hike could have been in the back of Sandburg's mind when he aired that thought; few other places in the dunes display with such drama the unrelenting effects of wind and water. The main attraction on this hike is a stunning dune ridge that runs between large areas hollowed out by lake wind.

You'll encounter several quick turns shortly after starting the hike (north) on Trail 9, to the right of the nature-center building. After 0.1 mile, turn right (south) on Trail 8. Immediately, you'll pass the junction with Trail 10 on the left before crossing the bridge spanning the east branch of Dune Creek. After the bridge, the trail reaches the

DISTANCE & CONFIGURATION: 4.5-mile loop

DIFFICULTY: Moderate due to a few short climbs on loose sand

SCENERY: Bottomland forest, marshland, Lake Michigan shoreline, dunes, ravines, and blowouts (large depressions created by blowing sand)

EXPOSURE: Mostly shaded

TRAIL TRAFFIC: Moderate

TRAIL SURFACE: Hard-packed dirt and loose sand

HIKING TIME: 2–2.5 hours

DRIVING DISTANCE: 51 miles from Millennium Park

ACCESS: Daily, 7 a.m.–11 p.m.; admission: $7/vehicle for cars with Indiana license plates, $12/vehicle out-of-state

MAPS: Available at guardhouse, at park office, and the website below; USGS *Dune Acres, IN*

FACILITIES: Camping, picnic shelters, beach, and restrooms open year-round; swimming, water, and concessions in summer

WHEELCHAIR ACCESS: None

CONTACT: 219-926-1952, in.gov/dnr /parklake/2980.htm

LOCATION: 1600 County Road 25 F., Chesterton, IN 46304

COMMENTS: Dogs must be on leash no longer than 6 feet. Bring waterproof footwear in spring.

Wilson Shelter and continues in the far left corner of the parking lot on the other side of the restrooms. Turn left (east) at the Trail 2 intersection, 0.2 mile after the shelter parking lot.

Trail 2 runs for nearly 2 miles through an exceedingly flat and sometimes wet bottomland forest. During summer, you'll be hiking under a thick canopy of oak and beech trees; occasionally, these large trees are sprawled on the ground with root systems jutting up 15 feet. As these trees fall, the canopy opens, allowing shrubs to take hold on the forest floor.

At 1.4 miles into the hike, the trail curves left before reaching a bench at the beginning of a half-mile-long boardwalk spanning a section of what is called the Great Marsh, a long, thin wetland that once ran parallel to nearly the entire shoreline of the Indiana Dunes. Now much of the marsh has been filled in. Through this section of the marsh, patches of open water and marsh grasses are interrupted now and then by stretches of dry land and the occasional small pond. Completing the boardwalk, turn right (northeast) on Trail 10, and then quickly turn left (north) at the connector path for Trail 9. When you finish the connector trail, turn right (southwest) on Trail 9 proper.

Trail 9 passes over gradual ups and downs and between small dunes rising on each side of the trail. After these minor dunes, Lake Michigan comes into view as the trail reaches the Furnessville Blowout. (A blowout forms when winds blow sand inland, carving out what looks like a large amphitheater of sand.) From the Furnessville Blowout, Trail 9 curves left, beginning the best part of the hike—traversing a dune ridge for 0.7 mile on the way to the next blowout.

The section between these two blowouts offers some of the most striking natural scenery in the Chicago area. Left of the trail are tall white pines and black oaks rising out of a plunging ravine. On the right, the dune drops to the shore of Lake Michigan.

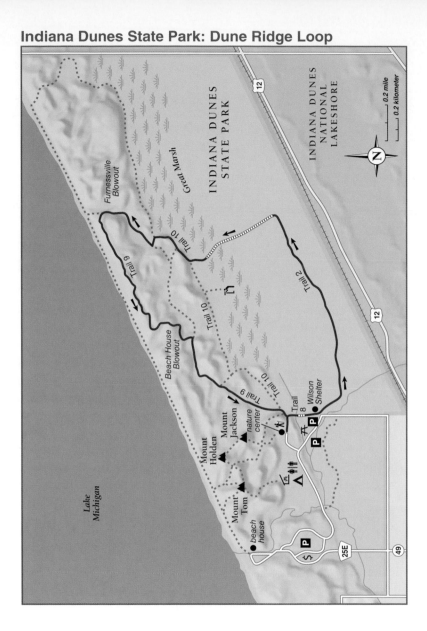

Indiana Dunes State Park: Dune Ridge Loop

Views along this squiggly ridge path are best when the leaves have left the branches: on a clear day, the Chicago skyline is clearly visible 30 miles to the northwest.

The trail reaches the edge of the Beach House Blowout at 3.4 miles into the hike. The bowl of the blowout, nearly 200 yards across, is mostly covered with marram grass. Also evident are the dead tree trunks, both standing and fallen, that are remnants of a forest that was swallowed and is now being uncovered by moving mounds of sand. You'll likely notice the illegal trails that zigzag this fragile sand canyon. To prevent further damage, the park requires hikers to stay on the marked trails. Continuing left along the rim of the blowout, be sure to avoid the steep and straight illegal trail on the left, and continue on the trail toward the high point that affords a great view of the bowl as well as the surrounding woods.

After dropping slightly from the high point, look for the post that marks a path meandering down the slope of the dune to the left. While hiking through these foredunes, as they're called, keep watch for the six-lined racerunner lizard. This lizard has yellow and brown stripes on a body about 9 inches long, including the tail. At 3.7 miles into the hike, after descending from the edge of the Beach House Blowout, take Trail 9 to the right (west), and follow it until the second junction with Trail 10 at the nature-center sign. Once you turn right (west) on Trail 10, the nature-center parking lot is just ahead.

NEARBY ACTIVITIES

Other great hiking opportunities abound at Indiana Dunes State Park. In particular, don't miss the big dunes on the west side of the park, near where this hike starts. **Mount Jackson, Mount Holden,** and **Mount Tom** (the highest dune, at 192 feet) provide stunning views of the lakeshore and the surrounding landscape. Much of the ascent up Mount Tom takes place on stairs, while the route up the other big dunes is mostly on loose sand. Oh, and don't forget to take a stroll (or perhaps a nap) on the park's lovely beach.

If you're looking for a restaurant or just a stroll through a charming small town, consider stopping in nearby **Chesterton.** Drive 3.5 miles south of the state park on IL 49, and then turn right (west) on Porter Avenue to reach the downtown area.

• •

GPS TRAILHEAD COORDINATES N41° 39.562' W87° 02.996'

DIRECTIONS From the junction of I-90 and I-94 in Gary, Indiana, head northwest on I-94 for 9.9 miles. Take Exit 26B to merge north onto IN 49 toward Indiana Dunes State Park, and continue 2.1 miles to the park entrance (IN 49 becomes County Road 25 East). After paying at the guardhouse, follow the signs to the nature-center parking lot.

PUBLIC TRANSPORTATION Take the **South Shore Line** to the Dune Park Station. Catch the short trail on the other side of the train tracks for a shortcut to County Road 25 East, which leads to the state park. Follow the trail north alongside this road for 0.8 mile. After paying at the guardhouse, follow the signs to the nature center. Even better, take your bike on the South Shore Line and ride the trail into the park. Plan your trip at mysouth shoreline.com.

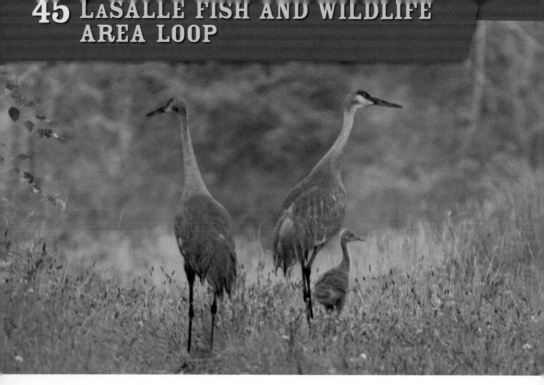

A sandhill crane family surveys its surroundings.   *Photo: Jed Hertz*

IF YOU LIKE riverside hikes and sprawling marshlands busy with birds, you'll find this to be one of the great undiscovered hikes in Chicagoland. Nearly every inch of this hike accompanies a river, a drainage ditch, a pond, or a marshland.

DESCRIPTION

About 150 years ago, the Grand Kankakee Marsh was the largest wetland in the Midwest, occupying nearly a million acres in northwest Indiana. Then in the mid-1800s, the marshes were drained, and the Kankakee River was deepened and channelized in order to use the flat, moist landscape for farming. Drainage tiles were installed, ditches were dug, and pumps were installed to push water away from the cropland. Also, an extensive levee system was built to reduce flooding near the waterways. According to the United States Geological Survey, only 13% of the Kankakee Marsh remains.

Grand Kankakee Marsh was named by the early French explorers who came through major waterways of the area looking for a water route to the Pacific Ocean. One of these explorers was Robert Cavalier, Sieur de La Salle, for whom the 3,797-acre fish-and-wildlife area is named. LaSalle Fish and Wildlife Area—one of the few original remnants of the Grand Kankakee Marsh—was first established as a state park in the 1960s.

DISTANCE & CONFIGURATION: 5.2-mile loop

DIFFICULTY: Moderate

SCENERY: Kankakee River, expansive marshland, prairie, savanna, woodland, numerous drainage ditches, and a stream

EXPOSURE: Mostly exposed

TRAIL TRAFFIC: Light

TRAIL SURFACE: Sand/dirt 2-track road

HIKING TIME: 3–3.5 hours

DRIVING DISTANCE: 61.5 miles from Millennium Park

ACCESS: Much of the west half of this hike is closed for waterfowl hunting October 1– December 1. If you're visiting during that time,

stick to the east half of the preserve. Otherwise open daily, sunrise–sunset; no fees or permits.

MAPS: Posted at park office and available at the website below; USGS *Illiana Heights, IL,* and *Schneider, IN*

FACILITIES: Boat launch at parking area

WHEELCHAIR ACCESS: None

CONTACT: 219-992-3019, in.gov/dnr /fishwild/3088.htm

LOCATION: About 1 mile north of IN 10 at the Kankakee River, Lake Village, IN 46349

COMMENTS: Dogs must be on leash no longer than 6 feet. Because this wildlife area is largely undeveloped, you're likely to be all alone once you get away from the prime fishing spots.

Start the hike in Parking Area 3A, situated at the edge of a vast wetland called Black Oak Bayou. (If it's after August 15 and waterfowl season is under way, you may have to park in Parking Area 3B, which is just south of Parking Area 3A. If parking in 3B, you can easily start the hike at its midpoint. Visit in.gov/dnr/fishwild/2344 .htm for more information on waterfowl-hunting season.) Facing the Kankakee River, take the gravel two-track road to the left (west) as it runs along the levee. The levee— which is about 15 feet above the surrounding landscape—provides a bird's-eye view of the river on the right and the marshes and woodland to the left. At 0.2 mile, a large, swampy pond covered with algae and speckled with dead trees opens on the left. Many of these riverside ponds are shaped like short, wriggling worms—indicating their former life as the curves or perhaps the oxbows of the Kankakee before it was channelized. After a brief stretch of cottonwoods and oaks growing in a wet savanna on the left, you'll encounter more marshland alive with swallows soaring among the dead trees, turtles plopping off logs into the water, and lily pads tilting in the breeze.

Once you've logged nearly a mile of hiking, the trail turns left and passes over a bridge spanning a waterway between the marshes on each side of the trail. As the small, open marsh on the right turns into an algae-covered ditch and the marsh on the left fades into stands of cattails and willows, the trail turns left again. Prairie grass and compass plants fringe the trail, while willows and cottonwoods hang over the algae-covered drainage ditches on each side of the two-track road. Beyond the foot- bridge on the right that provides a connection to Parking Area 4B, you'll see some cropland peeking through the trees on the left as the trail enters a savanna.

After crossing the road at 2.25 miles into the hike, you'll pass a wet, shrubby prairie with a backdrop of oak woodland on the left. At the point where two-track roads come from both sides, continue straight ahead (southeast) as the trail angles

LaSalle Fish and Wildlife Area Loop

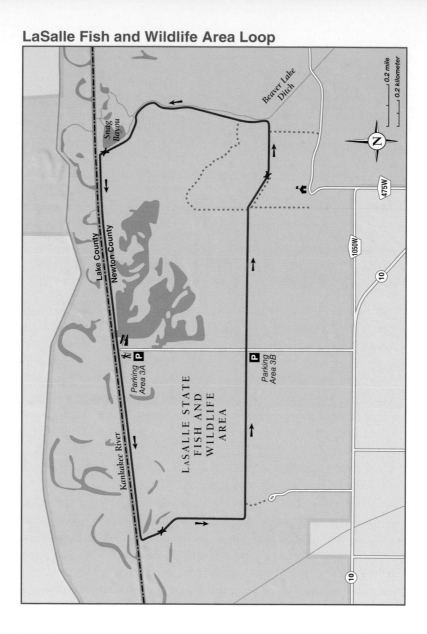

slightly to the right. Soon, two successive footbridges cross the continuous ditch on the right. Stay on the two-track road as you cross a gravel road and then swing left.

As the trail curves left, Beaver Lake Ditch splits to the right and left, running under the road. Continuing ahead, the trail accompanies a pleasant stretch of the sandy-bottomed creek that gently meanders through wet savanna and woodland. The damp, shady sides of the trail are thick with horsetail grass, the stems of which come apart at their black-fringed joints. After you pass a marshy area through the trees on the left, Beaver Lake Ditch flows into Snag Bayou, which is bordered by quaking aspen and oak. Once you cross a bridge, the trail hits the Kankakee River.

Turning left, finish off the hike with a mile-long stroll between the straight, fast-moving river and the immense bayou with stands of dead trees jutting upward and patches of green algae on the surface. In recent years, the park decided to lower the water in this 240-acre bayou by about two feet so that it will become a more welcoming spot for water birds. While the fishermen have been ticked off about the lower water level, the results have been good so far for bird-watchers. New species have been observed along with such existing species as bald eagles, pelicans, ospreys, kingfishers, and a variety of ducks and geese. The view of the marsh is obscured now and then with berry bushes, small trees, and full-size cottonwoods. Continue ahead on the levee until you reach the parking lot.

NEARBY ACTIVITIES

Ten miles northwest of the LaSalle Fish and Wildlife Area is the **Grand Kankakee Marsh County Park Hike** (Hike 38, page 186). Thirteen miles south of LaSalle is the **Iroquois County State Wildlife Area Hike** (Hike 52, page 248).

• •

GPS TRAILHEAD COORDINATES N41° 10.110' W87° 29.821'

DIRECTIONS From the southern end of the Tri-State Tollway (I-294) in South Holland, Illinois, exit south onto IL 394 toward Danville. Drive 4.8 miles; then exit east onto US 30/East Lincoln Highway. In 2 miles, turn right (south) to continue on US 30, shortly passing into Indiana; then, in 3.8 miles, turn right (south) on US 41/Indianapolis Boulevard, and continue 24 miles until you reach IN 10. Turn right (west) on IN 10, and proceed 2.4 miles until you see the FISH & WILDLIFE AREA sign on your right—here, turn right and follow the road north until it dead-ends at Parking Area 3A.

The mowed trail carves its way through tallgrass prairie.   *Photo: Heather Millsap*

OAK RIDGE PRAIRIE County Park allows visitors to sample a variety of appealing environments within a fairly small area. During the hike, the landscape swiftly moves from lakeshore to woodland to prairie to marshland.

DESCRIPTION

Tucked in between the northwest Indiana communities of Griffith and Merrillville, this 700-acre county park offers a pleasing mix of woodland, marshland, and prairie. On the east side of the park, you'll ramble along the shoreline of a popular fishing lake, through an oak and quaking aspen forest, and then along the edge of a large marsh. After hiking through a savanna dotted with stately oaks and then mounting a sledding hill in the recreation area in the middle of the park, you'll explore the park's west side. This section offers more savanna as well as an attractive tallgrass prairie, wet prairie, and an isolated lake with an observation deck.

Start the hike at the fishing pier by taking the sidewalk to the right (south) as it leads over the boardwalk and along the shore of the lake. Follow the wide mowed path along the south shore of the small fishing lake. At about the halfway point around the lake, turn right (southeast). As you follow this flat, winding trail through stands of oak, sumac, quaking aspen, and sassafras trees, you'll hear acorns crunching underfoot,

DISTANCE & CONFIGURATION: 3.15-mile loop

DIFFICULTY: Easy

SCENERY: Lakes, woodland, marsh, tallgrass prairie, savanna, and drainage canals

EXPOSURE: Mostly exposed

TRAIL TRAFFIC: Light

TRAIL SURFACE: Dirt, mowed grass

HIKING TIME: 1.5 hours

DRIVING DISTANCE: 38 miles from Millennium Park

ACCESS: Daily, 7 a.m.–sunset; admission:

$5/vehicle for Indiana residents, $8/vehicle out-of-state

MAPS: Available at the website below; USGS *Highland, IN*

FACILITIES: Picnic tables, pavilion, playground, restrooms, sledding hill, fishing pier

WHEELCHAIR ACCESS: None

CONTACT: 219-769-7275, lakecountyparks .com/245/oak-ridge-prairie

LOCATION: 301 S. Colfax St., Griffith, IN 46323

COMMENTS: Dogs must be on leash no longer than 6 feet

and you may hear whitetails bounding off through the thickets. Keep straight ahead at the trail junction.

Just ahead, a shrub-laden marsh sprawls out for a quarter mile to the left. On my early-morning visit to the marsh, a muskrat cruised through the drainage ditch that runs alongside the trail, while cedar waxwings swirled overhead feeding on berry trees.

After hiking 0.2 mile between the marsh on the left and shrubs and large cottonwoods on the right, the trail takes a sharp right turn. As the landscape changes from scrubland to savanna, you'll pass a short side trail on the left leading to West 58th Avenue. In the savanna, look for sand cherry, goldenrod, and blazing star growing beneath impressive 80-foot burr oaks. As the oaks multiply, you'll also see ferns and the occasional raspberry bush.

At the gravel road, continue straight ahead up the sledding hill; on its back side you'll see a set of train tracks and a savanna sprinkled with quaking aspen. Heading down the other end of the hill, follow the park road to the left (west), cross the bridge and take an immediate left turn (south) onto the mowed trail that runs alongside the hedgerow and an old drainage ditch. After crossing a bridge spanning a wooded ditch, stay left (south) as the trail twists and turns through stands of shrubs, berry bushes, quaking aspens, oaks, and cottonwoods, as well as a number of still-standing dead trees. Tall sedge grasses, willows, and ferns sprout from wet areas near the side of the trail. When you reach the tallgrass prairie, the trail swings back toward the park road and passes the other end of the trail you passed earlier.

Crossing the park road near several bluebird houses, the trail passes over a bridge and then accompanies a drainage ditch on the left and a cattail marsh on the right. You'll pass sumac, chokecherry, and waving shafts of goldenrod before the trail curves to the right alongside a wet prairie. On this stretch, you'll likely see and hear small planes taking off and landing on the single 4,900-foot runway at the Griffith-Merrillville

Oak Ridge Prairie Loop

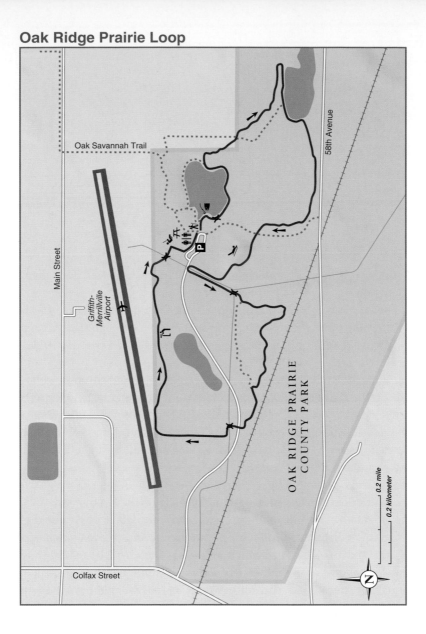

Airport on the other side of the fence. Soon you'll come to an observation deck with benches and interpretive signs that overlooks the wetlands and pond on the right. After walking through a bit more prairie, and passing through a cluster of small oak trees, cross the bridge that leads to the playground, picnic area, and the parking lot.

NEARBY ACTIVITIES

In Oak Ridge Prairie County Park, you can catch the west end of the **Oak Savanna Trail** as it heads east for 6.25 miles to the community of Hobart. The paved trail follows an old rail bed alongside savannas, remnant prairies, wetlands, lakes, and residential neighborhoods. Catch another local rail-trail—the **Erie Lackawanna Trail**—0.7 mile south of the entrance to Oak Ridge Prairie Park on South Colfax Street. This trail runs through several small towns and neighborhoods as well as grasslands and wetlands between Hammond and Crown Point. The map board at the trail's Colfax Street Parking Area will help you plot your journey.

• •

GPS TRAILHEAD COORDINATES   N41° 31.000' W87° 23.632'

DIRECTIONS From I-90/I-94, take the Chicago Skyway (I-90) toll road 7.8 miles southeast into Indiana; at the state line, I-90 becomes the Indiana Toll Road. In 9.6 miles, take Exit 10 north toward IN 912/Gary Road/Cline Avenue. In 1.4 miles, turn left (south) on Cline Avenue/IN 912. Proceed for 4.6 miles; then turn left (east) on Ridge Road and drive 1 mile to North Colfax Street, where you'll turn right (south). The entrance to the park is 2.2 miles ahead on the left. Follow the park road 1 mile east to its dead end at the parking area.

This book's only Michigan hike, Warren Dunes is well worth the trip.   *Photo: Ted Villaire*

ONE OF THE most beautiful spots on Lake Michigan's southern shore, Warren Dunes is the perfect place to combine a trip to the beach with a ramble through rugged wooded dunes and bottomland forest. About a quarter of this hike runs along a beach that looks like more-remote beaches farther north along the Michigan shoreline.

DESCRIPTION

Located 12 miles north of the Indiana border, Warren Dunes is one of Michigan's busiest state parks. Despite the popularity of the park, the trails are relatively quiet. Nearly all the visitors come for the park's 2.5-mile-long beach. Some also come to hurl themselves down Tower Hill. Among the many soaring sand dunes at Warren Dunes State Park, the highest and best known is Tower Hill. During the summer, Tower Hill hosts a steady stream of adults and children scrambling up it and then running—or often tumbling—down.

After starting the hike from the northwest corner of the parking lot, follow the sign to the right (northeast) pointing to the campground. Right away the trail leads

DISTANCE & CONFIGURATION: 4.2-mile loop with smaller side loop

DIFFICULTY: Moderate because of a few steep and sandy climbs

SCENERY: Lake Michigan beach, sand dunes, wooded bluffs, forested bottomland, wetlands, creek

EXPOSURE: Mostly shaded except for the stretch on the beach

TRAIL TRAFFIC: Moderate

TRAIL SURFACE: Dirt, loose sand, wood chips

HIKING TIME: 2–3 hours

DRIVING DISTANCE: 85 miles from Millennium Park

ACCESS: April–September, daily, 8 a.m.–10 p.m.; October–March, daily, 8 a.m.–sunset. Visitors need a Michigan Recreation Passport to enter the park: $16/year at the front gate or $11/year with license-plate renewal for Michigan residents, $9/day or $32/year for out-of-state (prices are per vehicle).

MAPS: On trail board near campground and available at the website below; USGS *Bridgman, MI*

FACILITIES: Concessions, beach, beach house, restrooms, water, campground, picnic areas

WHEELCHAIR ACCESS: None

CONTACT: 269-426-4013, michigandnr.com /parksandtrails/#list (choose "Warren Dunes State Park")

LOCATION: 12032 Red Arrow Highway, Sawyer, MI 49125

COMMENTS: Dogs are prohibited on the section of the trail that runs along the beach but permitted elsewhere on the trail (on leash no longer than 6 feet). Though it's farther than 60 miles from Chicago, this hike is worth the trip because of its remote lakefront beauty. Because the dunes can be easily damaged by unofficial trails, please remain on the designated trails.

you into a dense woodland and then climbs a dune through an area with rolling ravines on each side of the trail. The first part of this hike brings you over a series of old dunes. Unlike younger, exposed dunes, these dunes are no longer pushed about by the wind. These older dunes and the ravines between them are blanketed with maple, oak, and beech trees, as well as an assortment of shrubs and wildflowers. After a short climb on a staircase, the trail continues to ascend and sides of the dune just keep getting steeper. While catching your breath at the top, you may be able to see the bottom of the dune nearly 200 feet down. To the west, Lake Michigan peeks through the occasional break in the trees.

Heading down the dune, keep watch for the bowl-shaped ravine on the right and the clifflike exposed dune on the left. As the trail takes a series of small dips and climbs, you'll pass flowering plants such as columbine and Solomon's seal. Sassafras and beech trees mixed in with the many specimens of oak and maple also line the trail. Farther along, you'll have more fine views of a ravine on the right as it tumbles precipitously downward. The trail briefly levels out before passing an unofficial spur trail heading up the dune to the right. From this spot, you'll descend a sandy path into a large marshy area. Sprinkled between log-strewn patches of open water are stands of cottonwood and maple and clusters of shrubs. Shortly after the trail meets flat ground, you'll encounter a couple of junctions; skip the

Warren Dunes State Park Loop

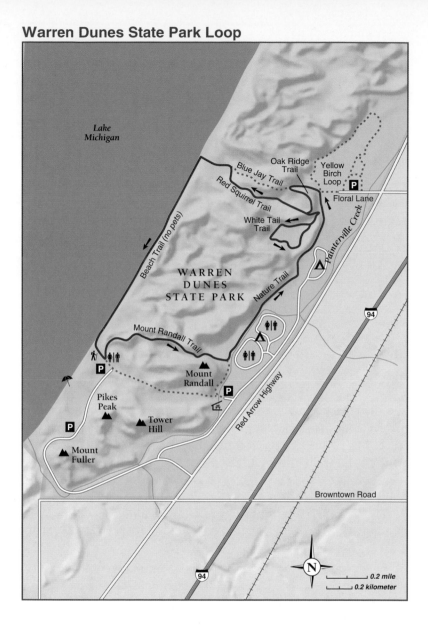

first left and take the second one (northeast) where the trail signs and map box are posted. You'll see that the trail to the right crosses Painterville Creek on a wooden bridge and enters the main campground.

In late summer and early fall, look for asters (clusters of small white flowers) lining the half-mile stretch of the trail that accompanies Painterville Creek. Follow the small spur trails on the right to get closer to the sandy-bottomed creek. While surveying the tannin-tinted creek, look for patches of watercress growing in the shallow spots. Unfortunately, it's not just the sound of the gurgling creek you'll hear on this stretch of trail. At this spot and other areas on the east side of the park, the hum of traffic announces the proximity of I-94 to the east.

Savanna gives way to woodland as you approach the concrete foundation of a former house. Stay left at a junction in front of the former house and pass through a grove of big maple trees, and continue straight ahead past the junction for the White Tail and Red Squirrel Trails on the left. Just ahead, take the next left (west) on the Blue Jay Trail.

The Blue Jay Trail wastes no time leading you out of the flat bottomland forest. The landscape changes quickly on the gentle sandy climb alongside a small ravine on the right. Just past an unofficial trail that heads up a steep incline on the right, the trail skirts the edge of a large area with open sand. At the junction, turn left (east) on the Oak Ridge Trail. The Oak Ridge Trail rises quickly and brings you on a switch-back climb through a maple forest. Peek down the steep left side of the dune to see the Blue Jay Trail below.

At the junction with the Red Squirrel Trail, turn left (east) and then, up ahead, turn right (west) for a quick loop on the White Tail Trail. The Whitetail Loop, surrounded by steep bluffs, occupies the flat bottom of a rounded ravine. The second half of the loop brings you by a grove of attractive hemlock trees growing on the side of a bluff. Finishing the White Tail Loop, stay to the left (west) on the Red Squirrel Trail, past the junction with the Oak Ridge Trail. (*Note:* If you're hiking with a dog, go right on the Oak Ridge Trail instead and retrace your steps to the traihead—the next segment heads to the beach, where pets are prohibited. There is, however, a designated dog beach past the northernmost swimming buoy, just north of this hike.)

As the Red Squirrel Trail gently roller-coasters through the wooded dunes, it runs through a small ravine and passes more hemlock trees. Once the trail leaves the woods and enters an open, grassy area, a great view of Lake Michigan appears in front of you. In the language of dune ecology, this area of mostly grass and patches of open sand is known as a blowout. It's like an amphitheater of sand, often with little vegetation growing within it because the sand is still on the move. This massive blowout is mostly covered with marram grass and the occasional sprinkling of oaks. As you journey down into the blowout, you'll pass the junction with the Blue Jay Trail.

Continuing straight ahead toward the beach, the trees thin out considerably and soon disappear, leaving just the hearty marram grass holding onto the sand. Once you've reached the wide, sandy beach, all that's left is turning left (southwest) and hiking 1 mile back to the parking area. On the walk back, however, you may want to take a closer look at several more blowouts (the largest by far is the one you just walked through). To get closer views of these strange and awesome sculpted sandscapes, follow the well-used trails from the beach, and try to retrace your steps as much as possible when you return.

NEARBY ACTIVITIES

If the weather is warm enough, consider a swim and a picnic somewhere along Warren Dunes' 2.5 miles of beautiful sandy beach. Or check out some of the restaurants, antique shops, and galleries that have sprung up in recent years along the **Red Arrow Highway** between the Indiana border and St. Joseph.

For more hiking in Warren Dunes, consider the **Yellow Birch** and **Golden Rod Loops** in the far northeastern corner of the park. Most of the Yellow Birch Loop runs along the edge of a large wetland (these trails may get mucky in the spring). Another option is to hike along the Warren Dunes beach north to **Weko Beach,** which is operated by the town of Bridgman. A round-trip hike between the Warren Dunes day-use area and Weko Beach is 5 miles.

Another nearby hiking option is **Warren Woods State Natural Area,** 3 miles north of Three Oaks. The park is home to the last mature beech–maple forest in southern Michigan. The 3.5-mile trail network runs through the forest and follow the Galien River.

• •

GPS TRAILHEAD COORDINATES N41° 54.575' W86° 36.193'

DIRECTIONS From the junction of I-90 and I-94 in Gary, Indiana, head northeast on I-94 into Michigan. In 41.7 miles, take Exit 12 west onto Sawyer Road. Proceed 0.6 mile; then turn right (north) on Red Arrow Highway, and drive 1.3 miles to the park entrance, on the left. Follow the park road to the beach, and park in the lot that's farthest north along the beach. The trail starts from the northwest corner of the parking lot.

OPPOSITE: An overcast sky softens the Lake Michigan shoreline at Warren Dunes.
Photo: Hank Erdmann/Shutterstock

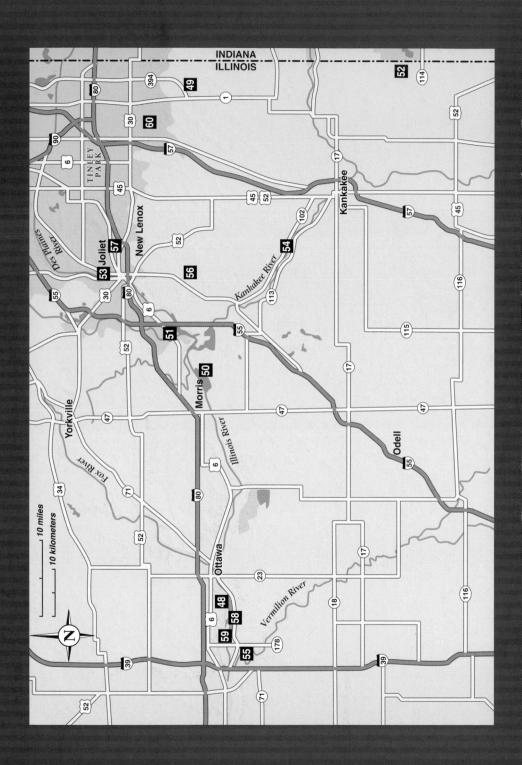

INDIANA
ILLINOIS

SOUTH CHICAGOLAND AND THE ILLINOIS RIVER VALLEY

Visitors explore the giant outdoor sculpture high above the Illinois River.   *Photo: Leslie Adkins*

LOCATED ON A bluff overlooking the Illinois River, this small but charming park is home to an enormous outdoor sculpture. Mounds representing five different creatures invite visitors to walk around and explore this engaging homage to an old Native American practice. Though it's more than 60 miles from Chicago, I've included this hike for the cultural interest.

DESCRIPTION

On a 90-foot-high mesa above the Illinois River, a 2,000-foot-long snake slithers along a rocky ledge, its head hovering on the riverbank. Nearby, an 18-foot-tall frog looks ready to spring over the high sandstone cliff into the river. Made from earthen mounds, these and three other creatures at Buffalo Rock State Park are part of an immense outdoor sculpture called *Effigy Tumuli*. Paying homage to the 4,000-year-old practice of mound building among Native Americans, artist Michael Heizer decided to depict creatures native to Illinois; the frog and the snake are accompanied by a catfish, turtle, and water strider. Commissioned in 1983 as part of an effort to reclaim 150 acres of strip-mined land polluted by toxic runoff, *Effigy Tumuli* is one of the largest sculptures in the nation since Mount Rushmore.

The signs posted for each mound reveal that each creature's shape is fairly geometric, as if each were covered with flat plates. Visualizing the sculptures as a whole requires some off-trail exploration as you put the pieces together and notice a leg here and an antenna there. The view from above can only be imagined once you have a

DISTANCE & CONFIGURATION: 2.5 miles

CONFIGURATION: Double balloon

DIFFICULTY: Easy

SCENERY: Cliffs and bluffs above the Illinois River, woodland, prairie, and giant mounds in the shape of a catfish, a turtle, a snake, a frog, and a water strider

EXPOSURE: Mostly exposed

TRAIL TRAFFIC: Light

TRAIL SURFACE: Dirt, gravel

HIKING TIME: 1.5 hours, plus extra time for exploring the mounds

DRIVING DISTANCE: 88.5 miles from Millennium Park

ACCESS: Daily, 8 a.m.–sunset; no fees or permits

MAPS: Available at the park office and the website below; USGS *Starved Rock, IL*

FACILITIES: Playground, restrooms, water, baseball diamond, vending machine

WHEELCHAIR ACCESS: None

CONTACT: 815-433-2224, www.dnr.illinois.gov /parks/pages/buffalorock.aspx

LOCATION: 1300 N. 27th Road, Ottawa, IL 61350

COMMENTS: Dogs must be leashed. Wear long pants if you intend to explore the mounds. Few paths exist on the mounds, and the grass grows several feet high. Kids will enjoy seeing the park's two American bison.

sense of what's on the ground. The best times to see the mounds are spring and early summer, when the grasses are short or matted, better revealing the shapes and lines.

As you enter the park on the steep park road, you'll pass a 40 to 50 foot sheer sandstone wall decorated with lichens, moss, ferns, and vines. Jewelweed and wild quinine grow near the base. At the top of the mesa, pull into the first parking lot on the left. The trail starts just beyond the restrooms at the bluff overlooking the river.

Before following the sign for the River Bluff Trail to the right, pay a visit to the observation platform and the short segment of trail at the top of the bluff off to the left. The rocky ledge 90 feet above the river provides a great view of the river to the east. While it's tough to tell from the overlook, the woodland on the opposite side of the river is actually a large island positioned at a wide point in the river. After following the bluff a bit farther to the left, turn around and begin the River Bluff Trail as it heads down a set of steps into an oak and hickory woodland. Shortly after passing a small ravine on the right, you'll notice a short connector trail to the parking lot on the right. Passing two more junctions on the right, you'll arrive at the edge of a prairie with a bench situated at another overlook. From here, a couple of islands are visible to the west in the river.

The trail continues between the heavily wooded bluff on the left and the prairie on the right. Along with big bluestem, Indian grass, and goldenrod, the prairie is peppered with thick stands of tasseled sedge grasses in the wet spots. At 0.6 mile, the trees disappear on the left, providing a great view of the river and the farmland and woods on the opposite shore. Continuing on, cottonwoods, quaking aspen, and varieties of pine rise up again on the bluff and then disappear.

At 0.8 mile, stay to the left at the junction, and you'll see the sign for the catfish, the highest of the five earthworks in the park. Although not all of the mounds have

Buffalo Rock State Park Hike

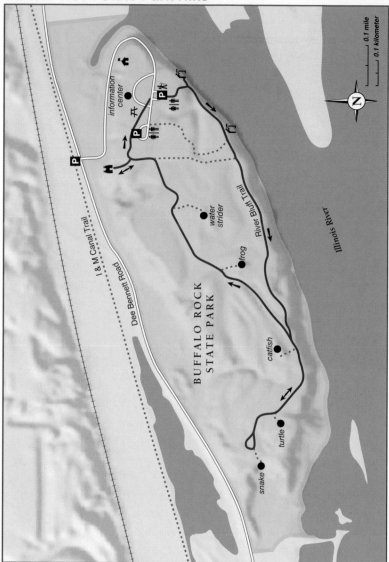

trails going up on top of them, visitors are invited to walk on and around them. Hiking to the top of the earthwork helps to provide a better view of the entire sculpture and gets you a little closer to the ideal vantage point—about 100 feet straight up.

After the catfish, the trail brushes next to the turtle's back left leg and its tail as it slides down the slope and into the river (based on the size of its tail, this turtle is a snapper). The artist incorporated the existing bluff to serve as the turtle's shell and preexisting mounds by the river to serve as the turtle's front legs.

Like the turtle, the snake appears as if it's heading over the bluff and into the water. Climbing up on the zigzagging back of the snake provides a nice view of the nearby sandstone cliffs and the river beyond the thick stands of cottonwoods. The name of the park came from the Native American practice of running buffalo off these cliffs. With seven different parts, the snake is the most complex of the mounds. If bushwhacking sounds appealing, you can get to the head of the snake by following the body of the snake to the right nearly to the tip of its tail. At the bottom of the bluff, head left toward the river and look for the 150-foot-wide head on the little promontory sticking into the river.

Heading back toward the parking lot, take a left at the catfish. As you get deeper into the prairie, the number of trees dwindles and the patches of sedge grasses grow larger and more frequent. Climbing up the gently rising back of the frog provides a nice view of the prairie and a view of the water strider just to the east. After passing through a grove of locust trees, you'll begin to see the patchwork of little ridges surrounding a low hump, which is easily accessible by following one of the water strider's two slender legs that come close to the trail.

After passing the water strider and returning to the woodland, turn left at the junction. This trail brings you to a platform with interpretive signs about the effigies. Continuing ahead, take the wood-chip trail to the left for a short walk to an overlook of the deep wooded ravine occupied by Dee Bennett Road and the Illinois & Michigan Canal. From the overlook, you'll see evidence of mining operations in the area. After the overlook, you can walk through the picnic areas to get back to the parking lot where you started the hike.

· ·

GPS TRAILHEAD COORDINATES N41° 19.601' W88° 54.600'

DIRECTIONS From the junction of I-55 and I-80 west of Joliet, drive 35.5 miles west on I-80 to Exit 90. Turn left (south) on Columbus Street, and proceed for 1.3 miles. Turn right (west) on US 6, and drive 1.2 miles to Boyce Memorial Drive, where you'll turn left (south). After 1 mile, veer right onto Ottawa Avenue. Buffalo Rock State Park is 4.6 miles ahead on the left. As you get closer to the park, the name of Ottawa Avenue changes to North 27th Road/Dee Bennett Road.

Crowds are light on the trails at Goodenow Grove.   *Photo: Maggie Wolff/magmilerunner.com*

IF YOU ARRIVE early, you'll likely have these rolling hills, open grasslands, wooded ravines, and winding creek all to yourself. This delightful forest preserve remains undiscovered by people outside of the immediate area.

DESCRIPTION

The 700-acre Goodenow Grove Forest Preserve has a lot to offer. Along with hiking and picnicking, there is primitive camping and a nature center with a number of exhibits to engage kids. In winter, the preserve clears a pond for ice skating and provides inner tubes for a sledding hill in the center of the preserve.

You might start this hike with a quick trip up the sledding hill for a view of the surrounding area. On the way down the hill, take the paved path to the right (west) leading into the next parking area. Stay to the right (north), and you'll enter dense oak woods. (Continuing straight will take you on the new 3.15-mile, crushed-limestone Plum Creek Greenway Trail, which runs through the southern and western parts of the preserve.) Take a left (north) on the dirt trail leading into a dense and lush woodland beside Plum Creek. Stay to the right (west) at the fork; the trail gains elevation and passes a few large oaks and scattered deadfall. A ravine containing bottomland forest and a section of Plum Creek opens on the right. As the trail takes a sharp turn left, it roughly follows the edge of this picturesque wooded ravine.

Returning to the gravel trail, head left (northeast) as the trail rises. Eventually, after crossing the park road, take the crushed-gravel Plum Creek Greenway Trail to the left (south). Stay on this crushed gravel trail as skirts the perimeter of the campground. Once you're away from the campground, take the first left (northeast).

As you climb a wooded hillside, the trail turns into a wide, mowed path and then passes a few buildings on the right. After the buildings, the trail curves left,

DISTANCE & CONFIGURATION: 2.9 miles, several connected loops

DIFFICULTY: Easy

SCENERY: Wooded ravines, creek, grassland, savanna, and ponds

EXPOSURE: Mostly shaded

TRAIL TRAFFIC: Light

TRAIL SURFACE: Dirt, mowed grass, pavement

HIKING TIME: 1.5 hours

DRIVING DISTANCE: 37 miles from Millennium Park

ACCESS: Daily, 8 a.m.–sunset; no fees or permits

MAPS: Available at nature center and online at map.reconnectwithnature.org/publicwebmap; USGS *Dyer, IN*

FACILITIES: Nature center, restrooms, water fountains, picnic tables and pavilions, rustic camping, and a wheelchair-accessible trail

WHEELCHAIR ACCESS: Only the initial paved trail

CONTACT: 815-727-8700, reconnectwithnature.org/preserves-trails /preserves/goodenow-grove

LOCATION: 27064 Dutton Road, Beecher, IL 60401

COMMENTS: Dogs must be leashed. In winter, the hill serves as a premier sledding destination. The Plum Creek Nature Center at Goodenow has exhibits that kids will enjoy.

drops into a short but steep ravine, and then enters an open space sprinkled with pines, oaks, apple trees, and shrubs.

Climbing a gradual hill, you'll have a nice view of the landscape that includes shrubs, thickets, and woods. From the hill, the trail swings left and then drops down next to goldenrod plants and sumac trees, and then runs through a wooded stretch before returning to the camping area. Once you reach the ring road around the camping area, follow the road to the right (west). After passing the parking area, take the spur trail right (west), which will take you back to the Plum Creek Greenway. Take a right (north) on the greenway. Staying left at the next couple of junctions will take you to the final section of this hike, called the Trail of Thoughts. Stay right as you follow the paved path over a boardwalk, past a few benches and a wet prairie. You'll see that the trail gets its name from the nature quotations posted on signs along the way. The scenery gets wetter as the trail continues past a small pond and past viewing platforms at the edge of a cattail marsh and Snapper Pond. Complete the loop and follow the trail back up the hill to the parking lot.

NEARBY ACTIVITIES

About 8 miles west of Goodenow Grove, 46-acre **Monee Reservoir** (708-534-8499, reconnectwithnature.org/preserves-trails/preserves/monee-reservoir) is popular with anglers, boaters, and picnickers and offers 2.5 miles of adjacent mowed-turf trails. Just east of the reservoir, on the other side of the Illinois Central Gulf Railroad tracks and Governors Highway, is the 210-acre **Raccoon Grove Forest Preserve** (815-727-8700, reconnectwithnature.org/preserves-trails/preserves/raccoon-grove). Its half-mile trail leads through gently rolling woodland and along the shore of Rock Creek.

Goodenow Grove Hike

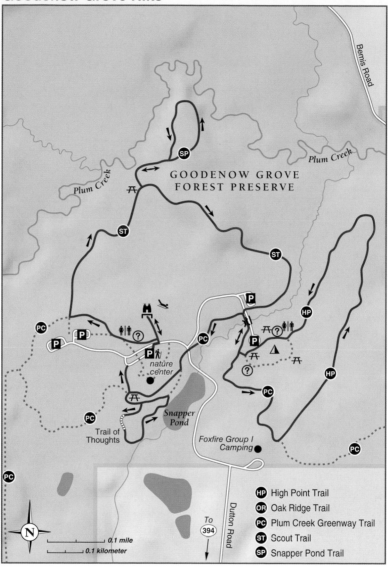

GOODENOW GROVE
FOREST PRESERVE

Plum Creek

Plum Creek

Bemis Road

nature center

Snapper Pond

Trail of Thoughts

Foxfire Group I Camping

Dutton Road

To 394

N

0.1 mile
0.1 kilometer

HP High Point Trail
OR Oak Ridge Trail
PC Plum Creek Greenway Trail
ST Scout Trail
SP Snapper Pond Trail

GPS TRAILHEAD COORDINATES N41° 24.119' W87° 36.359'

DIRECTIONS From the southern end of the Tri-State Tollway (I-294) in South Holland, exit south onto IL 394 toward Danville. Drive 14 miles; then turn left (east) on West Goodenow Road, and proceed for 1.2 miles. Turn left (north) on Dutton Road, and follow the signs to Plum Creek Nature Center.

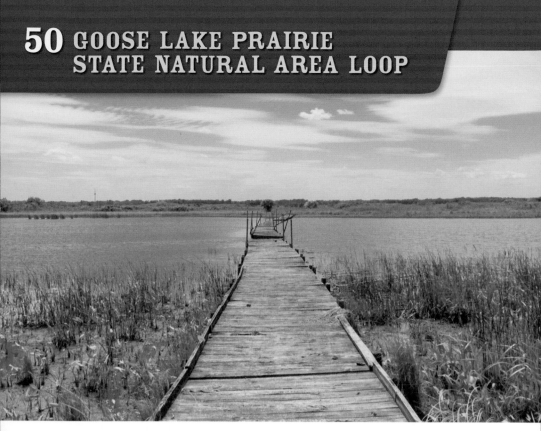

An interpretive boardwalk juts into the marsh.   *Photo: Brian Woolman/Shutterstock*

WHILE MAKING YOUR way through this hypnotic tallgrass prairie, you'll skirt the edges of several marshes and ponds active with birds. For those interested in improving their prairie-plant identification skills, this hike showcases a variety of grasses and flowers, as well as some interpretive signs to get you started. Near the end of the hike, the trail passes a reconstructed version of one of the earliest log homes in the county.

DESCRIPTION

Goose Lake Prairie is one of the few places left in Illinois where you get a sense of the expansive grassland that was so common here 150 years ago but was subsequently decimated by farming. This prairie was spared from the plow because of the stubbornness of the land: as far back as 1890, farmers tried to make this land conducive to agriculture by draining 1,000-acre Goose Lake; then, 35 years later, they dug drainage ditches to drain the water that remained in the marshes and ponds. Still, natural springs kept the ground too wet for farming.

With no chance for growing crops, farmers instead brought in livestock and allowed occasional mining. Along with coal, clay was pulled out of the former site of Goose Lake. The clay deposits attracted what was likely the first mass producer

DISTANCE & CONFIGURATION: 2.4-mile loop

DIFFICULTY: Easy

SCENERY: Tallgrass prairie, marshes, ponds, historic cabin, observation deck

EXPOSURE: Completely exposed

TRAIL TRAFFIC: Light–moderate

TRAIL SURFACE: Mowed grass

HIKING TIME: 1.25 hours

DRIVING DISTANCE: 64 miles from Millennium Park

ACCESS: Daily, sunrise–sunset; no fees or permits

MAPS: Posted outside visitor center; USGS *Coal City, IL*

FACILITIES: Restrooms, picnic areas, vending machine, and visitor center

WHEELCHAIR ACCESS: None

CONTACT: 815-942-2899, www.dnr.illinois .gov/parks/pages/gooselakeprairie.aspx

LOCATION: 5010 N. Jugtown Road, Morris, IL 60450

COMMENTS: Dogs must be leashed

of pottery in the state. Local-history buffs will enjoy an exhibit in the visitor center highlighting Jugtown Pottery Works, which started in 1856 and lasted for about 10 years in what is now the southwest corner of the park. Another exhibit at the visitor center displays plant and animal fossils from 300 million years ago that were dug up at a mining operation at Mazon Creek, south of the park.

Before you start the hike behind the visitor center, take in the view from the observation platform attached to the back of the building. If it's July, the prairie will be exploding with wildflowers of all shades; if it's September, goldenrod and compass plants will form a yellow carpet over the landscape. A few miles to the northeast, you'll see the Dresden Nuclear Power Plant; as you're hiking, you'll also notice another power plant, the Midwest Collins Generating Station, a couple miles to the west.

From the map board at the bottom of the platform's ramp, take the mowed trail on the right (east) winding through the prairie. In the wet areas, you'll see Indian grass, prairie cordgrass, and sedge grasses. Big bluestem grass, perhaps the most common of tallgrass prairie plants, lines the trail. Sometimes called "turkey foot" for the arrangement of its seed heads, big bluestem grows most attractively in the late summer, when it reaches heights of up to 10 feet and takes on various colors, from steely gray to wine red to muted lavender. In earlier times, livestock happily munched on big bluestem within this prairie. At 0.2 mile into the hike, you'll see evidence of the grazing that once took place here in the old windmill stand that pumped water out of the ground for the livestock.

Continuing on you'll pass a couple of smaller, cattail-fringed marshes—one with open water. Soon, take a right (east), and you'll come to the edge of a marsh where a rebuilt covered wagon with a bench inside is situated on a slight rise above the open water. Given the scarcity of trees near the pond, the wagon's canopy provides a welcome shady spot when the sun is hot overhead. In the vicinity of this marsh, I've seen great blue herons, a kingfisher, and a foot-long snapping turtle that became utterly peeved when I attempted to touch its shell.

Goose Lake Prairie State Natural Area Hike

During the warmer months, you'll see red-wing blackbirds perched on the tallgrasses and swallows swooping overhead. With the absence of trees, it doesn't appear that deer have many places to hide on the prairie. Keep alert, however, and you'll see how quickly they can disappear into the stands of bushes and taller grasses.

From the pond, stay to the right as you start the large rectangular loop. During the summer, tall compass plants grow on this section of trail, as do small crab apple trees and an attractive grass called Canada wild rye, which has a large, bushy, nodding seed head. Also, black-willow shrubs grow near the patches of open water on the left side of the trail. As the path curves left, a cattail marsh with open water appears on the right. The enclosed photo blind provides benches and small viewing doors that allow you to discreetly observe wildlife in the marsh. After passing another marsh on the right, look for obedient plants during late summer. (Obedient plants have lavender tubular flowers lined up on their stalks; if you bend the stalk, the plant "obeys" by temporarily staying bent, similar to a pipe cleaner.) This northern section of the park is dominated by Indian grass, which is often hard to identify until August, when the reddish-brown tassels and small yellow stamens come into bloom.

To finish the rectangular loop, turn right (west) on the gravel trail, which leads along the back side of the Cragg Cabin, a replica of one of the first homes in Grundy County. The next left takes you to the cabin. Originally built by the Cragg family in 1830 and located south of the park along the Mazon River, the cabin became a stopover for travelers and for cowboys who herded cattle from St. Louis to the stockyards of Chicago. The cabin, which sits at the edge of this pleasant pond bordered by a quaking aspen and willows, has been reconstructed a couple of times, most recently in 1980 by the Youth Conservation Corps. The small interior of the cabin is laid out much as it would have been 175 years ago, with a bed frame, a fireplace, and a ladder leading up to a second-floor loft. Stay to the right (west) after the cabin, and you'll hike along the edge of the pond back to the visitor center.

NEARBY ACTIVITIES

Adjacent to Goose Lake Prairie is **Heidecke State Fish and Wildlife Area,** a 2,000-acre cooling pond for Midwest Collins Generating Station. During fishing season, you can walk along the dikes accessible on the east side of the lake. Heidecke Lake hosts a variety of water birds and is a reliable spot for seeing bald eagles, particularly during winter.

• •

GPS TRAILHEAD COORDINATES N41° 21.666' W88° 19.079'

DIRECTIONS From the junction of I-55 and I-80 west of Joliet, head south on I-55 for 9.5 miles. At Exit 240, take Pine Bluff–Lorenzo Road to the right (west) for 2.9 miles. Turn right (north) at the sign for Goose Lake Prairie State Natural Area (North Jugtown Road). Proceed ahead for 1 mile, and then turn right (east) at the sign for the visitor center. Follow the park road 1 mile to the visitor-center parking lot.

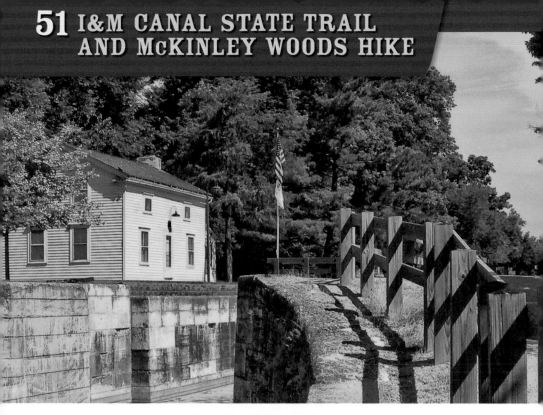

51 I&M CANAL STATE TRAIL AND McKINLEY WOODS HIKE

Lock tender's house at Channahon State Park   *Photo: Hank Erdmann/Shutterstock*

FOLLOW A SECTION of the historic Illinois & Michigan (I&M) Canal towpath along a sliver of land between the mighty Des Plaines River and the canal. Then, at the halfway point, leave the canal and explore the ravines and wooded bluffs at McKinley Woods, a Will County forest preserve.

DESCRIPTION

In 1848, the I&M Canal provided the final shipping link between the East Coast and the Gulf of Mexico. From Chicago, the canal angled southwest, running beside the Des Plaines River and the Illinois River halfway across the state to where the Illinois River was deep enough for boat traffic. Thanks to the 96-mile-long canal, Chicago quickly became the largest and most efficient grain market in the world.

From 1848 until 1900, the canal bustled with commerce. Channahon, which once claimed six grain elevators along the canal, is one of the many towns that were built up alongside the waterway. During most of the canal's lifespan, 150-ton canal boats were pulled along the towpath by mules or horses, usually guided by boys. Now, the towpath is an impressive 79.5-mile multiuse trail.

This hike runs along a section of the I&M Canal State Trail, southwest of Joliet where the DuPage and Des Plaines Rivers come together. After confluence of these

DISTANCE & CONFIGURATION: 8.1 mile out-and-back with double loop at the McKinley Woods end

DIFFICULTY: Moderate due to length plus some steep sections at McKinley Woods

SCENERY: I&M Canal and locks, Des Plaines River, wooded bluffs, marshy areas

EXPOSURE: Mostly exposed along the canal path, shaded at McKinley Woods

TRAIL TRAFFIC: Moderate

TRAIL SURFACE: Crushed gravel, dirt

HIKING TIME: 4 hours

DRIVING DISTANCE: 51.5 miles from Millennium Park

ACCESS: The Channahon State Park parking lot is open daily, sunrise–sunset; McKinley Woods is open daily, 8 a.m.–sunset; no fees or permits

MAPS: Available at the Channahon State Park office and at map.reconnectwithnature .org/publicwebmap; USGS *Channahon, IL*

FACILITIES: Water, restrooms, visitor centers, picnic tables, grills, camping

WHEELCHAIR ACCESS: None

CONTACT: 815-467-4271, www.dnr .illinois.gov/parks/pages/channahon .aspx (Channahon State Park); 815-727-8700, reconnectwithnature.org/preserves-trails /preserves/mckinley-woods (McKinley Woods)

LOCATION: Canal Street at Story Street, Channahon, IL 60410 (Channahon State Park)

COMMENTS: Dogs must be leashed

rivers, the Des Plaines and the canal arc around a series of steep bluffs and plunging ravines. This is where you'll leave the canal and enter the unusually rugged landscape of McKinley Woods.

From the Channahon State Park parking lot, head up a small hill to the white house that is one of only two lock tender's houses remaining along the canal. Lock tenders had to be available day or night to keep boat traffic moving by raising and lowering boats in the 12-by-100-foot locks. Fifteen locks, made from limestone blocks, were needed along the canal to raise and lower boats for 141 feet of elevation change between Chicago and the Illinois River.

From the lock tender's house, head left (south) over a footbridge that spans a small dam in the DuPage River. To the right is the dam's backwater, fringed with cattails and wetland. In several places along the canal, when the builders encountered another waterway, they constructed aqueducts for the canal to flow over streams. In Channahon, the builders had a different solution: here, the canal runs right through the DuPage River.

After crossing the river, the trail accompanies the canal under Bridge Street and then passes a parking area with restrooms. On the opposite shore of the canal, you'll see a few houses, a small stream that empties into the canal, and pastures for sheep and cows. On the left across the DuPage River is the site of the largest American Indian mounds in northern Illinois. The two mounds on the site were built between 1200 and 1500 A.D. The mounds were excavated in 1964, revealing 16 bodies. While the site is currently undeveloped, the state hopes to build a visitor center there in the future.

At about 0.75 mile into the hike, you'll pass the entrance to a new Will County preserve called Kerry Sheridan Grove. Until fairly recently, the preserve was a

I&M Canal Trail and McKinley Woods Hike

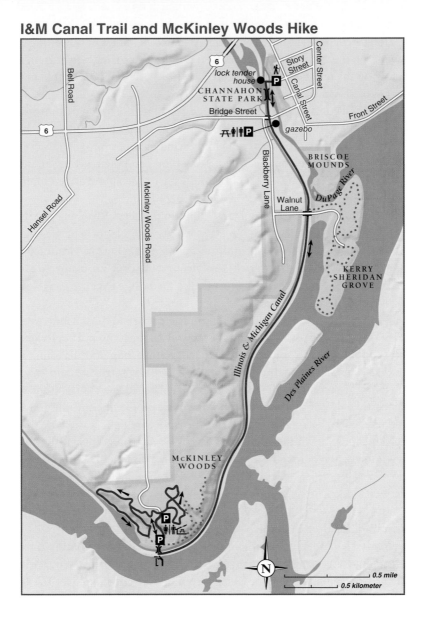

private resort on 525 acres jutting out into the Des Plaines River. Officially part of McKinley Woods, Kerry Sheridan Grove now contains 2.3 miles of mostly paved trails that run through open prairie and some wooded areas. Anglers love the many waterside spots in this park to cast a line. If you wanted to add some mileage to your hike, this would be a good place to do it: just turn left at the trail before the I&M Canal State Trail goes under Walnut Lane.

Continuing south on the I&M, the trail turns to gravel, and you begin a beautiful journey along a 15-foot-wide strip of land between two bodies of water: the 30-foot-wide canal is on the right, and the broad and mighty Des Plaines River is on the left. At the eddy on the left, look for waterbirds such as egrets and great blue herons, as well as signs of beaver activity.

Every half mile or so, squat limestone ledges appear on the left; these are great places to take a rest. With good weather, expect to see plenty of pleasure boats on the Des Plaines River. Barges may come lumbering by too, some as long as a couple of city blocks. After passing under a set of power lines and then passing an industrial plant on the far shore of the Des Plaines, you'll start to see the wooded bluffs rising on the right.

McKinley Woods is situated at a large bend in the river. Reaching the tip of the bend at 3.2 miles into the hike, you'll see a stone viewing platform at the edge of the river. The viewing platform, as well as the stone picnic shelters in McKinley Woods, were built by the Civilian Conservation Corps, which set up camp at McKinley Woods in the 1930s. Opposite the platform, take the bridge over the canal leading to the McKinley Woods picnic area.

From the picnic area, head up the hill on the park road for 0.2 mile to the next picnic area. Just past the parking area, take the trail to the right and keep right. You'll encounter footbridges and some ravines. Start another loop after finishing the first one, making your way through a flat landscape dense with shrubs and small trees. After finishing the second smaller loop, cross the park road and continue ahead. Soon you'll reach the edge of the bluff overlooking the Des Plaines and the I&M Canal. Large old oaks abound along this section of the trail. Stay right at the fork.

Before heading down the bluff, take a look at the landscape—if the leaf cover permits—immediately across the Des Plaines River. This was the location of another archeological site: a village of early Native Americans containing nine mounds and more than 50 lodges. Archaeologists report that the village was occupied as early as 500 B.C. and as late as A.D. 1675. Sadly, most of the village remained unexcavated by the time it was destroyed by a gravel-quarrying operation.

As you descend the bluff, a stream flows through the ravine on the right. After dropping about 60 feet, the path swings left alongside the canal. During springtime, look for the bright-pink flowers of Eastern redbud trees hanging over the water. A dock on the right provides a view of a wide, marshy part of the canal, frequented by birds such as herons, egrets, and kingfishers.

Eventually, the trail swings back up the bluff. (If you'd like to take a shortcut, you can cut through the campground you'll see on right for a quicker trip back to the I&M.) After returning to the picnic shelter, descending the park road, and then reconnecting to the I&M Canal State Trail, you'll enjoy a reverse view of the river on the way back to Channahon State Park.

NEARBY ACTIVITIES

Both Channahon State Park and McKinley Woods have small primitive camping areas. The best sites, operated by the state park, are the secluded walk-in sites between the canal trail and the Des Plaines River near McKinley Woods.

The 79.5-mile-long I&M Canal State Trail runs from Lemont to LaSalle. From end to end, the route wanders through a variety of landscapes: dense woods, marshes, prairies, riverbank, agricultural land, and small towns. Continuing west on the trail from McKinley Woods brings you to Dresden Dam and the only mule barn left standing along the canal (when the canal was built, mule barns were situated every 10–15 miles so the mules and horses could eat and rest before their next haul). The bluffs at McKinley Woods continue along the canal nearly all the way to Dresden Dam. Detailed maps of the trail are available at Channahon State Park, iandmcanal.org, and tinyurl.com/iacanalmap, among other sources.

• •

GPS TRAILHEAD COORDINATES N41° 25.384' W88° 13.675'

DIRECTIONS From the junction of I-55 and I-80 west of Joliet, head south on I-55 for 2 miles. At Exit 248, head right (southwest) on US 6 for 2.7 miles; then turn left (south) on South Canal Street. The entrance to Channahon State Park is three blocks ahead on the right.

A lush tree canopy shelters this stretch of trail. *Photo: John Baxter*

GLORIOUSLY REMOTE, IROQUOIS COUNTY State Wildlife Area offers a serene place to stretch your legs. During the summer, wildflowers decorate the sides of the trail, while bluebirds and woodpeckers dart among the stately oak trees in the savanna.

DESCRIPTION

The State of Illinois first started acquiring land at the Iroquois County State Wildlife Area in the 1940s in an effort to prevent the decline of the prairie chicken, a grouse-like bird that, despite the state's preservation efforts, disappeared from the Chicago region by 1974. While the prairie chicken didn't survive, the wildlife area did, largely as a hunting preserve. Surrounded by fields of corn and soybeans, this 2,480-acre wildlife area consists mostly of wetland and prairie in its southern half, while the northern and eastern sections are mostly woodland with patches of former cropland.

This hike starts in Hooper Branch Savanna Nature Preserve, a nearly 500-acre expanse within the wildlife area. Look for the wide, grassy trail heading north into the nature preserve directly across the road from Parking Area 8. Entering the preserve, you'll immediately notice the sandy soil left here by a glacial lake that receded

DISTANCE & CONFIGURATION: 2.15-mile barbell

DIFFICULTY: Easy

SCENERY: Oak savanna, prairie, wet prairie, marshland, woodland

EXPOSURE: Mostly exposed

TRAIL TRAFFIC: Light

TRAIL SURFACE: Grass

HIKING TIME: 1 hour

DRIVING DISTANCE: 81 miles from Millennium Park

ACCESS: Daily, sunrise–sunset except during hunting season (October–December); no fees or permits

MAPS: Available outside the headquarters building (corner of County Roads 3300 and 2800)

and at the website below; USGS *Donovan, IL-IN,* and USGS *Leesville, IL-IN*

FACILITIES: Picnic table, grill, and pit toilet at the parking area

WHEELCHAIR ACCESS: None on this hike, but a 1.2-mile trail near the headquarters building has an accessible 0.3-mile paved section

CONTACT: 815-435-2218, www.dnr.illinois .gov/parks/pages/iroquoiscounty.aspx

LOCATION: 2803 County Road 3300, Beaverville, IL 60912

COMMENTS: Dogs must be leashed; call before you go to check when access will be restricted

some 14,000 years ago. Near the beginning of the trail, you'll see a small mound rising on the right. Farther into the savanna, a dense layer of 5- to 6-foot-tall oak shrubs and smaller sumac shrubs blanket the sides of the trail. Rising above the shrubs are 40- to 60-foot-tall black and pin oak trees, many of which are shaped like funnels: wide at the top and narrowing quickly. A number of still-standing dead oak trees seem appealing to bluebirds, red-headed woodpeckers, and flickers.

Indian, porcupine, and big bluestem grasses grow in the open spaces on the sides of the trail. Mixed in with the prairie grasses are flowers such as partridge pea, thistle, goldenrod, and round-headed bush clover. Before turning right at the beginning of the loop, look for a large marsh 100 feet off to the right. Once you've started the loop, the oak canopy thickens, and the savanna briefly looks like a woodland landscape. After you pass open grassland on the right, the shrubs become thick on the sides of the trail. Once you've completed the loop, retrace your steps to the parking lot.

Continue the hike on the other side of the road in back of the picnic area. Taking the trail to the right brings you into a shrubby savanna and through stands of pine. At 0.4 mile into this section of the hike, you'll pass a trail junction on the right and see an enormous wet prairie through stands of shrubs. If you feel like doing a bit of bushwhacking, it's well worth a short walk out into this prairie, which is dominated by bluejoint grass, cordgrass, and sedges.

According to the Illinois Department of Natural Resources, the Iroquois State Wildlife Area contains one of the largest networks of wet prairie, sedge meadow, and marshes in Illinois (on the continuum of wetness, wet prairies are the driest, while marshes are the wettest). During the summer, the edges of this prairie are thick with yellow-flowered compass plants. Back on the trail, stay to the left (east) as you pass

Iroquois County State Wildlife Area Hike

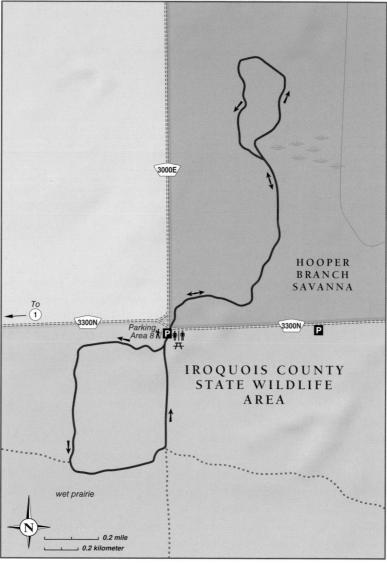

through groves of quaking aspen, and then stay left (north) again at the next junction. On the way back to the parking lot, the trail passes dense oak woodland speckled with ferns.

Note: As you hike the established trails mentioned here, you'll encounter a number of other wide, grassy trails along the way. While none of the trails in this wildlife area are marked, curious hikers with GPS devices handy can find plenty of pathways to keep them busy.

NEARBY ACTIVITIES

Just to the east and across the state line in Indiana is the enormous (10,000-acre) **Willow Slough Fish and Wildlife Area.** While it has no established trails, it does have plenty of doubletrack roads that you can explore on foot; pick up a map at the office, but call ahead at 219-285-2704 to find out when access is restricted due to hunting season. To reach Willow Slough from the trailhead for this hike, head north on County Road 3000 for 2 miles; then turn right (east) on CR 7000. In another 1.8 miles, turn right (south) on State Line Road (the Illinois–Indiana state line). The Willow Slough entrance is 3.4 miles ahead on the left.

You'll also find a few short hikes just north of Willow Slough at **Kankakee Sands,** a Nature Conservancy preserve that encompasses 30,000 acres straddling Indiana and Illinois. More trails will likely be built here in future years on this land that is slowly being returned from cropland to native prairie and savanna. On County Road 400 North just east of US 41, the preserve has a birding overlook and a bison-viewing area (in 2016, The Nature Conservancy reintroduced a herd of bison here to help restore the prairie). Go to tinyurl.com/kankakeesands for maps and more information.

• •

GPS TRAILHEAD COORDINATES N40° 59.707' W87° 33.668'

DIRECTIONS From the junction of I-57 and I-80 in Tinley Park, head south on I-57 for 32.6 miles. Take Exit 312 east (left) onto IL 17 (East Court Street). In 5.7 miles, turn right (south) on IL 1, and proceed 9.1 miles through the community of St. Anne. At County Road 3300N, turn left (east). The wildlife area's headquarters is 6.9 miles ahead on the right; the trailhead is 2 miles farther at the edge of Parking Area 8, also on the right.

These ruins provide a glimpse into Joliet's industrial past.   *Photo: Jeremy M. Farmer*

THE JOLIET IRON WORKS Historic Site provides a snapshot of how large-scale iron-making worked in the late 19th century. By reading the interpretive signs and wandering among the crumbling remains of buildings, you can trace the practice of iron-making from raw materials to the casting bed.

DESCRIPTION

In the 19th century, Joliet was known as the City of Steel and Stone. The stone was quarried from the nearby banks of the Des Plaines River, while the steel was produced at the Iron Works. Constructed in the 1870s, the Joliet Iron Works employed some 2,000 workers when production reached its peak at the turn of the century. Much of the steel made in Joliet went toward barbed wire and train-rail production.

For decades after the factory closed in the 1930s, the Iron Works lay forgotten. In the early 1990s, the Will County Forest Preserve bought the property and then opened the 51-acre site to the public in 1998. While much of the immediate area around the Iron Works is wooded, you'll see that the general location has maintained its industrial character; the railroad tracks on the right, which once served the steel mill, are still used today.

About 50 yards north of the parking lot, the first stop on the tour is the stock house, where the raw materials—iron ore, limestone, and coke—were stored. A sign

DISTANCE & CONFIGURATION: 1.3-mile loop

DIFFICULTY: Easy

SCENERY: Concrete-and-brick remnants of the historic Joliet Iron Works, wooded surroundings

EXPOSURE: Nearly all exposed

TRAIL TRAFFIC: Light–moderate

TRAIL SURFACE: Paved

HIKING TIME: 1 hour

DRIVING DISTANCE: 47.5 miles from Millennium Park

ACCESS: Daily, 8 a.m.–sunset; no fees or permits

MAPS: Posted at the south and north ends of the site and available online at

map.reconnectwithnature.org/publicwebmap; USGS *Joliet, IL*

FACILITIES: Bike racks, map board, benches, restrooms, interpretive signs

WHEELCHAIR ACCESS: Yes

CONTACT: 815-886.1467, reconnectwithnature .org/preserves-trails/preserves/joliet-iron-works -historic-site

LOCATION: Joliet, IL

COMMENTS: Dogs must be leashed. Keep a close eye on children and pets due to crumbling ruins. At the hike's halfway point, you can follow the Joliet Iron Works Heritage Trail to the left. This segment of the 11.4-mile Heritage Trail takes you to a lock in the historic I&M Canal (see previous hike).

along the path explains that the raw materials were transported by elevator nearly 100 feet up to be dropped in the top of the furnace. The next stop is the site of a blast furnace where the iron was made by heating raw materials to 3,500°F for 8 hours. After passing the casting bed, where the iron was molded for transporting, you'll see foundations of four more blast stoves.

Many of the explanatory signs along the path describe the often-dangerous jobs laborers performed at the mill. There are also plenty of photos of men who served in jobs such as stove tenders, clay busters, ladle liners, and cinder snappers. A few of the signs describe the laborers' lives outside of work. One sign displays a map of where the different ethnic groups lived in relation to the mill: the Western Europeans often lived farther away from the grime and noise of the mill, while the Eastern and Southern Europeans lived closer to the mill and tended to have the lower-paying jobs.

As you continue ahead, you'll see a series of octagonal and rectangular foundations that are remnants of the gas-washing plant, where gases were purified before they were burned in the furnace engines. Next, you'll see four-pass stoves that heated the air for Blast Furnace 4. After passing the doghouse, where workers monitored the stoves and the iron flow, the path heads up a set of stairs to Blast Furnace 3, a big bowl-shaped depression on the left. After Blast Furnace 4, follow the ramp down as you pass a large tunnel that penetrates layers of brick and concrete.

Across the railroad tracks, you won't miss the Illinois State Penitentiary, built by convict labor with locally quarried limestone in 1858 and codesigned by the same architect who designed the famous Water Tower in Chicago. The 25-foot walls of the penitentiary are 5 feet thick at their base. Closed since 2002, the castlelike prison was featured in *The Blues Brothers,* among many other films and TV shows. The next stop on the Iron Works tour looks more like the ruins of a lost city than part of a

Joliet Iron Works Hike

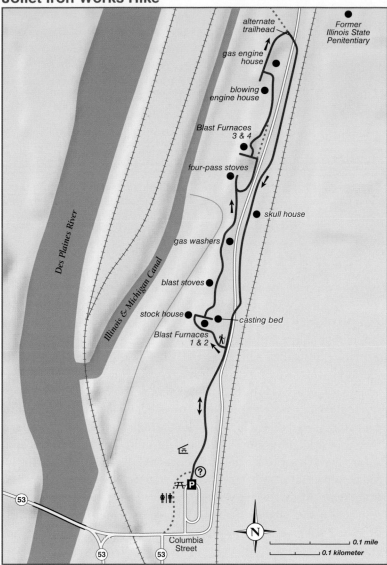

former factory. The large concrete footings at this site served as mounts for the enormous gas engines that powered the plant.

At 0.7 mile into the hike, turn right (south) and follow the gravel-surfaced Joliet Iron Works Heritage Trail back to the parking lot. You can also add some extra mileage to your hike by taking the Heritage Trail to the left. This multiuse crushed-limestone trail runs north along the Illinois & Michigan Canal for 11 miles to the town of

Lockport. A half mile north of the Iron Works, the Heritage Trail crosses a couple of bridges that span two former locks, which were used to raise and lower boats in the canal. Also along this section of trail you'll see another one of the state penitentiary's imposing guard towers.

Following the Heritage Trail to the right toward the parking lot leads you across a gravel road and close to the train tracks until it reaches the skull house. This is where workers known as ladle liners would clean the ladle cars, which transported molten iron around the plant for processing. After breaking up hardened iron residue with hammers and chisels, the ladle liners would reline the cars with fire bricks and clay so that the cars could be used again. From the skull house, the parking lot is 0.3 mile ahead.

NEARBY ACTIVITIES

For a thorough introduction to the Joliet area, visit the **Joliet Area Historical Museum** (204 N. Ottawa St.; 815-723-5201, jolietmuseum.org). The museum's main gallery covers seven distinct thematic areas: River City, the Canal, City of Steel and Stone, Metropolitan City, World War II, and the All-American City.

• •

GPS TRAILHEAD COORDINATES N41° 32.232' W88° 04.784'

DIRECTIONS From the junction of I-57 and I-80 in Tinley Park, head west on I-80 for 18.7 miles. At Exit 132, follow US 52/South Chicago Street left (north) for 1.7 miles through downtown Joliet (US 52 becomes IL 53/US 6/North Scott Street along the way). The Joliet Iron Works Historic Site will be directly in front of you at the T-intersection where Columbia Street heads left and right; turn right and immediately turn into the parking area on your left.

PUBLIC TRANSPORTATION Take **Metra**'s Rock Island District Line or Heritage Corridor Metra Line; both lines end in downtown Joliet. From the Joliet Station, follow Jefferson Street west for half a block, and then proceed 0.7 mile north on IL 53/North Scott Street to the historic site.

54 KANKAKEE RIVER STATE PARK HIKE

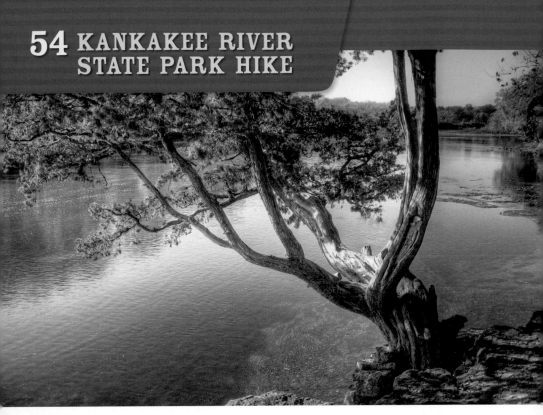

A tree perches precariously at the edge of the bluff. *Photo: Jason Sheputis*

THE FIRST SECTION of this river hike takes you along the wooded bluffs above wide sections of the Kankakee River. After crossing a pedestrian suspension bridge, you'll follow Rock Creek along a dramatic canyon to a gentle waterfall.

DESCRIPTION

The focal points of Kankakee River State Park are the craggy cliffs and vertical walls of Rock Creek Canyon as it gently curves toward the Kankakee River.

This beautiful and dramatic canyon has been captivating visitors for many generations. At the time of the first European contact, the Miami Indians were numerous along this part of the Kankakee River; by 1770, Indians from the Potawatomi, Chippewa, and Ottawa tribes—known as the Three Fires—dominated the area. The last Indian settlement at the confluence of Rock Creek and the Kankakee River was a sizable Potawatomi village. Most of the Potawatomi had been removed by the end of the decade, except for Chief Shawanasee, who lived the rest of his life here and whose grave is commemorated with a boulder along a trail in the northern section of the park. Established in 1948, the park was greatly expanded over the years largely from land donated by Commonwealth Edison. Now Kankakee River State Park is 11 miles long and encompasses 3,932 acres, straddling both sides of the Kankakee River.

DISTANCE & CONFIGURATION: 4.8-mile out-and-back

DIFFICULTY: Easy

SCENERY: Kankakee River, bluffs, limestone canyon along Rock Creek

EXPOSURE: About half exposed and half shaded

TRAIL TRAFFIC: Moderate

TRAIL SURFACE: Paved path, dirt

HIKING TIME: 2.5–3 hours

DRIVING DISTANCE: 61.7 miles from Millennium Park

ACCESS: April 1–October 31, daily, 7 a.m.–10 p.m.; November 1–March 31, daily, 7 a.m.–6 p.m.; no fees or permits

MAPS: Available at the park office and the website below; USGS *Bourbonnais, IL*

FACILITIES: Picnic areas, concession stand, bike and canoe rentals, camping, restrooms, visitor center, water fountains

WHEELCHAIR ACCESS: None

CONTACT: 815-933-1383, www.dnr.illinois.gov /parks/pages/kankakeeriver.aspx

LOCATION: 5314 W. IL 202, Bourbonnais, IL 60914

COMMENTS: Dogs must be leashed. Exercise caution when looking out from the ledges along Rock Creek, especially if you've brought kids or pets along. The seasonal concession stand offers ice, vending machines, bait, and canoes and bicycles for rent.

Before you start out from the Warner Bridge Road parking lot, I suggest taking a short walk to the right along the river to see the limestone pillars built to support a train bridge in the late 19th century. The bridge was never finished, however, because financiers ran out of money before the railroad was completed. Heading back toward Warner Bridge Road, the trail runs under the bridge before turning left and making a steep climb. At the top of the hill, you'll pass a farm and an agricultural field on the left before the trail turns right toward the river. For the next mile the trail glides along the side of this wooded bluff about 40–50 feet up from the river's edge. In some places, the drop to the river is steep enough for the park to have erected steel fencing along the trail. The season that you're hiking will determine how well you can see the river: if the leaf cover is heavy, look for occasional openings in the shrubs that will allow you to see shorelines in the distance and the low islands. Shortly after passing a picnic table with a shelter overlooking the river, the trail curves left up a hill toward the suspension footbridge spanning Rock Creek.

The bridge offers a great vantage point from which to enjoy the beginning of this dolomite rock canyon. The stone walls—sometimes vertical, sometimes slanted or steplike—become even more pronounced as you head upstream. On the other side of the bridge, at 1.6 miles into the hike, turn left (north) to cross IL 102. On the other side of the highway, continue ahead, ignoring the old EMERGENCY ACCESS sign.

Approach the cliffs on the left with care: there are no guardrails between you and a 50- to 70-foot drop to the water. Oak trees are often thick at the top of the cliff, but there are dozens of spots that allow for viewing the dramatic canyon and the river. At 0.3 mile after crossing the highway is a sign indicating that the waterfall is a half mile ahead. Just beyond the sign, the dilapidated pavement ends and the wide dirt path begins. To the right, a line of pine trees starts to run parallel to the trail. In a

Kankakee River State Park Hike

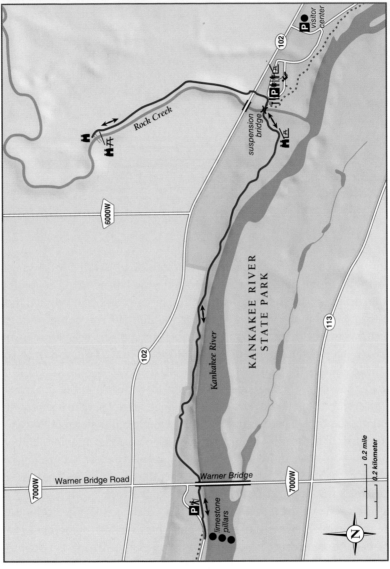

few places, you'll see horse trails heading off to the right into the shrubby woodland. While these trails are on park-owned land, hiking on them is not encouraged.

At the next picnic table, look upstream for a view of the waterfall, which makes a sloping descent for about 8 feet. Enjoy the view while you can: according to the Illinois State Geological Survey, the waterfall is moving upstream at a rate of 3 inches per year. If you continue ahead, there's another perch where you can look out directly above the falls. This is also where you'll see the chain-link fence signaling that it's time to turn around and head back toward the highway.

Back across IL 102, the park visitor center is 0.15 mile to the left. Along with a few mounted animal and bird specimens, the visitor center hosts an impressive collection of fossils and arrowheads—nearly all of which were found in the park.

Heading toward the Kankakee River from the visitor center, you'll come upon a paved path that runs next to the river. To the left, the path runs 1.8 miles through riverside picnic areas, near the community of Altorf, and next to the site of an old mill and distillery. From there, the path's surface turns to crushed limestone and runs for 3.7 miles near the park's Potawatomi Campground and through a secluded wooded area with a few scattered marshes, streams, and savannas. The trail, which is a great route for biking or hiking, ends at the Davis Creek Group Camping Area.

Heading to the right along the Kankakee River and back toward the beginning of the hike brings you past a couple of lookout platforms above the river. Near the covered pedestrian bridge is a knoll with a fenced-off cemetery at the top. Most of the graves are those of infants and children from the Smith family, who died from yellow fever at the turn of the century. Heading back toward the suspension bridge brings you past the log-cabin concession stand and the restrooms. From the bridge, retrace your steps 1.6 miles back to the parking lot on the other side of Warner Bridge Road.

NEARBY ACTIVITIES

The park offers canoe rentals; staff can drop you off in the town of Kankakee for a 10-mile paddle back to the park. Call 815-932-6555 for reservations. Learn about the park's riding stables by calling 815-933-1383.

In addition to the trails described here, there's a long equestrian loop that can be hiked on the other side of the river, and there are trails in Area A in the western tip of the park; check in at the visitor center to find out if hunting season is under way at either of these spots. For information about the park's two campgrounds, call 815-933-1383 or visit reserveamerica.com.

• •

GPS TRAILHEAD COORDINATES N41° 12.548' W88° 00.825'

DIRECTIONS From the junction of I-57 and I-80 in Tinley Park, proceed south on I-57 for 22.7 miles. At Exit 322, head west on County Highway 9/West 9000 North Road) for 8.2 miles. Turn left (south) on North County Highway 20/Warner Bridge Road/North 7000 West Road, and proceed for 2.7 miles. Shortly after you cross IL 102, the signed parking lot is on the right, just before the bridge over the Kankakee River.

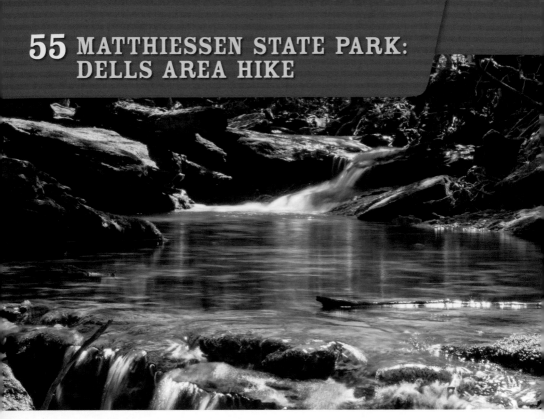

This small cascade is fed by spring rains.   *Photo: Eddie J. Rodriquez/Shutterstock*

FORMERLY A PRIVATE retreat for a local industrialist, Matthiessen State Park features a narrow, mile-long canyon carved in sandstone by a stream. Beginning at the dam and lake at one end of the canyon, you'll encounter a couple of dramatic waterfalls while exploring the moist and shady canyon floor and the wooded bluffs above.

DESCRIPTION

Overshadowed by the far more popular Starved Rock State Park 2 miles to the north (see Hikes 58 and 59, pages 272 and 276), Matthiessen State Park is often unjustly ignored by the many visitors to this area. Although the 1,938 acres at Matthiessen State Park don't offer as many miles of trails nor as many canyons as Starved Rock, they still have plenty of geological charm—plus a much quieter atmosphere.

A LaSalle businessman named Frederick William Matthiessen, who reportedly employed some 50 people to build the trails, bridges, stairways, and dams, first developed the area as a private park. Matthiessen also built a not-so-modest summer home with 16 bedrooms and 9 baths, along with a smaller mansion for one of his children. While Matthiessen's structures no longer remain, visitors will see the handiwork of his grounds crew in the dams, stairs, and soaring concrete footbridges. By 1940, 22 years after Matthiessen's death, his heirs donated the property to the state.

DISTANCE & CONFIGURATION: 2.2-mile loop with out-and-back segment

DIFFICULTY: Easy–moderate

SCENERY: Sandstone canyons, waterfalls, wooded bluffs, lake, high footbridges over creek

EXPOSURE: All shaded

TRAIL TRAFFIC: Moderate

TRAIL SURFACE: Gravel, dirt

HIKING TIME: 1.5–2 hours

DRIVING DISTANCE: 97.5 miles from Millennium Park

ACCESS: Daily, 8 a.m.–sunset; no fees or permits

MAPS: Available at trailhead and the website below; USGS *LaSalle, IL*

FACILITIES: Picnic tables, pavilion, water, flush toilets

WHEELCHAIR ACCESS: None

CONTACT: 815-667-4868, www.dnr.illinois.gov /parks/pages/matthiessen.aspx

LOCATION: Utica, IL

COMMENTS: Cross-country ski rentals are available December–March when weather permits. Maps at horse-trailer parking areas show the routes for 13 miles of equestrian trails available at Matthiessen. Horse rentals are available on IL 71, a half mile west of IL 178.

Similar to those at Starved Rock, the beautiful sandstone walls at Matthiessen were carved out by centuries of flowing water. The mile-long canyon at Matthiessen is nearly 100 feet deep in places and ranges from 50 to 140 feet wide. The section closest to the dam and Matthiessen Lake is called the Upper Dells, and the path of the canyon closest to the Vermilion River is called the Lower Dells. A dazzling 40-foot waterfall separates the two sections of the canyon.

From the parking lot, head toward the small log fort, which is a replica of forts the French built in the Midwest during the 1600s and early 1700s (the French constructed one of these forts on Starved Rock in 1683). Start the hike by heading down the stairs and taking the first trail to the right (east). This elm-lined, wide gravel trail follows the bluff above the creek deep within the sandstone canyon on the left. At 0.2 mile, as the path starts to curve, you'll begin to see rock on the other side of the canyon and hear a couple of waterfalls down below. Stay to the left as you pass over the creek flowing through a culvert under the trail (the trail to the right leads to the horse-trailer parking area).

Continuing on the other side of the canyon underneath a canopy of sugar-maple trees, the trail soon becomes paved. Before crossing the bridge over Lake Falls, pay a visit to the overlook on the left for your first view of the Lake Falls as it drops 40 feet from the top of a dam to the floor of the canyon. This might be the most attractive human-made waterfall in the state of Illinois. After crossing the bridge, which provides a nice view of the wooded banks of Matthiessen Lake and the falls underneath, the first trail on the left brings you down closer to the falls and then descends to the floor of the Upper Dells.

On the canyon floor, you can gingerly step through a mix of sandstone, rock, and mud to get a better view of the falls. Mosses, liverworts, and ferns grow on the damp, shady, 30- to 40-foot walls of the canyon. Farther along in the canyon, solid

Matthiessen State Park: Dells Area Hike

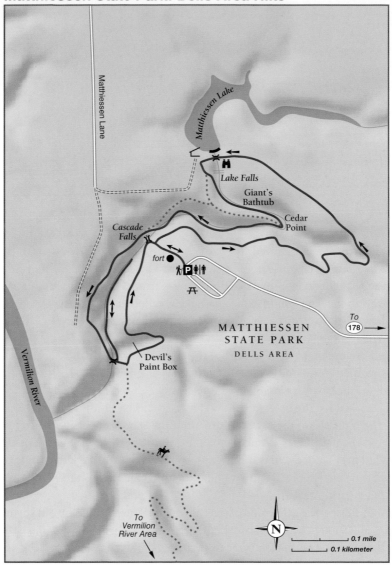

sandstone channels the stream over a small waterfall that empties into the pool called the Giant's Bathtub. Geologists say these pools develop and grow larger by the action of rocks and pebbles getting swirled around. As you continue ahead, several places require using boards and rocks to cross the stream. As the canyon curves to the right at a place called Cedar Point (due to the abundance of cedar trees), continue ahead past stairs leading up to the bluff.

Farther ahead, take the stairs out of the canyon and then follow the sign for the Lower Dells and proceed along the bluff, passing Cascade Falls on the left. After walking along the bluff, cross the bridge and follow the stairs to the Lower Dells. The short box canyon on the right is called the Devil's Paint Box, because the walls are decorated with swaths of yellow, orange, and brown, formed by minerals seeping out of sandstone. In the main canyon, look for spots where lichen has changed the rock to light green. Look for changes in the texture of the walls, too: some sections are smooth and flat, while others are rough, pitted, and almost grotesque. The cracks in the walls form much like the cracks in pavement during the winter, growing bigger and chipping apart when water freezes inside.

Similar to the trails at the Upper Dells, the trail here alternates between mud and rock and requires stream crossing via large rocks and concrete blocks. More trees grow in this canyon, particularly sugar maples, some of which are draped with vines. At the end of the canyon, listen for the soothing echo created by the 40-foot natural waterfall.

Heading back up the stairs, turn left at the sign for the fort and parking lot. Turning right at this junction leads to the Vermilion River Area within the park (see Nearby Activities section). Heading toward the parking lot, the trail rises and then curves left. Complete the hike by climbing the stairs back up to the parking lot.

NEARBY ACTIVITIES

South of the Dells Area, the **Vermilion River Area** within the park offers 1.9 miles of hiking along the wooded bluffs above the river. While there are no canyons in this section of the park, there is exposed rock in places, and there is a striking view from a high bluff. Drive to the Vermilion River Area by heading south on IL 178 from the Dells Area entrance.

• •

GPS TRAILHEAD COORDINATES N41° 17.765' W89° 01.555'

DIRECTIONS From the junction of I-55 and I-80 west of Joliet, drive 45 miles west on I-80. Take Exit 81 south (left) to Utica. Proceed south along IL 178 for 5.1 miles, passing through North Utica and over the Illinois River. The signed entrance to the Matthiessen State Park Dells Area is on the right.

These old ammo bunkers seem eerily out of place in this peaceful prairie setting.   *Photo: Darius Norvilas*

ONCE THE LARGEST munitions plant in the world, Midewin National Tall-grass Prairie is now the biggest—and most tranquil—piece of protected land in northeastern Illinois. While the adjacent farmland isn't terribly scintillating, there are plenty of other parts that make up for it: a pioneer cemetery, a lovely pond with a picnic area . . . and dozens of ammunition bunkers.

DESCRIPTION

Established in 1996 as the first National Tallgrass Prairie in the United States, Midewin is an enormous work in progress. Converting the former Joliet Army Ammunition Plant into what will be the largest swath of tallgrass prairie in the country is a multidecade project with a goal that is reflected in its name: in the Potawatomi language, *midewin* means "healing."

Today, about half of Midewin's 20,000-plus acres are open to the public. The property includes some 34 miles of trails, most of which are multiuse trails for hikers, bikers, and horseback riders; many of these trails, including the ones on this hike, are former roads from the days of the arsenal. At its peak, the Joliet arsenal employed some 10,000 people and produced 5.5 million tons of TNT a week. In operation from World War II through the Korean and Vietnam Wars, the arsenal was shut down in 1975, leaving 1,300 structures, 200 miles of roads, 166 miles of rail bed, and 392 concrete bunkers that were used to store the TNT.

While there's plenty of natural beauty to enjoy on this hike, be aware that the infrastructure left from the arsenal can feel a tad postapocalyptic—as if it were a battleground in a war against the zombies. The removal of old infrastructure has

DISTANCE & CONFIGURATION: 8.6-mile loop with out-and-back section

DIFFICULTY: Moderate–strenuous

SCENERY: Wooded areas, farmland, multiple streams, pond, prairie, and abandoned munitions bunkers

EXPOSURE: Mostly exposed

TRAIL TRAFFIC: Light

SURFACE: Gravel doubletrack, mowed grass, pavement

HIKING TIME: 3.5–4 hours

DRIVING DISTANCE: 56 miles from Millennium Park

ACCESS: Daily, 4 a.m.–10 p.m.; no fees or permits

MAPS: Available at Midewin Welcome Center and the website below; USGS *Elwood, IL*

FACILITIES: Restrooms and picnic tables near the parking lot and at Turtle Pond

WHEELCHAIR ACCESS: First mile only

CONTACT: 815-423-6370, www.fs.usda.gov /main/midewin/home

LOCATION: Just south of Hoff Road at South Chicago Road, Wilmington, IL 60481

COMMENTS: Dogs must be on leash no longer than 8 feet. Midewin is changing as the U.S. Forest Service slowly develops a more-extensive network of trails. Watch out for heavy farming equipment in the area. A herd of bison roams 1,200 acres in the central portion of Midewin.

progressed slowly due to the complexity of the project and limited funding. In the eastern section of the park, where this hike takes place, the government leased out land to local farmers; this farmland is slowly being converted back to tallgrass prairie or various types of bird habitat.

Start the hike by passing through the chain-link fence and heading straight ahead (south) on the old asphalt road. As you pass under the high-tension power lines and get farther into the park, farmland opens up on both sides of you, occasionally interrupted by small stands of trees. Soon you'll start to notice that the only thing you hear are the calls of birds and the sound of the wind. Unless you're hiking in July, in the middle of the winter wheat harvest, or in October, when it's time for the soybean harvest, you may notice that Midewin is one of the quietest places in the Chicago region. Enjoy the silence. Relish it. Squeeze it dry.

The serene ambience gets even better when you arrive at Turtle Pond, 1 mile into the hike. Created for the enjoyment of the arsenal employees, Turtle Pond is pleasantly fringed with cattails, sedge grasses, and trees hanging over the water. On one trip here, the peaceful atmosphere at the pond prompted me to take an alfresco nap. When I awoke, I watched a line of wild turkeys pecking their way across a recently harvested field of winter wheat.

After making the short loop around Turtle Pond and passing through the small picnic area, head right on the Twin Oaks Trail as it shoots straight east. Soon you'll cross a small winding creek, the first of many that you'll see snaking through this landscape. As the Twin Oaks Trail turns left, keep straight ahead on the Bailey Bridge Trail. This is where you'll catch your first glimpse of the concrete bunkers rising from the ground. The roofs and sloped sides are covered in dirt and grass, giving the appearance of wrinkles in a vast green carpet. Placing earth on top of the bunkers served the dual purpose

Midewin National Tallgrass Prairie Hike

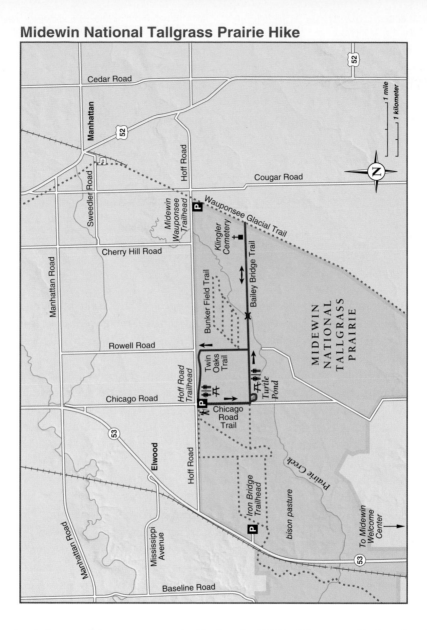

of maintaining a stable temperature inside for the TNT while camouflaging the sites from aerial view. The bunkers were specifically designed with thin roofs and thick walls so that if one blew, it would blow upward, preventing a chain reaction of explosions.

Just ahead, another bridge crosses another small creek, followed by a much larger structure, called a Bailey bridge, spanning the larger Prairie Creek. Built with prefabricated parts according to a standardized design, Bailey bridges first gained popularity during World War II because they could be assembled and positioned with common hand tools. This Bailey bridge, built in 2006 according to an interpretive sign, looks like a tank would have no trouble crossing it.

Less than 1 mile ahead, the trail runs through an area dense with bunkers. Piles of railroad ties appear now and then as a reminder of the many miles of railroad tracks that once crisscrossed the arsenal. This is also where the farmland gives way to grazing land, which is why barbed wire fencing lines both sides of the trail. At one point, you'll encounter steps going over the fence, offering access to the bunkers. While none of the doors are open on these bunkers, you can get a closer look at the structures. If cows are grazing nearby, give them plenty of space.

As you leave the bunkers behind, tiny Klingler Cemetery soon appears ahead on the side of the trail. You can enter the gates to inspect the 50 or so gravestones set within a small grove of pine trees. Started by a settler from Pennsylvania in 1877 as a place to bury his family and neighbors, the cemetery is one of six pioneer cemeteries within Midewin. Before reaching the end of the Bailey Trail about 0.3 mile ahead, you'll cross three more bridges straddling scenic winding creeks.

The end of the Bailey Bridge Trail roughly intersects the halfway point of the Wauponsee Glacial Trail, which runs from the outskirts of Joliet to the Kankakee River. (For a full description of this 22-mile rail-trail, see my book *Best Rail Trails Illinois,* published by FalconGuides.) At the Wauponsee Glacial Trail, it's time to turn around and retrace your steps 2.3 miles to the Twin Oaks Trail.

After returning to the Twin Oaks Trail and turning right (north), you'll soon have another opportunity to explore the bunkers. A second set of steps over the fencing leads to a several-mile-long trail that traces the perimeter of the bunker field. As you continue north on the Twin Oaks Trail, small clusters of trees come and go, and as the trail curves to the left for the final stretch of the hike, big silver grain silos rise from the farm operating across Hoff Road. The trail curves slightly as it parallels Hoff Road and runs alongside acres of shrubby greenery on the right and intermittent marshy spots and small stands of trees on the left. When you reach the asphalt road that you started on, the parking area is just to the right.

· ·

GPS TRAILHEAD COORDINATES N41° 23.608' W88° 04.660'

DIRECTIONS From the junction of I-355 and I-80 in New Lenox, head west on I-80 for 7 miles. At Exit 132, go right (south) on US 52/IL 53. In 6 miles, at the CHICAGO ROAD/ BROWN CEMETERY sign, turn left (east) on Brown Road; then immediately turn right (south) on South Chicago Road. The trailhead parking lot is 2.2 miles ahead on the right, just across Hoff Road.

Pilcher Park's Bird Haven Greenhouse   *Photo: Lotzman Katzman/Flickr*

PILCHER PARK OFFERS an appealing mix of graceful ravines, lush bottom-land forest, and small winding streams. Toward the end of the hike, you'll see a couple of area landmarks from the 1920s: a still-used public water well and the Bird Haven Greenhouse.

DESCRIPTION

Harlow Higginbotham, an important figure in Chicago during the late 19th century, once owned Pilcher Park. Higginbotham was the president of Chicago's 1893 Columbian Exposition, a world's fair commemorating the 400th anniversary of Columbus's arrival in the Americas. After the exposition, Higginbotham used many of the trees that were part of the exhibits to establish a private arboretum on this property. Specimens such as Southern magnolia, sweet gum, cypress, tulip tree, pecan, black birch, and various hickories were added to a park that already contained about 75 native species of trees.

In 1920, Higginbotham sold the arboretum to Robert Pilcher, a businessman, self-taught naturalist, and "sturdy pioneer," according to the inscription on his statue near the park's nature center. Eventually, Pilcher donated his 327 acres of virgin woodland to the city of Joliet, with the stipulation that the land be left wild. Higginbotham's name is preserved across the road from Pilcher Park in a natural area called Higginbotham Woods (see Nearby Activities).

Your first stop at Pilcher Park ought to be the attractive log cabin–style nature center. Outside stands a large, colorful totem pole, built in 1912. Inside, kids will enjoy the

DISTANCE & CONFIGURATION: 3.3-mile loop

DIFFICULTY: Easy

SCENERY: Bottomland forest, ravines, streams, river, a historic well, and an impressive public greenhouse

EXPOSURE: Mostly shaded

TRAIL TRAFFIC: Moderate

TRAIL SURFACE: Dirt with sections of new pavement and deteriorating asphalt

HIKING TIME: 1.5 hours

DRIVING DISTANCE: 43 miles from Millennium Park

ACCESS: The park is open daily, sunrise–sunset; the nature center is open June–August, 9 a.m.–

4:30 p.m., and September–May, 9 a.m.–3 p.m.; no fees or permits

MAPS: Available at the nature center and the website below; USGS *Joliet, IL*

FACILITIES: Nature center, restrooms, picnic tables, and shelters

WHEELCHAIR ACCESS: None

CONTACT: 815-741-7277, jolietpark.org /pilcher-park-nature-center

LOCATION: 2501 Highland Park Drive, Joliet, IL 60435

COMMENTS: Dogs must be leashed. To find out about special flower shows at the Bird Haven Greenhouse, call 815-741-7278.

turtle pond and several habitats containing fish, snakes, and birds. Also inside is a large window where you can watch the park's birds (and squirrels) dine at a cluster of feeders.

To begin the hike, follow the sign for the Green Trail at the nature center. After the trail dips down to meet the edge of a small pond, continue on the Green Trail to the right (north). Just ahead, the trail passes over several drainage culverts before crossing a gravel path and then the park road. On the other side of the park road, the landscape starts to rise.

Reaching the hilltop, the terrain levels, and the trail curves left and runs above a pleasant wooded ravine containing an intermittent stream. At 0.6 mile into the hike, where several asphalt trails come together, follow the sign for the Purple Trail on the right (east). Right away, the Purple Trail enters a flat and dense woodland with a few intermittent streams. After passing an open area where a number of small- and medium-sized trees have been cut, the path starts to lose elevation. Just after crossing a stream, you'll see the beginnings of an expansive wooded ravine on the left. Farther ahead is a nicely situated bench where you can pause and take it all in.

From the bench, the trail descends gradually through a mature oak forest before curving right and passing a trail junction. When you reach the gate at the park road, keep straight ahead on the park road and look for the Light Blue Trail (also called the Artesian Trail). After crossing the wooden footbridge, you've suddenly entered a flat bottomland forest. Up ahead, beyond the paved service road, the Woodruff Golf Course appears on the left. Taking a right at the fork leads you over a footbridge, across the park road, and into a picnic area with tables, a shelter, an open grassy area, and the Flowing Well, drilled in 1927 to a depth of 207 feet. You'll likely see people filling their water bottles here; according to the park district, the water's mineral content and 51°F temperature have remained constant since the well was first

Pilcher Park Loop

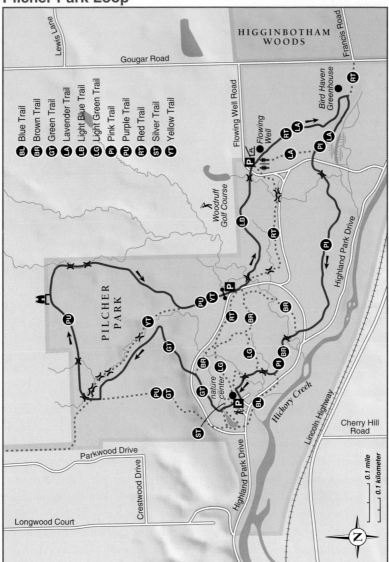

dug. If you don't mind the slight taste of iron and other minerals common in well water, take a drink.

From the well, follow the paved Pilcher Interpretive (Lavender/Red) Trail to the left of the restrooms heading southeast for 0.3 mile to the Bird Haven Greenhouse, which hosts indoor plants and flowers, outdoor formal gardens, seasonal flower shows, and a children's garden. The greenhouse, designed by the same architectural firm that designed the Central Park Greenhouse in New York City, was built in 1929 and underwent a major renovation in 2003. Displayed in front of the greenhouse is the original clock face from the Will County Courthouse, built in 1887 in Joliet.

Proceeding with the hike, find the Pink/Lavender Trail heading west at the back of the greenhouse just to the left of the paved path. A quarter mile from the greenhouse, continue on the Pink Trail as it passes a small pond and a marshy area thick with shrubs on the left. Soon the trail crosses a park road and a footbridge, then heads back into the bottomland forest; here, you may see wildflowers such as jack-in-the-pulpit, spring beauty, mayapple, and red trillium. Crossing the park road again, keep straight ahead, soon reaching a footbridge over a small rocky stream. After crossing another footbridge, the trail runs next to the park road and Hickory Creek. At the junction with the Trail of Oaks, bear left (west), and the nature center should be visible through the trees. Cross one final footbridge, and then turn left on the Pilcher Interpretive Trail, which runs toward the back side of the nature center.

NEARBY ACTIVITIES

Higginbotham Woods, also owned by the Joliet Park District, is across Gougar Road from Pilcher Park. You can walk an old gravel road that traverses the preserve from east to west. It's accessible from a parking area on the north side of Francis Road, about 0.6 mile east of Gougar Road. At the entrance to the parking area is a large boulder with an inscription describing a French fort that was allegedly built on this land in 1730. Archeological studies show, however, that the supposed remnants of the fort are actually earthworks created by Native Americans of the Hopewell Period (200 B.C.–A.D. 400).

• •

GPS TRAILHEAD COORDINATES N41° 31.980' W88° 01.339'

DIRECTIONS From the junction of I-355 and I-80 in New Lenox, head west on I-80 for 2.1 miles. At Exit 137, head northwest on US 30/Lincoln Highway for 2.4 miles. Turn right (north) on South Gougar Road, and follow it 0.3 mile until you see the signed entrance for Pilcher Park on the left. Here, turn left and, in 0.3 mile, turn right (north) at the intersection. In 0.6 mile, keep right at another intersection, and drive 0.5 mile farther. Turn left on Highland Drive, and shortly turn left again into the signed parking lot for the nature center.

PUBLIC TRANSPORTATION Pilcher Park is 2.5 miles from the New Lenox Station on **Metra**'s Rock Island Line. From the station, head north on North Cedar Road; then turn left on West Francis Road, which ends at Gougar Road. Just after you cross the road (be careful of traffic here), the Pilcher Interpretive Trail heads west just left of the parking lot; follow it about 1 mile to the nature center.

A small waterfall flows in shaded Ottawa Canyon.   *Photo: Eddie J. Rodriquez/Shutterstock*

THE EASTERN SECTION of Starved Rock State Park offers canyons galore, each with slightly different shapes, sizes, and colorings. Cool and shady, overgrown with ferns, trees, and flowering plants, the numerous canyons on this hike are a delight to explore. You'll also encounter scenic overlooks 100 feet above the Illinois River.

DESCRIPTION

Though Starved Rock State Park is more than 60 miles from Chicago, I'd be remiss in leaving it out: not only is it the most popular state park in Illinois, it's a must-hike destination. While the views from atop its bluffs and cliffs are spectacular and well worth a visit, the real showstoppers at Starved Rock are the numerous sandstone canyons that were carved deep into the bedrock as upland streams drained into the Illinois River. During the wet seasons, waterfalls cascade through some of the canyons. In the winter, dramatic ice sculptures take the place of the waterfalls.

The hike starts with an exploration of the longest and one of the widest canyons at the park. At the east end of the parking lot, follow the wide dirt trail south as it heads underneath a canopy of cottonwoods. After a short way, you'll notice cliffs rising up beyond the trees on both sides of the trail. The farther you hike, the closer

DISTANCE & CONFIGURATION: 6.4-mile out-and-back with short loop

DIFFICULTY: Moderate

SCENERY: Numerous deep sandstone canyons; several rocky cliffs overlooking the Illinois River and surrounding woodland

EXPOSURE: Shaded

TRAIL TRAFFIC: Very busy at popular times

TRAIL SURFACE: Dirt

HIKING TIME: 3–4 hours

DRIVING DISTANCE: 93.5 miles from Millennium Park

ACCESS: Daily, 5 a.m.–10 p.m.; no fees or permits

MAPS: Available at the visitor center and starvedrockstatepark.org; USGS *Starved Rock, IL*

FACILITIES: Restrooms are available in nearby parking areas; otherwise all facilities, including the visitor center, are at the western end of the park.

WHEELCHAIR ACCESS: None

CONTACT: 815-667-4726, www.dnr.illinois.gov /parks/pages/starvedrock.aspx

LOCATION: IL 71, Utica, IL 61348

COMMENTS: Dogs must be leashed. Exercise caution on the rims of the canyons. This section of the park tends to be quieter compared with the western end. When the weather is wet, these trails can become flooded and muddy.

the walls come to the trail—in some places, the sandstone walls are streaked with yellow on what looks like a bleached-white background. Sugar maples and basswood thrive on the wide canyon floor, and jewelweed grows thickly on the edges of the shallow creek that accompanies the trail. Watch your step while crossing the creek on a jumble of logs, rocks, and concrete blocks. A large fallen cottonwood may offer a pleasant spot to sit and admire the scenery like a small waterfall emptying into a serene pool. Heading back toward the parking lot, you may consider exploring parts of the canyon off the main trail; getting closer to the sides of the canyon will enable you to see some of the small cavelike openings at the base of the sandstone walls.

Continue west at the other end of the parking lot. From here, the trail runs through another parking lot and then crosses a bridge over a stream. After the bridge, stay left (south) and head up a small hill, following the sign for the Council Overhang. The overhang is an impressive white sandstone cavern 40 feet high and 30 feet deep. Following the sign for Kaskaskia Canyon to the left brings you to a narrow trail winding along a streambed that turns into a series of puddles during the summer. The walls of this canyon are sometimes craggy and in places shaded with bluish-green lichen. At the end of the canyon, in springtime, water flows from a moss-covered shelflike opening that sits above a small shallow pool. Continuing on to Ottawa Canyon, you'll notice that the tall, straight walls create a darker and damper atmosphere. If you're hiking on a hot day, you'll notice the moist air and cooler temperatures upon entering the canyons.

Back at the junction on the other side of the Council Overhang, stay to the left (west) as you navigate a steep, rough section of the path, and then mount a flight of stairs leading up to the park road. On the other side of the park road, another flight of stairs takes you up to a trail that leads along the bluff. At 2.4 miles into the hike,

Starved Rock State Park: East Hike

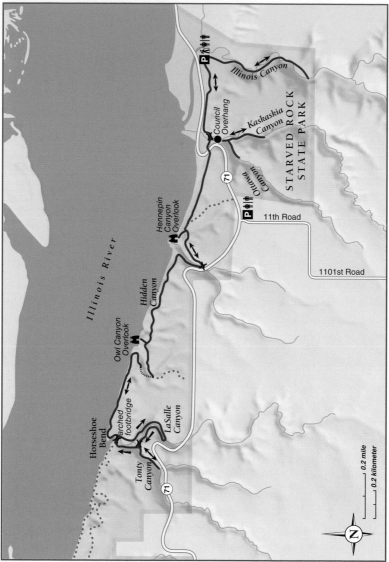

pass a trail on the left that branches to a parking lot, and then follow a side trail that leads to the Hennepin Canyon Overlook. At the overlook, the Illinois River is almost a mile wide; nearly 2 miles to the left is Starved Rock Lock and Dam. From the overlook, the trail turns inland and moseys along the bluff above Hennepin Canyon. The park road is right above as you pass over a bridge crossing the stream that drops into the canyon.

After the bridge, the trail runs between a fence and a concrete embankment and then back out to the bluff's edge. Just beyond the steep cliffs of Hidden Canyon, you're afforded another great view of the Illinois River at the Owl Canyon Overlook. Passing a trail leading to another parking lot, you'll descend a bluff and drop to the river's edge via a long set of stairs. Watch for the thick, knotty roots that emerge from the surface of the trail on this stretch along the riverbank. Just before the arched footbridge, turn left into LaSalle Canyon. As the trail runs along a terrace at the base of the wall, the canyon narrows, and the sandstone surface becomes pitted and lightly grooved. Farther along, the beige stone takes on a gold color and pits become potholes. At the end of the canyon, a steady waterfall pours off an overhang and into a small basin before flowing out toward the river.

Heading out of LaSalle via the terrace on the opposite wall, you'll cross a bridge and then turn left before crossing a longer bridge. Coming into the next canyon, Tonty, feels a bit like you're entering a jungle: the air is damp, while ferns and vines grow on the canyon walls. Jewelweed and sedge grasses grow beside the slow-moving stream on the canyon floor. At the end of the canyon, instead of a waterfall, there's a steady drip coming down from the overhang, with caverns underneath. If you decide to climb around on the low-banked walls, you'll notice that the sandstone is wet with the consistency of sugar and is easily scratched with a fingernail.

Retrace your steps out of Tonty Canyon, taking a left at the bridge and then crossing a couple more bridges and several short flights of stairs before arriving back on the riverside trail. Once you reach the river, turn right and cross the arched bridge over the 20-foot-wide creek flowing out of the two canyons. From the bridge, stay to the left for (east) 2.2 miles back to parking lot.

• •

GPS TRAILHEAD COORDINATES N41° 18.527' W88° 56.314'

DIRECTIONS From the junction of I-55 and I-80 west of Joliet, head west on I-80 for 35.4 miles. At Exit 90, turn left (south) on IL 23/Columbus Street, and proceed 2.7 miles, passing through the community of Ottawa. Then turn right (west) on IL 71/Hitt Street, and drive 4.1 miles. Continue past the Lone Point Parking Area on the right and the Salt Well Parking Area on the left, and park in the Illinois Canyon Parking Area, the next parking area on the left.

French Canyon on an early-fall morning   *Photo: Eddie J. Rodriquez/Shutterstock*

AFTER HIKING THROUGH deep sandstone canyons, you'll encounter a series of overlooks from the wooded bluffs and rocky cliffs high above the Illinois River. This classic northeastern Illinois hike requires considerable stair climbing.

DESCRIPTION

While there are dozens of points of interest throughout Starved Rock State Park, the dominant feature is a narrow bluff that runs 4 miles along the south bank of the Illinois River between Ottawa and LaSalle. Carved deeply in the sandstone of the bluffs are narrow canyons of varying lengths. In the western section of the park, where this hike takes place, visitors can't help but notice what is perhaps the most popular attraction in the area: the sandstone pedestal from which the park gets its name. Topped by white pines and cedar, Starved Rock towers 125 feet above the river, offering a commanding view of the nearby islands, the surrounding wooded landscape, and the river, particularly to the east, where it swells to a width of nearly a mile.

Artifacts such as human bones and weapons reveal that different groups of Native Americans lived on and used the rock for nearly 10,000 years. In 1682, the French took advantage of the easily defended location on the rock and built a fort as part of their plan to keep the British from gaining control of the Mississippi River Valley. (On display in the park's visitor center is a miniature model of this fort built

DISTANCE & CONFIGURATION: 2.9-mile loop, with options for increasing or decreasing the distance

DIFFICULTY: Strenuous, primarily because of the number of stairs

SCENERY: Sandstone canyons, wooded bluffs, rocky cliffs—all at the edge of the Illinois River

EXPOSURE: Nearly all shaded

TRAIL TRAFFIC: Can be heavy at popular times

TRAIL SURFACE: Dirt, sand, wooden boardwalk and stairs, and short paved sections

HIKING TIME: 2 hours

DRIVING DISTANCE: 93.5 miles from Millennium Park

ACCESS: Daily, sunrise–sunset; no fees or permits

MAPS: Available at the visitor center and starvedrockstatepark.org; USGS *Starved Rock, IL*

FACILITIES: Visitor center, snack shop, campground, picnic areas

WHEELCHAIR ACCESS: None

CONTACT: 815-667-4726, www.dnr.illinois.gov /parks/pages/starvedrock.aspx

LOCATION: IL 71 at IL 178, Utica, IL 61348

COMMENTS: Dogs must be leashed. This is the most popular part of the most popular state park in Illinois. Avoid the crowds on summer weekends by visiting very early in the day. Exercise caution on the canyon rims. When the weather is wet, trails along the river can be flooded and muddy. A 133-site campground is a couple of miles southeast of the visitor center.

by a group of students and teachers in Aurora.) The formation got its name from a legend about a group of Illinois Indians who fled to the rock for protection while being pursued by Fox and Potawatomi Indians. The Fox and Potawatomi were seeking revenge because one of the Illinois Indians had killed their leader, Chief Pontiac. Unable to escape, the Illinois Indians eventually starved to death.

Start the hike on the paved path that runs on the left (east) side of the visitor center, and follow signs for French Canyon and the lodge. Soon the trail runs alongside a ravine that grows into a canyon featuring 50- to 60-foot-high moss-covered walls. Before taking the stairs up toward the lodge, be sure to follow the trail farther into the French Canyon, where it dead-ends in a rounded chamber of layered sandstone. In French Canyon and in other canyons throughout the park, you'll see variety in the surface of the stone: in some places the sandstone is deeply pitted and ridged, while in others it's smooth and flat. The sandstone takes on different colors, too—sometimes it's green and moss-covered, or bleached and nearly white, or it may be covered in various shades of blue and green lichens.

After you climb the stairs out of French Canyon, the trail offers a great view from above the rocky walls as it follows the canyon's upper lip. Once you've passed the trail on the right leading to the lodge, take the next left (south) on the East Bluff Trail as it crosses a bridge, which spans the now-intermittent stream that once carved out French Canyon. From the bridge, the trail winds along on the opposite side of French Canyon and then traverses a high bluff. Along the bluff, the elms, oaks, and conifers open in places to provide striking views of the river and the opposite bank. After reaching a high point and then following a flight of stairs and a boardwalk, stay to the right at the junction, heading toward Wildcat Canyon.

Starved Rock State Park: West Hike

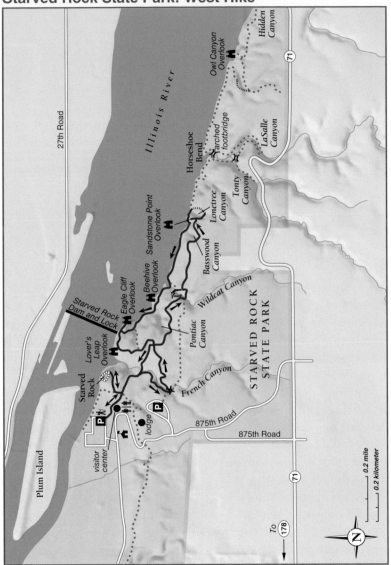

On the way to Wildcat Canyon, you'll encounter the smaller Pontiac Canyon and take in sweeping views of the Illinois River before mounting more stairs and boardwalks. Soon you'll arrive at a lookout platform that offers a stunning view of Wildcat Canyon as it opens to the river. As you follow the boardwalk to the viewing platform on the opposite side of the canyon, look for the cliff swallows entering and leaving their mud nests built under the rocky overhangs.

From Wildcat Canyon, follow the signs for Sandstone Canyon. Not long after passing Basswood Canyon, the trail arrives at Sandstone Point, the final overlook before the trail descends to the river. After the overlook, the trail skirts the edge of Lonetree Canyon and then leads you down a long series of steps.

At the bottom of the stairs, take the trail to the left along the wooded riverbank (taking the trail to the right leads to trails on the east side of the park; see previous hike). As the junctions come and go along this busier section of the hike, keep following signs to Starved Rock.

Soon you'll head up a set of stairs to Eagle Cliff, which provides a great view high above the dam. On a cold day in January, during my first visit to this spot, I saw a half-dozen bald eagles soaring above the river, waiting for dead fish to turn up in the open water by the dam. (Attracted to the open water by the dam, bald eagles begin to arrive in November and grow in numbers into January and February.) Continuing on, the platform at Lover's Leap provides a great view of the rocky pedestal of Starved Rock.

Getting closer to the visitor center, follow the paved road through the woods and the stairs up to Starved Rock. On the west side of the observation platform, look for Leopold Island No. 1 on the right and the larger Plum Island on the left. (In recent years, Plum Island was spared from a massive development plan that would have eliminated prime habitat for bald eagles during the winter.) From Starved Rock, the visitor center is just a couple of signposts away.

NEARBY ACTIVITIES

The stone-and-log **Starved Rock Lodge** on the park property was built by the Civilian Conservation Corps in the 1930s. The hotel offers 72 rooms and 22 cabins, along with an indoor swimming pool, saunas, a whirlpool, and an outdoor sunning patio. The lodge's original great room is a comfortable space centered around a massive stone fireplace. The restaurant, open seven days a week, serves a number of house specialties. For rates and reservations, call 800-868-7625 or visit starvedrockstatepark.org.

• •

GPS TRAILHEAD COORDINATES N41° 19.278' W88° 59.631'

DIRECTIONS From the junction of I-55 and I-80 west of Joliet, head west on I-80 for 44.5 miles. At Exit 81, turn left (south) on IL 178 and proceed 3.3 miles, passing through the town of Utica. The entrance to Starved Rock State Park is on the left, about 0.4 mile after you cross the bridge over the Illinois River. Follow the signs to the visitor center.

This 156-year-old church houses Thorn Creek Woods' nature center.   *Photo: Rich Whitehead*

THIS LIGHTLY USED nature preserve is a gem: after exploring the ravines, the pine plantations, the wooded hills, and the streams surrounded by bottomland forest, you may enjoy a visit to the former country church that now serves as a nature center.

DESCRIPTION

Considering how much it has been hauled around the neighborhood, the little wooden country church that serves as the Thorn Creek Woods Nature Center is in surprisingly good condition. An Emmanuel Evangelical Lutheran congregation built the church in 1862 several miles northwest of its present location. After 100 years, Emmanuel Lutheran gave the church to Village Bible Church of Park Forest, which moved it just north of the nature center off Monee Road. Ten years later, when the Village Bible Church built a new structure, the congregation passed the

DISTANCE & CONFIGURATION: 2.5 miles, 2 connected loops

DIFFICULTY: Easy–moderate **SCENERY:** Ravines, bottomland/upland forest, pine plantations, creeks, pond

EXPOSURE: Nearly all shaded

TRAIL TRAFFIC: Light

TRAIL SURFACE: Dirt, some gravel

HIKING TIME: 1 hour

DRIVING DISTANCE: 37 miles from Millennium Park

ACCESS: Trails open daily, sunrise–sunset; nature center open Friday–Sunday, noon–4 p.m.; no fees or permits

MAPS: Posted at all trail junctions, available at the nature center, and online at map.reconnectwithnature.org /publicwebmap; USGS *Steger, IL*

FACILITIES: Restroom, water, picnic tables

WHEELCHAIR ACCESS: None

CONTACT: 708-747-6320, reconnectwithnature.org/preserves-trails /preserves/thorn-creek-woods

LOCATION: 247 Monee Road, Park Forest, IL 60466

COMMENTS: No dogs allowed. A bird checklist is available for free at the nature center.

old church to the Village of Park Forest. The village spruced it up and put it on a new foundation in its present spot.

Inside, where generations of churchgoers came to hear ministers preach, school-kids now sit in the pews while park naturalists explain the features of the Thorn Creek Woods Nature Preserve and surrounding areas. The large pulpit, elevated 8 feet above the pews, now contains an action-packed taxidermy scene of a red fox chasing a Canada goose through a cattail marsh. Visitors of all ages will enjoy touring the nature center's displays of preserved animal specimens; lichens found in the area; bones, skulls, and arrowheads; photos of animals and plants found in the preserve; and a small nature library in the gallery upstairs. There are also photographs of the farm that occupied the preserve in the early 1900s.

Currently comanaged by the state, the county, and two nearby villages, the nature preserve was formed in the 1960s when private and governmental organizations joined forces to save the property from development.

The hike starts in the backyard of the nature center, on a gravelly path that immediately crosses a bridge over an intermittent stream. As the trail starts to descend a slight hill, watch for the logs half-buried on the trail surface that serve to direct runoff away from the trail. Stay right (east) at the first junction, and you'll soon enter a bottomland forest of black walnut, swamp white oak, basswood, ash, and slippery elm. After passing a second junction on the left, the trail mounts a bridge over Thorn Creek—which may dry up into a series of isolated pools during the summer. Following a short boardwalk, the trail flattens out and winds through a grove of maples.

Soon a shallow ravine develops on the left, and a much deeper 50-foot ravine plunges down on the right. Dominated by maple, ash, and red oak, this ravine contains a tributary of Thorn Creek. As you proceed, listen for wind whispering through

Thorn Creek Woods Hike

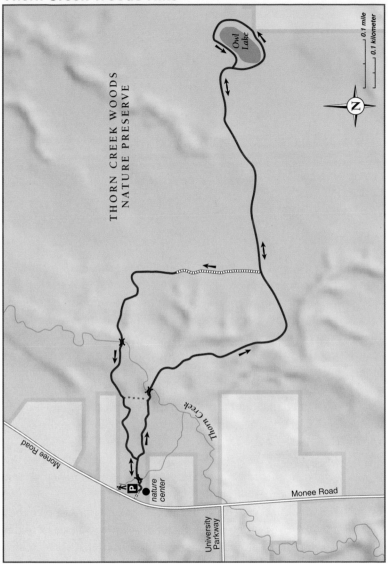

groves of red and jack pines planted by farmers in the 1950s (both red and jack pines' needles are in clusters of two, but the red's needles are up to 6 inches long, while the jack's are only 1.5 inches long). According to the bird checklist available at the nature center, these pine plantations provide some of the best bird-watching spots in the 880-acre preserve.

As the path curves left, the landscape flattens and the woods are unwrapped from the dense canopy. In these upland areas, you'll see white and red oak; shagbark hickory; and, after passing the junction with the boardwalk on the left, white pine (needles in clusters of five). On this straight and flat route to Owl Lake you'll see a small cattail pond, pasture roses, and open fields beyond the trees on the right.

After circling Owl Lake (really more pond than lake), head back to the junction where the boardwalk starts on the right (north). While traversing the 0.2-mile board-walk, you may notice a variety of fern species growing in the wet soil on the sides of the platform. Leaving the boardwalk behind, you'll head back toward Thorn Creek and notice that the landscape begins to drop down on the left. After passing an enormous section of a concrete drain duct, the trail takes a sharp left, drops down the slope, crosses a bridge, and then enters a bottomland forest along a 50-foot section of board-walk. For the remainder of the hike, look for thick trunks belonging to 150-year-old white and red oaks: the white oaks tend to grow in flat spots, while the reds often grow on the slopes. Stay right at the next two junctions to return to the parking lot.

NEARBY ACTIVITIES

Crete is a pleasant village with tree-lined streets and tidy front yards planted with flowers. The village is home a number of antiques shops and some charming restau-rants. Farther south on IL 1, horseracing fans are drawn to the **Balmoral Park Race Track.** To reach Crete from Thorn Creek Woods, head left (south) on Monee Road 0.9 mile; then turn left on University Parkway and drive 3.6 miles.

• •

GPS TRAILHEAD COORDINATES N41° 27.547' W87° 41.942'

DIRECTIONS From the junction of I-57 and I-80 in Tinley Park, head south on I-57 for 7.1 miles. At Exit 339, turn right (east) on West Sauk Trail, and proceed 0.9 mile. Then turn right (south) on South Cicero Avenue and, in 1.9 miles, turn left (east) on University Parkway/Stuenkel Road. In 1.65 miles, turn left (north) on Monee Road; the nature pre-serve is 0.5 mile ahead on the right.

PUBLIC TRANSPORTATION The University Park Station on **Metra**'s Electric Line is 1.5 miles from the start of this hike. From the station, head east on University Parkway. At Monee Road, turn left. The Thorn Creek Woods Nature Center is just ahead on the right.

BASS PRO SHOP
basspro.com

Bolingbrook, Illinois
709 Janes Ave.
630-296-2700

Gurnee, Illinois
6112 W. Grand Ave.
847-856-1229

Portage, Indiana
6425 Daniel Burnham Drive
219-787-6800

CABELA'S
cabelas.com

Hammond, Indiana
7700 Cabela Drive
219-845-9040

Hoffman Estates, Illinois
5225 Prairie Stone Parkway
847-645-0400

DICK'S SPORTING GOODS
dickssportinggoods.com

Algonquin, Illinois
1816 Randall Road
847-960-7700

Arlington Heights, Illinois
401 E. Palatine Road
847-577-1283

Bloomingdale, Illinois
328 W. Army Trail Road
630-351-0823

Chicago (North)
1538 N. Clybourn Ave.
312-489-2136

Chicago (South Loop)
1100 S. Canal St.
312-448-2184

Deer Park, Illinois
21830 W. Long Grove Road
847-550-1527

Geneva, Illinois
618 Commons Drive
630-943-4100

Glenview, Illinois
1900 Tower Drive
847-730-7400

Lombard, Illinois
810 E. Butterfield Road
630-317-0200

Niles, Illinois
5601 Touhy Ave.
847-779-8800

Orland Park, Illinois
1 Orland Park Place
708-675-3100

Schaumburg, Illinois
601 N. Martingale Road
847-995-0200

Vernon Hills, Illinois
700 N. Milwaukee Ave.
847-573-8240

EREHWON MOUNTAIN OUTFITTER
udans.com

Bannockburn, Illinois
2585 Waukegan Road
847-948-7250

Kildeer, Illinois
20505 N. Rand Road
847-726-1301

Naperville, Illinois
47 E. Chicago Ave.
331-215-6900

MOOSEJAW MOUNTAINEERING
moosejaw.com

Chicago, Illinois
1901 N. Clybourn Ave.
773-529-1111

THE NORTH FACE
thenorthface.com

Chicago
875 N. Michigan Ave.
312-337-7200

PATAGONIA
patagonia.com

Chicago
1800 N. Clybourn Ave.
312-951-0518

REI
rei.com

Chicago
1466 N. Halsted St.
312-951-6020

Northbrook, Illinois
888 Willow Road
847-480-1938

Oakbrook Terrace, Illinois
17W160 22nd St.
630-574-7700

Schaumburg, Illinois
1209 E. Golf Road
847-619-0793

UNCLE DAN'S
OUTDOOR STORE
udans.com

Chicago (Lakeview)
3551 N. Southport Ave.
773-348-5800

Chicago (Lincoln Square)
4724 N. Lincoln Ave.
773-271-1000

Evanston, Illinois
700 W. Church St.
847-475-7100

Highland Park, Illinois
621 Central Ave.
847-266-8600

Park Ridge, Illinois
25 S. Prospect Ave.
847-720-4105

Titled *Arc of Nature,* this striking mural graces Openlands Lakeshore Preserve, adjacent to Fort Sheridan Forest Preserve (see Hike 28, Nearby Activities, page 143).   *Photo: Ted Villaire*

REI
rei.com

Chicago
1466 N. Halsted St.
312-951-6020

Northbrook, Illinois
888 Willow Road
847-480-1938

Oakbrook Terrace, Illinois
17W160 22nd St.
630-574-7700

Schaumburg, Illinois
1209 E. Golf Road
847-619-0793

UNITED STATES GEOLOGICAL SURVEY
nationalmap.gov/ustopo,
store.usgs.gov
888-ASK-USGS (275-8747)

APPENDIX C: Hiking Clubs

On the trail at Goodenow Grove (see Hike 49, page 236).   *Photo: Maggie Wolff/magmilerunner.com*

CHICAGO HIKING, OUTDOORS, AND SOCIAL GROUP
meetup.com/chicagohos

CHICAGO GROUP OF THE SIERRA CLUB
illinois.sierraclub.org/chicago
200 N. Michigan Ave., Ste. 505
Chicago, IL 60601
312-251-1680

FOREST TRAILS HIKING CLUB
foresttrailshc.com
2025 Sherman Ave., Ste. 407
Evanston, IL 60201

STARVED ROCK WALKERS CLUB
Meets at Starved Rock Lodge, starvedrocklodge.com
815-220-7386

WINDY CITY HIKERS
meetup.com/hiking-169

INDEX

Ted Villaire is the author of *Best Bike Rides Chicago, Best Rail Trails Illinois, Road Biking Illinois,* and *Camping Illinois* (all for FalconGuides) in addition to this guidebook. He has worked as a reporter for numerous daily and weekly newspapers and is currently communications director for the Active Transportation Alliance, a nonprofit organization that advocates for better biking, walking, and public transport in the Chicago area. He also frequently gives presentations about local biking and hiking opportunities.

Ted holds a bachelor's degree from Aquinas College in Grand Rapids, Michigan, and a master's degree from DePaul University in Chicago. He and his wife, Christine, live on Chicago's Northwest Side. Visit his website, tedvillaire.com, or email him at ted@tedvillaire.com.

DEAR CUSTOMERS AND FRIENDS,

SUPPORTING YOUR INTEREST IN OUTDOOR ADVENTURE, travel, and an active lifestyle is central to our operations, from the authors we choose to the locations we detail to the way we design our books. Menasha Ridge Press was incorporated in 1982 by a group of veteran outdoorsmen and professional outfitters. For many years now, we've specialized in creating books that benefit the outdoors enthusiast.

Almost immediately, Menasha Ridge Press earned a reputation for revolutionizing outdoors- and travel-guidebook publishing. For such activities as canoeing, kayaking, hiking, backpacking, and mountain biking, we established new standards of quality that transformed the whole genre, resulting in outdoor-recreation guides of great sophistication and solid content. Menasha Ridge Press continues to be outdoor publishing's greatest innovator.

The folks at Menasha Ridge Press are as at home on a whitewater river or mountain trail as they are editing a manuscript. The books we build for you are the best they can be, because we're responding to your needs. Plus, we use and depend on them ourselves.

We look forward to seeing you on the river or the trail. If you'd like to contact us directly, visit us at menasharidge.com. We thank you for your interest in our books and the natural world around us all.

SAFE TRAVELS,

Bob Sehlinger

BOB SEHLINGER
PUBLISHER